Date Due

Demco 293-5

FURNITURE

of the

PILGRIM CENTURY

(OF AMERICAN ORIGIN)

FURNITURE
of the
PILGRIM CENTURY

(OF AMERICAN ORIGIN)

1620-1720

WITH MAPLE AND PINE TO 1800
INCLUDING COLONIAL UTENSILS
AND WROUGHT-IRON HOUSE HARDWARE
INTO THE 19TH CENTURY

BY
WALLACE NUTTING

ILLUSTRATED WITH MORE THAN FIFTEEN HUNDRED EXAMPLES

COMPLETELY REVISED
AND
GREATLY ENLARGED

OLD AMERICA COMPANY
PUBLISHERS
FRAMINGHAM   MASSACHUSETTS

THE PLIMPTON PRESS
NORWOOD · MASS · U · S · A

To

HENRY WOOD ERVING

WHO EARLY DISCERNED THAT THE
STRENGTH AND BEAUTY OF
PILGRIM FURNITURE
WAS AN EXPRESSION OF
PILGRIM CHARACTER

EXPLANATORY

THIS work, like the first edition, is essentially confined to American furniture and minor articles. Greater care has been taken in this edition to exclude pieces of doubtful American origin. The few exceptions to this rule are noted in the text.

The first edition being exhausted the author was faced with the question whether to reprint or revise. The publication of the first edition elicited information of the existence of many previously unknown but important pieces. For instance, a court cupboard of supreme interest was called to the attention of the author by the owner. It had never been known to the public. By one means or another so much material, in regard to interesting articles, came to the attention of the author, that it appeared to be wiser to undertake a complete new edition. Practically every page has been rewritten and about six hundred additional articles have been illustrated so that the total number shown, numbered and un-numbered, approaches two thousand. Many articles appearing in a decorative form as, in one case, about a hundred pieces of pewter on an open dresser are not taken account of and are not even referred to again. We have thought it wiser to pass over the partial consideration of any class of subjects, and to treat in a very full manner those classes called for in our title page. Thus in the matter of iron: cast iron, though certainly used more or less for five hundred years, is shown in only one or two examples.

As there appear to be no known American clocks of the Pilgrim Century, or at least not enough examples to merit treatment here, it has been thought best to exclude all clocks, leaving that class of objects for possible treatment in a separate work.

Advantage has been taken of the opportunity to make a few corrections and to omit a few pieces which, owing to their similarity to others, or for other competent reasons could be spared. It should not, however, be inferred that the omission of any piece casts a reflection on its authenticity.

Greater attention has been paid to dimensions, to dates, and to the woods employed. The matter of ownership has been brought up to date so far as feasible, but the articles in the owner's collection are not, in the text, so designated. The curious may find them in the index. Some owners reserve their names.

All classes of subjects shown have been much increased in number. This is especially true of court cupboards, pine cupboards, chests and, most of all, of hardware. Here the additions are so numerous that they outnumber the old subjects many fold. In this department of the work almost every one of the objects shown is in the collection of the author or those of his friends.

Since so much English furniture has been coming to America, and so much study has been given to English works on the subject, the opinion had been pretty generally established that, so far as grace and charm and quaintness are concerned, American furniture before the mahogany period, in the turned styles at least, surpasses the old world patterns. Never before have exclusively American collections been so desired.

The author makes no pretence to exhaustive knowledge, and where any article is referred to as unique or as one of two or three of its class known, he would be understood as limiting these statements to his own or his friends' knowledge, as of the date of issue of this edition.

The increase of interest in the subjects treated has been startlingly rapid. A score of years since one might have gathered up most of the good old iron in America, and have been thanked for carrying it away. Yet this iron is now felt to be almost as important in giving a house the feeling of the period as the furniture itself, particularly if we take into account the fixed, as well as the lighting and fireplace hardware.

The best pieces of American furniture are certainly cherished as highly by us as are the best pieces abroad. Possibly this would be true irrespective of the comparative intrinsic merits of American and foreign articles. We want what our own ancestors made and used. It enriches life, and gives us the aroma of a past which is most delightful in retrospect, whatever may have been its strenuous reality. That which has been handled and used by six, seven or eight generations of our ancestors, is in a manner sacred, so that we avoid any financial appraisal of it. We think of it in terms of affection. The great war has stimulated our attention to it and enhanced our regard for it.

The great number of new plates and the increasing costs of material and labor, have worked hardships in the matter of books. But the publishers are to issue this work at the same moderate price as the first edition, encouraged by the reception of the first edition. Indeed, those who really know the extent of the labor required in this volume will also know that it is issued primarily as a labor of love.

WALLACE NUTTING

FRAMINGHAM, MASSACHUSETTS

CONTENTS

The references are to text pages only

FURNITURE

of the

PILGRIM CENTURY
(OF AMERICAN ORIGIN)

1. An Architectural Chest. 1640–60.

2. End of Chest.

3. End of Court Cupboard.

4. A Carved Oak Chest. 1650–70.

5. A Carved Three-Panel Oak Chest. 1650–70.

6. A Carved Oak Paneled Lid Chest. 1650–70.

7. An Oak Chest with "Rope" Carving. 1660–70.

8. A Carved Oak Four-Panel Chest. 1660–70.

9. A Carved Oak Five Panel Chest. 1660–70.

Furniture of the Pilgrim Century

.:.

CHESTS

CHESTS are the first form of furniture. We dig them out from Egyptian tombs. Even nomads find the need of chests, which mark the beginning, indeed, of a settled civilization. The word chest is of extremely ancient origin and in the Greek it is precisely the same as the form still heard among country people, chist. Cyst and encyst are of the same source and meaning, as is also chest applied to the human body. As ordinarily used, the word refers to a wooden receptacle with a lid. In its European form the chest was first an ecclesiastical appurtenance for the storage of sacred vessels. Indeed the ark of the covenant among the Hebrews was a chest. The use of the word tabernacle in conjunction with a small sacred receptacle is an interesting side light, since it also is applied to furniture.

The first known carving upon furniture was done on chests, some of the quaintest of which are still found in the churches of the old world. In the middle ages the nobles used chests for their valuables and clothing, and it was a custom for a king in his progress to carry chests with him. The use of the word box in England for our trunk is a curious survival of that ancient custom. It was a symbol of respectability and thrift to own a good chest. The custom of providing a young lady with a hope or dower chest marked the solid beginnings of her home life. The loose custom of applying the word dower to small chests-on-frames as special designation is wrong. Probably most dower chests were initialed and sometimes carried the initials of both husband and wife. There is no manner, however, of assuring ourselves that any chest is a dower chest, though the carving of interwoven hearts or of double initialing is usually to be regarded as the mark of a dower chest. As any family advanced in worldly gear it added to the number of its chests.

While chests vary greatly in size they most often perhaps approximate a length of forty-eight, a hight of thirty, and a depth of eighteen inches.

That is, the proportions are about eight by five by three. This would hold approximately for chests with one drawer. There are those who claim that a very nice and precise proportion was maintained in the dimensions of the chests and of all its panels, but this seems somewhat fanciful. The theory may have some basis when applied to a chest with a strictly architectural front.

While the chests of the wealthy were often carved with great elegance and elaboration, the poor, who also required chests, used the simplest forms, even the board chest perhaps dating back beyond the seventeenth century.

The early styles of chests were, like all things artistic, derived mostly, so far as we are concerned, from Italy, whence, through France, Flanders and Holland, and sometimes from Spain, those styles came into England, and at length in restricted and special forms were adopted in America. We, however, retain only the slightest reminiscences of Romanesque and Gothic shapes. We derive some painted styles from middle Europe, especially Moravia. For the most part the carving done in America was flat, linear or peasant carving, terms interchangeable in common use. Carving in the round or bas-relief is exceedingly rare among us. Indeed, possibly a dozen instances will cover all American examples.

We recognize that such peasant carving is a marked, even perhaps a complete degradation, from the forms of the middle ages. America was founded when a decline in the arts had already set in. We must, therefore, regard American furniture with mixed sentiments. Probably our taste for the quaint and our love for what our own ancestors left, and the admiration which we have for a people who paused in a wilderness to embellish their households, form a stronger stimulus for the American collector than any elements of pure art which are found in antique furniture.

With the going out of carving, and in conjunction with its later phases, came in the addition of applied ornaments, until, in the mid-eighteenth century, the artistic instinct had so far faded, that we reached a point where the merest molding was the only survival of decoration on chests.

The material of the earliest American chests was oak, in accordance with English traditions. But very quickly pine lids were introduced. The abundance and the size of " pumpkin " pine should have been, it would seem, an early and irresistible temptation. But curiously enough the pine adopted was the hard or yellow pine so largely vanished now from our local forests. The hard pine was almost as heavy and difficult to work as the oak. Following the use of it in lids it quickly came into use in panels and bottoms.

It is not until the eighteenth century that we begin to see much of the soft or white pine used, and then it is principally found in the board chests which have no claim upon our attention, unless they are in some manner decorated.

The joined, that is the mortise and tenon frame panels, is always the mark of good cabinet furniture in any age. The cabinet work of American chests seem to be not at all inferior to their English prototypes. The use of the draw bore pin to secure tight joints was first publicly noticed by Lyon in his invaluable pioneer work. The method consists in so boring the holes in the rails and the stiles that they shall not absolutely coincide but that the hole in the rail shall be nearer the shoulder of the tenon, so that the pin when driven shall draw the rail to form a very close joint with the stile. Thus an old pin, withdrawn, often shows in a crooked form. These pins are of white oak.

It is probable, at first, that the joiner was the same person as the cabinet maker. That is, the word carpenter is far less common in that time. The same person erected a dwelling and built its furniture. We have known such instances as late as 1800. The mechanic specially engaged as such by the Pilgrim Fathers was John Alden, who was followed by Kenelm Winslow in 1639. We shall have occasion later to refer to chests and cupboards which one or the other of them probably constructed.

The first chests were mere boxes without a drawer, and were therefore most inconvenient. The use first of one drawer, then of two and three, and finally the transition to a chest-of-drawers was easy. We do not wonder that the use of the chest went out. The peculiar features of the American chest, which distinguish it from its English cousin, are the simplicity of its hinges, the use of wood instead of iron for drawer handles, the usual presence of pine in some part, this last feature not being conclusive. The method of joining is by some regarded as a distinguishing feature but we are frank to say that we are not quite able to feel certain about this difference. Even as regards the oak there are those who are quite ready to distinguish between the American and English sort. It is usually easy to discern the difference in the oak. But when our best judges are at variance as to the very species of the wood, how much less able are they to separate, in every case, varieties of the same species? A very keen judge once mistook chestnut for plain oak. We do not mean to indicate scepticism on our part. We can only say that the best people are sometimes mistaken. The difference in color between American and English oak is not always conclusive. The English examples are sometimes as light as our own. Further, English oak is often as strongly featured as our own. Ordinarily, oak exposed to the smoke of an English apartment for several hundred years will be more or less creosoted, and of course dark. So far has this process gone that the term black oak is a common and apt description of that wood as seen in

English dwellings and furniture. To us it seems most sombre and altogether unattractive. The very late introduction of chimneys, and the discovery by an American, Count Rumford, of a method for preventing smoky chimneys are circumstances which have freed us from black oak. The American Indian, had he constructed chests, would soon have seen on them a complexion properly smoked by his wigwam.

There is a powerful, insidious, sentimental and prideful tendency to induce us to regard a piece of furniture as American. Its native origin makes it more attractive from every standpoint, even the pecuniary. But in a work of this kind certainly we cannot afford to lean toward judging a piece to be American unless we are obliged to do so. This position is an amusing shift from that of a few years since, when everyone who had a piece of old furniture was inclined to refer it to an English origin. Thus even now we find on Connecticut chests and Pilgrim cupboards, no trace of the style of either of which we find in England, labels affixed declaring that these pieces were brought over by English ancestors, if not in the Mayflower then in the Anne. But even in some recent instances the age of Anne has of necessity been repudiated. Almost as we write a chest of drawers with lapped joints has been in good faith represented to us as brought over by John Alden, and it is still in a family of his descendants. There are a few Americans who possess a sort of insight into the origin of furniture. This insight arises from long association with English and American examples, and is usually trustworthy. Unhappily, it is circumstantial evidence that we are, as a rule, obliged to follow. Only one or two of the makers of American seventeenth century furniture have been surely connected with the specimens they have left us. Traditions are unsatisfactory. It is easy to trace the process of their formation. A father may tell his son that a certain heirloom belonged to his great grandfather, and was probably handed down from their pioneer ancestors, and that perhaps he brought it from England. The next generation changes the perhaps to a probably and the generation following omits the probably. It is not a conscious misrepresentation. Indeed, the origin of traditions is often creditable to those through whom they are handed down, even when such traditions are not reliable. Documentary evidence is almost wholly lacking. Even when we find writings referring to furniture it is only by inference that we can connect a particular piece of furniture with the writing. Before the age of photography we lacked an easy and immediate method of connecting a piece of furniture with the comments upon it. Indeed, at the present time there is a loose method of referring to furniture in writings which are not directly connected with the objects described. The only precise method is to write legends directly upon the photograph of the piece concerned.

We are subjected to further difficulties in the establishing of authenticity in furniture by the repairs, wise or unwise, generally the latter, which have been made. More often than not the lid of an ancient chest wears out or splits and is replaced by a new one, so that we cannot certainly know whether the original lid was pine or oak. The old clinch or staple or cotter pin hinges, words which describe the same thing, are often replaced by modern, or at best by a different style of hinges. New panels and new pins are inserted. New bottoms are placed in the chest or its drawers. The legs are pieced. Sometimes the decorations or the moldings or the applied ornaments are restored or even hopelessly changed. This work is not always done by the unscrupulous. Our attention has recently been called to what would have been a remarkable court cupboard, the door of which has been replaced by a glass front! Its shelf also has been replaced by a marble substitute! Yet the piece is in the hands of the original family of owners who claim to cherish it with the utmost veneration. They would not part with it under any consideration nor would they let it alone.

We are using chests, the first great class in furniture of which we treat, as an opportunity for mentioning these difficulties which occur in our estimate of all alleged antique furniture, for in all classes of objects we meet the same principle. We find recently painted or varnished or wrongly restored pieces to such an extent that their value as examples is mostly lost.

Chests usually appear with three panel fronts. The four panel front is exceptional and the five panel front is very rare. The ends of the chests according to merit, age, or style, are arranged in one or two or more panels either sunk or raised. The backs of good pieces are mostly paneled. The legs of a chest are in earliest examples simply continuations of their corner stiles. These legs originally extended below the body of the piece from seven to eight inches. A present length less than those dimensions is almost invariably to be accounted for by cutting or decay. Pieces late in the seventeenth century often terminated in ball feet, which were not as long, but varied from three to perhaps four inches. In some instances the ball feet were applied on somewhat shortened stile legs. In most cases the ball feet were applied directly to the body of the piece by boring a round bottomed hole into the corner of the frame. A square bottomed hole indicates a modern auger rather than the ancient pod bit. The lids of chests when not attached by the clinch hinges were secured by cleat hinges. These were in the form of cleats fitted under the end of the lid where it projected beyond the chest. This cleat gradually widened towards the back, was bored, and attached to the body by a wooden pin. The cleats were ordinarily oak even when the lid was pine. The projection of the lid beyond the cleat was slight. Where there was no cleat the projection usually varied from three quarters of an inch to an inch and a quarter on the ends and on the front. Behind, the lid was sometimes flush and sometimes overhung, in such a manner that when it was raised, the overhang formed a stop to prevent the lid from falling back too far. The edge of the lid on the ends and the front, but almost never on the back, was finished in what is popularly called the thumb nail mold. In a few instances, however, the front and rarely the back has a somewhat more complicated mold with a bead or two, and the ends are left plain or they are finished with gouge carving. Two or three instances are known of paneled top chests which claim an American origin. There are a considerable number of instances of original plain oak tops. The great majority of original tops are yellow (hard) pine. In this volume the words yellow and hard as applied to pine are considered as interchangeable terms.

All the legitimate shapes of chest hinges known to the author are shown later in this work. So far as we have noted the strap, or strap and T hinges, are confined to the Pennsylvania chests of walnut or pine, or to the New England chests of pine. Even in this last instance the hinges are more likely to be mere cotter pins.

The usual practice in the making of chests was to rive not only the rails and stiles but often the panels. This method secured greater strength, because if a stick of oak would not split smoothly it was rejected. It was also far easier to rive than to saw. Our ancestors did not always do work in the slowest and the hardest way, although such an impression has their strenuous life made, that some authors seem to presume that the fathers preferred a hard way to an easy one. The riving of the wood is often apparent yet, on the unfinished interiors of the rails or stiles, and is quite frequent on the backs of the panels, and the under side of the drawers.

The oak used is referred to as white in all works that we have seen. We have, however, repaired with red oak certain chests, and the applied portions, of old wood of course, had precisely the texture and the color of the original. Red oak is easier to work than white oak, since its grain is more open. White oak is stronger, and better, and for practical purposes we may consider the early furniture as constructed of that wood.

The use of pine panels in the back came in very early, and in the case of cupboards this remark applies to the fronts as well. In the chests, pine panels seem to have been a little later on the fronts. There is no fixed rule of practice in this matter. Both customs existed side by side until finally the age of oak passed out entirely.

10.   A CARVED OAK FOUR PANEL CHEST.   1660–70.

11.   AN OAK THREE-TULIP-PANEL CHEST.   1660–80.

12. A Carved Oak Tulip Chest. 1660–70.

13. A Palm-Panel Chest. 1650–70.

The drawer was usually constructed with a solid one piece front. The drawer ornamentation was by applied moldings. Sometimes this application extended so far as to divide even a narrow drawer into minute false panels. The drawer ends were usually of oak and always grooved to fit oak runs which were secured to the frame of the chest by mortise or nail or both. The lack of the grooved end is, broadly speaking, a mark of eighteenth century work. The bottom and the back of the drawer may be of pine or rarely oak. But the drawer bottom is not attached in the eighteenth century style by being driven into a groove panel-wise, in the earlier examples, but is nailed on to the bottom, the drawer front being rabbeted to receive the bottom boards so that they shall not show. We give elsewhere an illustration of a drawer end, but would remark here that the earliest drawer construction showed no dovetailing. The drawer end was nailed against a rabbet. The first dovetailing appears, however, before the seventeenth century ends. This early dovetail is very broad and totally different from the numerous small dovetails which followed. The back of the drawer is usually nailed on in an absolutely plain form, the groove of the drawer end cutting through it also. The drawer bottoms vary in thickness. They may be an inch or more in the very earliest pine forms, and they may fall to a half inch. They often resemble, when of pine, a surface very like a shaved pine shingle. One should carefully note that the use of nails, so usual in drawer construction, was confined exclusively to that portion of the chest, which was otherwise constructed always entirely with pins of wood. In fact, this method of construction continued well into the nineteenth century and is not a mark of great age. The pins were square or roughly octagoned. In no instance has one been found turned. The figure of the oak was quite generally quartered, and this figure too often shows on carved surfaces. On such surfaces, to avoid a confusion of ornament, it is always better to find plain oak. We always prefer it although we by no means generally find it. Nor is the absence of plain oak in panels in any way a detriment to a piece as an antique. The chest usually contained a till of oak or pine molded on the edge of the lid in the same manner as the chest lid. The till lid is frequently made with small dowels, portions of the solid wood, as hinge pins, so that the lid put in place, as the frame was driven together, was henceforth permanently fixed in position. An instance comes to our attention of a little drawer beneath a till. Sometimes the till itself is decorated with die stamping and, in one instance that we recall, by a date so stamped.

The earliest chests had no drawer, but America was scarcely settled before the one drawer chest came in. The two drawer chest is very frequent. The chest with three drawers is very rare. Cabinet makers seemed to reason that if they were to go so far as to make three drawers it was as well to make a complete chest of drawers.

The locks of chests were usually attached on the interior. Most of such locks are lost. Their origin will be discussed later. We leave to particular chests the treatment in detail of the carving, the molding and the applied ornaments.

Chests are rarely found, as far as we know, with handles, except in the form of the seaman's chest of pine. Handles are restricted, usually, to two part chests of drawers or table cabinets.

The chest in its usual form, or as a miniature, to be used for valuable papers or a Bible, was the article of furniture most likely to be imported. It could be brought to America containing linen or apparel, and thus could be stowed in the hold without occupying much additional and valuable cargo space. There are apparently a few such pieces still left to us. Possibly a box at the Marblehead Historical Society, and others at Pilgrim Hall, Plymouth, and two or three chests, came over on the first ship or in one of those that followed within two or three years.

As to methods of construction, when the difference between English and American work is pointed out, we need to remember that at the very first this difference was negligible. It became wider with the passing years. It may have required fifty years to establish a distinct American type of construction or ornamentation. This difference arose partly from materials at hand, partly from the exigencies of the colonists, and partly from the natural variation that would arise on separation from the parent stock.

By 1700 pine became common as the principal structural wood in New England, while walnut, followed by pine, came in at the same period in Pennsylvania. When we speak of Pennsylvania we refer to the general type which existed on both sides of the Delaware River, and which is found to a considerable degree in New Jersey. The southern types of seventeenth century furniture are so rare that we can scarcely generalize upon them. The Dutch types proper are those contiguous to the Hudson River and are to be distinguished from the Pennsylvanian or German types, often loosely called Dutch.

Although the love for carving seems inherent in Hollanders, chests by them in a carved form are exceedingly rare. They were fond of painted decoration also, and nearly all our painted furniture of the colonial period is Dutch or Pennsylvania or from southern Connecticut where, as we shall see, it developed in a special style.

Chests in cherry are known. Possibly chestnut was rarely used.

14. An Oak Tulip-Panel Chest with Cross Panel. 1670–90.

15. A Connecticut "Sunflower" No-Drawer Chest. 1670–80.

16. A One-Drawer Sunflower Chest. 1660–80.

17. A Carved Oak Four-Panel Chest. 1660–70.

18. A Two-Drawer Sunflower Chest. 1660–80.

19. An Oak Three Panel Chest. 1670–80.

20. A Carved and Painted Chest. Dated 1704.

21. A Captain's Six-Board Sea-Chest. Dated 1677.

Nearly all of our best examples, however, are in oak, or pine which followed it at a great distance as to merit.

Old inventories mention also spruce; cypress and butternut has been found. The so called sea chest reputed to have belonged to one of the Pilgrim Fathers has inverted V or bootjack end, and is of board construction. A sea chest should properly sit flat on the floor without any legs. Otherwise it would overturn at sea. It is also made, as a rule, narrower at the top than at the bottom, to fit it against the ship's side in the forecastle. Its handles are of woven rope attached to a bracket. This sort of chest, together with the plain pine chest, has been broken up in great numbers for use in the repair of antique furniture. Unless such chests have some special sentiment connected with them they are of small account.

In this book all objects are designated by number, never by page.

No. 1 is called an architectural chest because the arches of the panel are structural and not simulated. The chest was found in a very ruinous condition on Long Island. It is owned by Mr. G. H. Buek of Easthampton, Long Island. His dwelling is that made famous as the inspiration of the poem " Home, Sweet Home." According to a tradition, the chest was brought from Lynn in 1649 by a family of Osbornes. It has been carefully restored, the feet of course being new. It is important as showing a true façade. It is also highly meritorious architecturally. The arrangement of two end-to-end drawers is scarcely found elsewhere in American chests except in the serrated Plymouth type.

No. 2 shows the end of the chest with its scratch or grooved carving, an obvious imitation of the heavier structural work of the front. The end carving is found very rarely on chests, only three or four other instances coming to our mind.

No. 3 is the end of the Virginia court cupboard shown in full later. We insert it here to afford an interesting comparison, since, in this instance also, the end is scratch carved, whereas the front is, in part at least, carved in the round. Thus we see an effort to carry out a slighter and less expensive decoration on the ends. In this instance, however, we have somewhat better carving on the top end rail. In all probability No. 1 was carved on the leg stiles below the frame but the restoration is proper, since it is not safe to surmise a design the precise character of which we cannot ascertain. The modillions opposite the ends of the drawers are extremely rare on chests. They show as projecting substantially in No. 2. Where we have seen them, they are more often opposite the upper rail, especially on cupboards. This chest shows in the upper rail a conventional foliated scroll which very commonly appears on chests. The tulip decoration in the panels is more unusual, especially in this excellent form. The rope carving of the arch is also of very rare character.

No. 4 is an elaborately carved oak chest owned by Mr. William B. Goodwin of Columbus, Ohio. It has been restored. It is fair to say that its American origin has been challenged. The very early date of the chest, however, which is conservatively given with its title, may fairly account for its resemblance to English designs. Made at so early a period, there was no reason for a marked divergence from the foreign pattern. The effect is that of a low relief carving, the edges being rounded and the foliage being of varying depths, following the styles of the previous century, and producing a handsome effect. The carving on the stiles and top rail depart very markedly from what we are accustomed to see, which is more in the nature of that on the bottom rail. The panels also are of high character, those at the sides being of the tulip blossom and bud design, whereas the central design shows in its upper part a three leaf pattern.

This chest came to Mr. Goodwin through the descendants of Kenelm Winslow, the official coffin maker of the Pilgrims of Plymouth. It is believed by Mr. Goodwin to have been made by Kenelm Winslow. The bottom, as found, was of butternut. The lid was of yellow poplar. It has been replaced with old pine. The body is believed to be of American white oak. Mr. Goodwin is the owner of a great number of interesting chests, each representing a special type or origin.

Size: $47\frac{3}{8}$ by $27\frac{3}{4}$ by $21\frac{3}{4}$ inches.

No. 5 is another very early chest whose special features are its rare paneled oak top, not looked for in an American piece. The carving is of a crude character on the panels, but the rails and stiles are better done, the inner stiles being palmated. The rope molding on the bottom stile is to be compared with that on No. 1.

Another feature of interest is the scrolled, scolloped, not engrailed bottom rail. We do not find this except on early chests, and then on those with no drawer or possibly with one drawer.

The bottom of this chest is pine but the back is oak. English chests of oak and also containing pine have come to our attention. The origin of this chest is not certain but it is presumably Connecticut. Size: 46 by $27\frac{1}{2}$ by 20 inches. Here as throughout this volume we name the long dimension first, that is, the length, or as some would call it the width across the front; then the hight from the floor to the top of the lid, then the depth from front to back. It is important to take note of these specifications as they will not subsequently be explained.

We have here a two panel end, as is frequent in chests of the earliest

22. An Oak Diamond-and-Arch Chest. 1660–80.

23. A Norman Tooth Carved Chest. 1660–80.

24. Serrated Plymouth Chest 1660–80.

25. Serrated Plymouth Chest. 1660–80.

type of the highest character. There is also a thumb nail molding of the lid.

No. 6, owned by Mr. George Dudley Seymour of New Haven, is supposed to be American, although its lid is of paneled oak, like that of No. 5, a feature which appears in only one other instance among the great number of chests here illustrated. The panels are carved in what is called a Runic design. The lower rail and the stiles are very slightly carved. The upper stile is outlined with scratches and prepared for intersecting lunettes. This is not the only instance of incomplete carving. A chest-on-frame in this work is similarly outlined. The chest was found in Portsmouth, New Hampshire, and is now in Wadsworth Atheneum, Hartford.

No. 7 is a four panel front chest, owned by Mr. H. W. Erving of Hartford. The ends are in single panels. The short stiles are plain, but the end stiles carry double rows of pencil and pearl carving. The top rail between rows of pencil and pearl ornament shows a scroll, and the bottom rail carries one row of the pencil and pearl ornament. The lid is oak.

To a student of structure this chest may serve to illustrate certain peculiarities. The molding on the inside of the leg stiles is worked from the solid, apparently, after the parts of the chest were assembled. That is to say, this molding runs out to nothing at the top and bottom, being chiseled rather than planed, and stops not abruptly but on a curve. Again the bottom rail is beveled or molded on its upper edge under each panel, which is not true on the lower edge of the upper rail. Sometimes the beveled edge was carried around all sides of a panel but always stopped before the corner was reached. The moldings on each side of the stiles here are, as appears, cut before the chest was put together. The back posts projecting as they did beyond the back top rail were often cut away for an inch or so, at the top, to allow the lid to open and to stop it, when it struck the shoulder, thus cut on the post. Otherwise the lid would have been strained.

The till within the chest at one end was framed in. In the earliest examples the till was of oak. Subsequently we often find it in pine even though the chest is oak.

Size: $47\frac{1}{2}$ by $26\frac{1}{2}$ by $20\frac{1}{4}$ inches.

No. 8 represents a very long chest. The decoration of the top rail is a series of lunettes and reversed lunettes, which we see also on various other chests of oak and even on one of pine in this work. The laureling which it bears on the short stiles resembles that on the Parmenter court cupboard, and also that on other chests. Wherever found it indicates an early date and strong English influence. The rosettes or asters in the panels resemble those on a Bible box shown later.

The initials P. W. are a somewhat early instance of initialing though the English practice in this respect was probably different. Here the most frequent dating and initialing is found on chests of the last decade of the seventeenth century.

Chests were usually made to order and we suppose them always to have been so made when they were initialed. It is this circumstance that gives individuality, romance and charm to old furniture. It is apparent that this furniture was designed for the house into which it was to go, and that it was to be used for a very specific purpose. It is a not altogether pleasing reflection that the names of the owners, even of initialed pieces, of early furniture, are almost always unknown. Their makers also are unknown. Although many stories accompany furniture, especially where it is found for sale in shops, it is practically impossible, more than once in a thousand times, to establish the precise origin of furniture in the Pilgrim Century.

No. 9 represents two extremely rare features in a chest, namely a five panel front and a carved end. The owner is Mr. George Dudley Seymour. The lid is a restoration as are also the feet. Of course the bottom should not show.

The chest is very handsome, and follows closely the analogy of some English models, and is similar in its diamond panel design to No. 10. The indentions above and below the panels are an interesting variant. The short stile on the two-panel end is also carved like those in front.

No. 10 shows a close cousin of the chest just discussed. The carving of the top rail has been called by some fluting, and the term is absolutely correct as a description. As in all cases of fluting the effect is enhanced by the curved line left at the bottom of the flute. The bottom rail has merely scratch carved lunettes. Both rails and stiles on the two-panel end are strongly molded, the moldings at the top and bottom being called channel molds. Flat panels like these are called sunken panels whereas those with the beveled edge which rise to a level with the surface of the stiles and rails are called raised panels. If the panels rise higher than the frame we name them block or highly raised panels. The lid of this chest is neither original nor proper. Size: 54 by 32 by 23 inches. The depth is very unusual but is evidently increased to correspond with the great length. The length of the feet is $7\frac{1}{2}$ inches, which is quite proper, showing only normal wear which is never very much on solid oak, unless a piece has stood in a wet place.

No. 11 is the first example we have thus far shown of applied orna-

26. A Serrated Plymouth Chest. Dated 1691.

27. A Serrated Plymouth Chest. 1660–90.

28. A Serrated Plymouth Chest. 1660–80.

29. Foliated Three Panel Chest. 1660–80.

30. A Carved Oak Chest, with Rosettes. 1670–80.

31. A Carved Oak Chest. 1660–80.

32. A Paneled-Lid Oak Child's Chest. 1670–1700.

ments in addition to carving. This construction points to a slightly later date than the pieces which are decorated by carving alone. True, there are individual instances of pieces that are carved, of later date than those that are both carved and otherwise decorated.

This chest also shows triangular blocks in the corners of the end panel. There are three tulip patterns in its panels, and in this respect it is, perhaps, unique. This chest also shows a heavy applied strip of molding about the base both at the ends and in front. It will be observed later that this molding often stops on the front when it is between drawers, and in some instances it is true also at the bottom, as in all the known examples of the serrated Plymouth chests.

The drops, also called split banisters, which appears to be the same word as balusters, are marked by great boldness in the turnings. The connection between the enlarged ends and the central portion is very small, so as to cause us to wonder how the crude early lathe could be coaxed into producing a result so delicate. It will be noted that these drops are in pairs on the inside stiles and appear in a larger form singly on the outside stiles. There is a strong affinity in shapes between all the patterns of drops. The rounded oval in the center of the end panel is called a turtle back, a boss or an egg. In this instance it will be seen that it is surrounded by four miniature bosses. These applied ornaments on chests and cupboards were almost always painted black, probably to simulate ebony. Their wood is often maple but sometimes beech, birch or pine though the last named is rare. They are attached by glue and in some instances wrought brads have reinforced the glue. Whether the brads were ever original, we have been unable to establish. The frames of the chests of the earlier type were as a rule put together without glue, the joiner depending upon his pin construction. Obviously when ornaments were attached he must follow a different method. Very rarely we have seen pins of wood used to attach ornaments but we cannot now name the instances. There seems to be a fatuous dependence by joiners upon the reliability of glue. Unhappily this dependence has been the cause of the loss of many fine decorations. It is the rarest thing to find a chest or a cupboard with all its original ornaments intact. In fact we know of only one such instance. Joiners today show the same simple faith in glue. In the ancient day when there was no dry heat such as we too often have in modern dwellings, glue was more likely to fulfil its function satisfactorily. Ornaments on an ancient piece will sometimes drop off like an unripe harvest when subjected to steam heat. There would seem to be no valid objection to securing these ornaments solidly by brads. The ancient cabinet makers are said to have used a far better glue than we have today, but that is a matter that is open to two opinions.

Our loss would not be so great were it not true that the moldings about the panels of old pieces were also often attached by glue, and hence have lost some of their members. The heavy skirt mold and other heavy molds we are happy to say was usually attached by pins of wood or by nails. The owner of this chest is Mr. George Dudley Seymour. The top is new and probably should have been of pine, not oak. The chest is otherwise original. It was found in the Capt. Charles Churchill house, Newington, Connecticut, about forty years ago. At that time it stood on end and was in use as a harness cupboard. In the same house was a Connecticut sunflower court cupboard which was rejected to " make room."

Size: 47 by 26 by 19 inches.

No. 12. This carved chest should be compared with the Hadley chest Nos. 33 to 42, and particularly with No. 41. It resembles the Hadley chest in being carved over the entire front and in showing everywhere the tulip blossom. In this case, however, instead of the narrow vine shown in No. 41 we have a highly conventionalized heavy rope. The style of carving is quite superior to that found on the ordinary Hadley chest, which is about as bad as anything can be, and scarcely worthy of the name carving.

There is a two drawer chest similar to the piece before us in the Connecticut Historical Society. The panels in that piece are more like the tulip pattern panels on the sunflower chest.

It will be noted that no moldings whatever appear on this or on the Hadley chests unless the chamfering around panels is to be called a molding, which is hardly allowable. Another feature of this carving is that a plain band is left all around the edges of the rails and the stiles before the carving begins.

As this is the first chest we have shown with a drawer, we may point out that American chests of this period had small wooden drawer knobs. They are much smaller than the Pennsylvania type of a later period, and very much smaller than the walnut knobs of the depraved Empire period. In English chests of this date we usually find an outline pear-shape iron drop handle, a thing we have never observed on an American chest.

Owner: Mr. H. W. Erving.

Size: 49 by 32 by 18½ inches.

No. 13. A rare four-panel chest with one drawer attractively carved in wheels, rosettes or geometrical figures, connected with grooved bands, and spaced by smaller similar circles. The palmated carving of the panels and

33. A One-Drawer Hadley Chest. 1690–1700.

34. Miniature Chest. 1700–10.

35. A One-Drawer Hadley Chest. 1690–1700.

36. A Six-Board Sunflower Pine Chest. 1690–1710.

37.   A One-Drawer Hadley Chest.   1690–1700.

38.   Miniature Chest,   c. 1700.

39. A Hadley Chest, with Full Name. 1690–1700.

the deep channel mold on the corner stiles are both noticeable. The chest has now had its legs pieced.

The lid is pine, a trifle too narrow, and bevels sharply outward and downward from the top, and is cut from a slab so as to give the benefit of the extreme width, a very amusing instance of adaptation.

The usual number of lunettes on such chests is five, as here, on the top rail. This chest has a three-panel end. A similar chest of Mr. Erving's has four panels. The old hasp remains.

Size: 52 by 34 by 21 inches.

The wood of this chest is very light white oak.

No. 14. An unusual Connecticut chest, has the side panels in the conventionalized tulip pattern, but instead of the aster or sun-flower pattern on the middle panel we have the diagonal cross often found on Connecticut cupboards. This is the first chest in which we find turtle backs on the front. The huge, ungainly handles are incorrect. They should be the usual moderate sized turned handles. We find on this chest the pairs of short drops on each side of the drawer and another pair in the center where the drawer front is divided in two parts by false panel work. In pieces of this kind, as usual, where there are moldings applied to the board which forms the front of the drawer, a plain thin piece, three eighths of an inch thick, more or less, is applied at the center to make the division between the two panels and on this the drops are applied. Thus the board forming the front is really recessed, or allowed to push in below the surface, and the surface is made flush by the applied blocks and moldings.

The blocks on which the stiles rest are not a part of the chest. This chest should be compared with No. 15.

It is from the Henry Stearns collection, formerly in Hartford.

No. 15. A rare example of which perhaps only one or two others exist of a Connecticut sunflower and tulip chest without a drawer. On this account it is probable that we should date the chest about ten years earlier than chest with drawers, although to do so is of course purely arbitrary. We observe in No. 14 a heavy molding carried around above and below the drawer, and here we have a similar mold on the bottom rail.

The carving on this notable class of chests is about an eighth of an inch deep, sometimes only three thirty-seconds deep. The background is pitted by numerous tool marks so as to form a pebbled or stippled surface. In many cases this ground is painted red. Perhaps this was always the case. In the process of years the red has faded or been washed away so that in some instances scarcely a trace of it remains.

The tulip and the sunflower are so highly conventionalized as to indicate at least a second stage of development. In fact the central and upper blossom of the sunflower is of a different character than the others, although all are supposed to grow on the same stem!

There are one or two score sunflower chests known. So far as we are able to trace them at all, as we are in a large majority of instances, we find that all came from Hartford County and many from Hartford itself. Lyon, who is very accurate, states that English collectors have never seen a chest of this character. Since his date, however, it is claimed that numerous oak pieces in England have pine in parts. Simmons, in an article on this subject, makes the same claim. If we are to generalize on these statements at all we may say that pine in English pieces of the oak period is very rare. We do, however, find it more frequently in the walnut and mahogany periods. There are those who claim that this pine is really Scotch fir and others who say that it was imported into England.

However, it not necessary to depend upon the presence of pine in oak pieces to establish their American character, in the case of the sunflower and various other chests. It is not at all credible that every English type of this sort should have been brought to America leaving none behind. The presence of so many in one city and county is evidence of the strongest character in favor of the conclusion that these chests were produced in Hartford.

The moldings on these chests are sometimes of red cedar, from which we infer that it was the intention to leave them in the natural wood so as to secure the color of the cedar. In instances, however, where a softer wood, or perhaps soft maple, is used, the moldings were painted red, which has now become an old red. At the time it is applied, however, we have evidence that it was very brilliant. Near the center of these molds there were small black parallel lines painted across the molding.

The owner of the chest is Mr. James N. H. Campbell of Hartford.

Size: 44¼ by 24½ by 18 inches.

No. 16. This one drawer Connecticut sunflower style is far more frequent, but the two drawer type is probably most often found, because it is a trifle later.

The piece before us has a pine lid, and two-panel ends. The upper end panel has beveled corners. The fashion of slanting the turtle backs on the drawer is an interesting characteristic.

Though the name sunflower chest has been bestowed on this style it is understood that there are side panels with conventionalized tulips.

Owner: Mr. H. W. Erving.

Size: 44½ by 31 by 19¼ inches.

No. 17. This four panel chest has its stile legs carved in the same fashion as No. 10. The bottom rail is also a lunette motive, only in this

40. A Two-Drawer Hadley Chest. 1690–1700.

41. TULIP-SCROLL HADLEY CHEST. 1690–1704.

42. A THREE-DRAWER HADLEY CHEST. 1690–1700.

43. Eight Paneled Oak Chest. 1660–90.

44. Oak Three Panel Chest. Dated 1693.

case it is doubled. Thus the bottom rail matches the top rail except that it is not so ornate. The double lunette here is of precisely the same outline as that in the pine chest No. 36. We may presume that the pine chest motives were copied from those on the oak chests. We have called this motive a shuttle pattern. The carving on the long stile has been characterized by carvers as a spade motive. The short stiles are carved in a manner like an inset split ball turning. It will be noticed that the bottom rail is not chamfered as is usual. This chest never had a drawer, but numerous chests, on careful examination, show that a drawer is missing. Sometimes the supports have been entirely removed but a trace of a framed rail for the drawer to slide upon can always be found, generally in the form of a rabbet on the back stile.

This chest is of extraordinarily large size, being $54\frac{1}{4}$ by $29\frac{3}{4}$ by $22\frac{1}{2}$ inches, about the size of No. 10. As these two chests have elements of carving in common and as their ends are almost precisely alike we may infer they may have been made by the same person.

Owner: The estate of William G. Erving, M.D., Washington.

No. 18 is a very good specimen of a two drawer sunflower chest. It was restored about forty years ago at the time when Connecticut cabinet makers, working in conjunction with Dr. Lyon, were first engaged on their pioneer work of finding and calling attention to this sort of furniture. This example has not lost any considerable portion of its feet; the top is original except the cleats; so also are most of the ornaments.

There is an interesting variation in these chests and in cupboards of the same period, which clearly indicates that they were made to order, and that the feeling of the cabinet maker and his patron coincided in the thought of giving individuality to each piece. Thus we observe that the carving, the ornaments, the size and many other particulars are varied slightly. A chest, especially when designed as a gift, was regarded properly as appropriately marked by some peculiarity. It is this variety, so natural to a good workman, and so fine a stimulus in all artistic production, that the seventeenth century had and we have not. It is this feature which must be introduced again into American life. It is one thing to standardize the mechanism of automobiles. That may be possible and is certainly desirable. But we ought to distinguish between mechanics and artisanship. Unless we are to revive individuality in our characters as well as in our surroundings, true progress will be at an end. There is no stimulus in thinking, and no character development, if every household is to be furnished with standard articles.

Size: 45 by 40 by $20\frac{1}{4}$ inches. The stile legs project six inches and were probably at least seven inches.

The top is hard pine. All the elements of this chest are quite correct.

No. 19 is an interesting variant. The owner is Mr. H. W. Erving. The foliated scroll on the center panel, bearing the initials W. B. differentiates the chest quite markedly. The absence of the drawer may probably call for an earlier date. There is a single panel end.

The channel or shadow molding in these chests is as a rule painted black to coincide with the applied ornaments. The maple used in turnings was the soft, swamp, or water maple, three names for the same variety. It was rather more common and easier to work than the rock or sugar maple. The birch used in turnings was often of the gray and rather frail and somewhat soft variety, not the heavy, hard mountain or salmon birch.

Size: 44 by 25½ by 18 inches.

No. 20. This unusual chest is a combination of carving with painted decoration, and is therefore probably earlier than the chests with painted decorations only. This piece is remarkable in giving not only the year, but the month and the day, on the central panel. The two drawers are also painted in the tulip bud and blossom, and the blossom is not as highly conventionalized as is usual. This is the first chest we show with decorated painting, the painting mentioned in the previous cases being in the nature of a background or relief to set off the carving. It will be observed that on this chest as well as on No. 18 the molding between the drawers stops on the front and is returned to the front. In the Plymouth serrated chests, however, while the moldings stop on the front, returns are seldom worked upon them. They are sawed off flush with the outside end of the carcass. Some have thought that this distinction in the manner of applying the molding indicates an earlier date for the Plymouth chests, and we incline to this opinion. It is entirely possible, however, to attribute the difference to the greater skill of the Connecticut craftsmen.

We feel quite certain that painting on Connecticut chests was a later decoration than the carving or the applied ornaments. It is found in southern central Connecticut. What inspiration it received from the Hollanders of New York and the Pennsylvania Germans is not clear, but we must presume a connection owing to the fact that the painted chests of Connecticut are found principally in the shore towns where connection with New Amsterdam was close.

Owner: Mr. Malcolm A. Norton of Hartford who also has chests like No. 18.

No. 21 a true seaman's chest. It is called a captain's chest, presumably because it is carved. Sailors had leisure and exercised it very frequently in the carving of small ornaments called scrimshaw work.

45. ALL OAK ARCH PANEL CHEST. 1660–90.

46. PINE BOARD INITIALED CHEST. 1700–20.

47. Oak Scrolled Skirt Chest. 1660–80.

48. Pine Miniature Chest. 1690–1710.

49. An Oak Two-Drawer Chest with Drops. 1670–80.

50. A CURVED MOLD CHEST. 1680–90.

They are a free hearted and generous lot. They seem to enjoy making something for wives and sweethearts more than for themselves. Hence we find surprisingly little in the way of carving by them on cabinet pieces. We accept with suspicion tales of their having done elaborate chairs on shipboard. In the instance of this board chest, the first by the way we have shown without a joined frame, the simplicity of the carving makes it seem reasonable to believe that it was done on shipboard. Nevertheless the hearts initialed M.S. would seem to point it out as a gift piece done for a sweetheart or a wife. That it was, however, made at sea or by a seaman is proved by the rope handles. Its lack of feet also indicates that it was for use at sea and may have been designed for the captain's wife. The material is pine, not the best for carving. Oak itself, though it is the classical wood for Gothic carving, is not susceptible of dainty cutting such as marked the work of Grinling Gibbons, whose favorite material was pear wood. The grain for the highest class of work should be close and hard and free from knots.

As has been pointed out before, the lids of sea chests are usually narrower than their bases owing to the forward slant of the back.

Owner: The estate of George F. Ives of Danbury, Connecticut. The date appears in no less than three places on the front, a curious repetition.

Size: the outside measurements including the lid, are 53 by 19 by 21 inches.

No. 22. This chest introduces a new element for our consideration, — the carved arch in combination with the panels we have already been considering.

The owner is Mr. H. W. Erving.

This American chest is very elaborate and has legs of unusual length indicating that good care must have been taken of it. The ends have three plain panels. The arch in this chest is also seen on English examples, and on No. 24 and No. 45 and on some court cupboards. The arch is quite precisely like the English, not only in its shape but in the projecting capitals and bases. One would hardly catch at first glance the great number of ornamental features, but to enumerate them is impressive: drops, bosses, nail heads, channel molds, diamonds, rosettes, blocked corners, incised ornaments, an arch, keystone and other arch-structure blocks and moldings about panels and drawer.

The wheel decoration rather than the flower type which appears in the diamonds may have been suggested by the wheel windows of the Gothic day. Of course the circle, as variously divided geometrically, is a primitive and obvious method of ornament.

Size: $45\frac{3}{4}$ by $33\frac{1}{2}$ by $19\frac{3}{4}$ inches.

No. 23 is a decided departure in ornament from the chests hitherto considered. Dr. Lyon showed a chest of this character. The series of square carved incisions running vertically on the stiles is called Norman tooth carving. The top rail is cut in foliated scrolls as often seen. The panels are done in a double scroll of the same character. The drawer is a restoration and the feet have been pieced. The chest presents a very handsome appearance and has a fine color. The lid is of thin oak with an unusual overhang.

Size: 36 by 33½ by 18.

No. 24 is our first example of a serrated Plymouth chest belonging to Mr. M. A. Norton.

These chests are of the highest importance for several reasons. They constitute, together with the serrated Plymouth cupboards, the main contribution of Plymouth Colony to our important and stately furniture of the seventeenth century. Eight or ten of these chests are known. The points of similarity between them are: first, serrations, like Norman carving, running across one or more oak molding bands the length of the chest. Second, two or four drawers arranged in sets of two on the same level. That is to say no drawer goes across the chests, but there are two side by side or end to end drawers. If more drawers are added they are in the same fashion. We shall notice later that this rule holds true also with the court cupboards of the same type. Third, narrow parallel gouges in pairs (pencil and pearl) running at intervals across one or more oak moldings on the front. Fourth, the molding stops on the top but does not return. It is sawed off flush with the ends. Fifth, all the pieces have applied turned decorations, both drops and bosses.

All have triglyphs on some one of the rails, perhaps always the top rail. Sixth, all have pine drawer bottoms, pine drawer fronts and probably all have pine panels in front and in some cases at the end. Seventh, all are paneled in the backs, sometimes with oak, sometimes with pine. Eighth, all are traced, as far as they can be traced at all, to Plymouth Colony or to Plymouth itself. The piece before us is peculiar in that it possesses an arched panel, which is the only instance we recall among the Plymouth serrated chests. This fact has the more importance since it bears on the question whether American chests and cupboards with arched panels may not be challenged as old importations. There is such a strong American feeling in these Plymouth pieces that we feel this arch settles the matter.

The shape of the notching is really in the form of pointed dentils on the highest member of the chest. The drawer moldings are, we believe, uniformly slanted back to the outside edges rather than slanting

51. HEAVY TWO-DRAWER BALL-FOOT CHEST. 1670–90.

52. OAK THREE PANEL CHEST. 1670–90.

53. OAK AND PINE THREE PANEL CHEST. 1670–90.

54. Plain Panel Oak Chest. 1670–90.

55. A One-Drawer Molded Oak Chest. 1680–90.

56. An Oak Chest, with Three Repeated Panels. 1670–90.

57. An Oak Six-Board Chest. 1690–1700.

inward like most chest moldings. We believe that this character of a molding, other things being equal, is the older of the two, since it follows the style of the seventeenth century looking-glasses.

This chest was found in Connecticut in a family which had possessed it for many generations. Yet the migration of Massachusetts people to Connecticut and the definite knowledge of Plymouth origin in other cases need not stagger us in relation to this chest. Though it has lost something from the feet it is a rich example of the type.

No. 25 is another chest of the same general character except that it has turned feet in front. The moldings of the panels are also more elaborate than we have seen on any other of the type. It is an exceedingly handsome piece. The side panels we think finer than the square blocking in the corners, although this of course is a matter of taste.

We have said that all these chests have two drawers. This chest being small scarcely breaks the rule, the shortness of the drawer not calling for its division.

Owner: Mr. M. A. Norton, the same as in the preceding example.

No. 26 presents many interesting variations and has the special flavor of a precise date. The till of this chest is of white oak divided down the center with a row of stamping, and then having the halves of the top each bearing an X of similar stamping. The face of the till is also stamped. Below the till are short side runs of oak which indicate that there was once a small sliding drawer under the till. The date is stamped by the same tool which executed the rest of the work, 1691.

Another exceedingly interesting mark of change with the progress of the years is the fact that a half of the old drop handle on one drawer was in place showing it to have been a brass ring drop. The handles therefore as shown are reproductions. This piece was found in an attic in Scituate, according to a report. It is, anyway, a Plymouth Colony piece.

The thin applied blocks at the center of each side of the middle panel and on the side panels were stamped in double rows with an interesting device. Some of these applied pieces were missing and also some of the moldings, as we would naturally suppose would be the case. But the most remarkable fact in regard to the condition of the piece was that every one of the applied turnings was intact. It is important to notice that these applied ornaments appear on the feet also, in this case in pairs. In two of the cupboards found, as we shall see, there is a single large turning, simulating to some degree a ball foot. The interesting question arises whether all chests and cupboards of this design should not have applied turnings on the feet. We incline to the belief that they did all have such turnings originally.

Another feature of odd interest in this chest is the fact that the lid, which is original, is of hard pine but is faced with a piece of oak, front and back, wide enough to admit the molding. This is an amusing circumstance since the panels are pine. Why they should have attached the strip in the back is difficult to say. We may presume that wide oak could have been found since the writer discovered a house constructed of two inch plank many of which were twenty-four inches in width, and ran for many feet without a knot. It is true that these planks were red oak, which perhaps is found in larger boles than the white. Nor could the choice of yellow pine, as in this case, have been dictated by a lighter weight since the difference is not great.

The mystery of these pieces is further hightened by the fact that we have in this example and in some others four oak panels in the back whereas the front panels are pine! Had oak been considered more desirable we cannot understand the failure to use it, because the panels are never very wide.

The ends are three panels, and of oak. The drawer bottom and drawer back are of pine, and like every example of this type we have examined they show the rive or cleaving marks, here and there, on the under side. We hardly think this could have been an English custom. It is fair to say that several excellent mechanics have pronounced this wood spruce. The difference between spruce and pine on the smooth grain is very slight. One of our friends became much alarmed at the statement about spruce, and warned us that our pieces would be slightly thought of if we mentioned the matter. There seems to be a kind of bigotry in relation to woods as well as in religion. All the bottoms of this class of pieces are of a very smooth even grain which split with an agreeable smoothness, and we believe that the material is pine.

A structural detail is that the drawer ends are nailed directly through from the fronts. The nails are then covered by the molding. This method is the opposite from a very early type in which the nails were driven from the drawer ends into the rabbet of the drawer front.

The presence of the drop handles on this piece, as distinguished from the wooden knobs found in all the other pieces of this type which come to our attention, undoubtedly indicates a considerably later date for this piece. We notice that the earliest highboys, which we date about 1690, all had brass drop handles, and from that date on no fine furniture, except possibly the drawers of gateleg tables, used wooden knobs. We shall later point out the certainty of an earlier date for the court cup-

58. An Oak Center Block Panel Chest. 1680–90.

59. A Pine Carved Chest. c. 1700.

60. Oak Chest with Drops, Plain Panels. 1660–80.

61. Oak Block Panel Chest. 1660–80.

62. OAK ORNAMENTED PANEL CHEST. 1680–90.

63. BALL-FOOT OAK PANEL CHEST. 1680–90.

64. Turnip-Foot Pine Chest. 1690–1710.

65. Arch Carved Walnut Chest. Dated 1776.

board of this type. The stamping which appears on this piece is also a decoration which seems to have come in about 1690. The piece is therefore marked by transitional ornaments, and notwithstanding its beautiful construction it really stands for the beginning of a decline.

Size: $52\frac{1}{2}$ by 34 by $20\frac{1}{4}$ inches. These dimensions as usual are given on the body, technically called the carcass, except that the vertical measurement is from the floor and includes the feet. Here the feet are only $4\frac{1}{2}$ inches long and have probably lost three inches. The oak strip on the lid is $\frac{3}{4}$ inches behind and $1\frac{1}{8}$ inches in front, and the thumb nail molding is carried around front and ends. The large oak moldings are $1\frac{1}{4}$ inches thick, and, in this solitary instance, we believe, the mold over the drawer in front is returned.

The love of individualism appears in this chest which has diamonds in the end panels and block corners in the middle panel, a decoration which is reversed in various other pieces of the type. All end panels in this style are sunk, we believe. The top molding under the lid is varied by a diagonal cut running up from the pairs of cuts which form a crude pencil and pearl ornament.

While mentioning dimensions we may say that the till has an extraordinary width being $9\frac{1}{4}$ inches. It also has a lock, now lost.

No. 27 is another of the same type of chests from the collection of Mr. B. A. Behrend of Brookline. A peculiarity here is the scratch carved serrations on the feet, both at the top and the bottom, which would indicate the general rule of applying ornaments to the feet was in this case dispensed with, and that the carved serrations on the moldings above were merely suggested on the feet. This piece is also peculiar in having four "beam ends" instead of triglyphs. It will be noticed also that the panel work on this chest is precisely the reverse of that on the one preceding it.

No. 28 belonging to Mr. H. W. Erving, is still another of these important chests. In this case we have the interesting variant already referred to of the large split turning on the feet which was also found on two recently discovered court cupboards of this type. We do not understand the lack of the third applied piece on the ends of the top rail, to make the triglyph, but we presume it to be correct as Mr. Erving is very accurate. There are other instances of two instead of three strips.

We have here the unusual thing in these chests of quartered oak panels instead of pine. The effect of the lighting does not show the quartering of the grain, on the left panel, but it is also, of course, of oak. It may be that the possession by a cabinet maker of a fine quartered piece induced him to use the oak rather than the pine.

In this connection there is a strong light thrown on the reason for using pine on the drawer fronts in this style. That part of the front which was not covered by the cedar molding was painted black. Thus there was no call to show a grain. Painted furniture may as well be pine as anything else. There still remains, therefore, only the problem of the true panels.

Size: 50 by 33½ by 21¼ inches.

We have now shown five of the Plymouth serrated chests. There is another one in Pilgrim Hall, Plymouth, and we believe several others known, which we cannot just now place. We consider these pieces among the most important of our American chests, especially when their character and their source are considered together.

No. 29 represents an oak chest the three panels of which are identical, being a doubled foliated scroll in the flat carving. The chamfering on all sides of the panels is clearly seen here. It is also clear that the chamfering on the short stiles was done on the bench, and all the rest was done after the chest was assembled, or at least with reference to the manner in which it must assemble. The panels including those on the ends, and the three on the back are of oak, and those on the back still show the rough riving. The lid is of pine molded with a bead on the front, and with pin hinges through the cleat. The chest was painted red and after the removal of all of the color possible it still has a strong tinge. Both upper and lower rails and all the stiles have a simple, doubled channel mold.

Size: 42 by 27½ by 18 inches. The legs are now 6¾ inches long. The chest has a one panel end. The till is missing but the mortise grooves where it existed appear.

No. 30 is a very elaborate and handsome chest belonging to Mr. James N. H. Campbell, of Hartford.

This very rich front exhibits numerous unusual features: One peculiarity is the very wide bottom rail, the like of which we do not remember to have seen in any other chest having a drawer, because the use of that portion of the chest is lost. The arrangement of the end panels is quite unusual; there being as a rule one, three or four. Here we have two, the lower one conventional, and above, instead of the two usual panels long vertically, we have a more decorative panel with triangular blocked corners. The front of the chest exhibits two styles of rosettes or asters or sunflowers, — we never are certain which term we should apply, and as these flowers are always conventionalized it is not a matter of importance. For the first time we have here, cut in the stile feet, similar flower blossoms to those found on other parts of the front. There is also a

66. Miniature Painted Chest. 1700–10.

67. Painted Oak Chest. Dated 1705–6.

68. A Painted Chest, with Two Drawers. 1690–1710.

69. Painted Oak Chest. 1680–1700.

70. Sunburst Painted Oak Chest. 1680–1700.

71. PAINTED WHITEWOOD CHEST. 1690–1710.

72 & 73. MINIATURE PINE CHESTS OF DRAWERS. 1700–20.

peculiar little scratch carving on the top rail which we could perhaps dispense with without loss to the feeling. Very peculiar members of the carving are those which, shaped like a bending corn leaf, either single or double, fill the spaces between the rosettes. It is probably the copy of the end of a palm leaf. Another peculiarity is the division, superficially, of course, of the side panels into four smaller panels. The drops are also shorter than we usually find.

Size: 48 by 37½ by 20 inches.

No. 31 is an unusual chest. The owner is Mr. George Dudley Seymour. It originates in New England. The front and end panels are of oak. It has the original pine lid. The carving of the stiles and top rail is similar to that of a copper-plate frontispiece fly leaf of an old Bible. It is a Renaissance type. The carving of the top rail also resembles that on chests already treated being in fact almost precisely like that of No. 23. This chest was sold many years ago at an auction of the effects of Josiah Herricks, of Antrim, New Hampshire, and, therefore, called the " Antrim Chest."

In this and other parts of this work it will be understood that the frames of chests and boxes are oak unless otherwise stated and that their lids are pine unless otherwise stated.

Size: 45 by 26½ by 22⅜ inches, the last dimension being the width of the top. Ordinarily speaking we are giving the frame size only, to which the overhang of the top should be added.

No. 32 is a miniature chest, also belonging to Mr. George Dudley Seymour. It is presumed to have been made for a child. It is of oak including the paneled lid. It is also the only miniature chest in oak of this date, so far found, in America. The front rail has been charred, perhaps by rush lights, a common thing in English chests, it is said. It is to be noted that there is also a wide dentil carving across the bottom rail and that this is repeated on both top and bottom rails on the end.

Size: 20⅞ by 14⅞ by 12½ inches, the first and the last dimensions being the outside measurements of the lid.

No. 33. With this chest we come to an interesting but perhaps overrated and certainly later series of chests to which the name Hadley has been given, due to the fact that Mr. H. W. Erving found a chest of this character which originated in Hadley, or at least was found there. The special characteristics of these pieces is that the entire front is carved, stile and rail and drawer front, and that the carving is even carried down the stile leg to a point near its bottom. There is a considerable difference in the merit of the carving but it is all poor. The main element is the tulip blossom, the bud seeming to be somewhat neglected. The carving is not even worked back to a ground in many instances but is merely scratched or outlined on the surface. This is always true of the veins from the stem to the leaf. The other motives in these chests are the introduction in many instances of the heart, in which case we suppose them to have been dower pieces. In addition to that they are, we believe, without exception initialed. They have the further peculiarity which appears also on one of the court cupboards in the author's possession, not however of this style, that the ends of the drawer fronts are mitered. We scarcely understand the origin of this detail but its effect is obvious. It prevents the drawer from pushing in too far, and keeps it just flush with the rails and stiles without the need of a stop in the rear. These chests, in the one drawer type, generally have a small horizontal panel at the bottom of the end and two small vertical panels above it. These panels are always sunk so far as noted. They are also surrounded by beaded molds and they are chamfered on all sides. On the two drawer and three drawer types there are usually four end panels, these being longer below and slightly shorter above. The lids of all the pieces we have examined were of pine. Other details we take note of under the separate numbers. No. 33 is one formerly in the B. A. Behrend collection. It is attractive in color having some of the old red in the ground work of the panels. Of course, it has lost a part of its feet but we believe is otherwise original.

No. 34 is a miniature chest belonging to the estate of J. Milton Coburn, M.D., of South Norwalk. It is the first example we have had of ball feet, which began to come in about 1680, but did not become fully established as a style for ten or fifteen years after that date. It has the double arch molding, which is a trifle later than the single arch. The use of these miniature chests was either for children or for placing on tables to contain more valuable or smaller articles than were placed in the large chests. We have here also the use of the brass drop handle, sometimes called the bell tongue or tear drop. The plates on the handles were cast with various ornamentations. The English were past masters in the production of beautiful brasses. It is supposed that in most cases elaborate early hardware was imported. We cannot, therefore, state with certainty the origin of brasses even on pieces which are distinctly American.

No. 35 shows another Hadley chest varying only slightly from No. 33. The feet have been pieced to the upper length. Those inclined to see the image of George Washington on the contour of cliffs may pick out his grotesque head on the drawer. Probably this resemblance was unintentional since it is formed of the foliation of the tulip. The initials

74. CARVED BOARD CHEST. 1698.

75. PANELED PINE CHEST. 1700–10.

76. A One-Drawer Carved Pine Chest. 1680–1700.

77. One-Drawer Pine Chest. 1710–20.

78. YELLOW PINE ALL-CARVED CHEST. 1700–10.

79. SHEATHED BRACKETED CHEST. 1700–10.

80. A Six-Board Round Panel Pine Chest. 1710–20.

81. Pine Chest on Shoes. 1710–20.

on these chests are so obvious that they will not be referred to except for special reasons. The lid on this chest was wrongly replaced by oak. It has now been changed again to pine. The chest was found in southwestern New Hampshire in the hands of an owner who doubtless carried it up the Connecticut river from its place of origin.

Size: $41\frac{1}{2}$ by $35\frac{1}{4}$ by $18\frac{7}{8}$ inches.

No. 36 is the first instance we show of a carved pine chest. It is now owned by the Pennsylvania Museum and was in the author's former collection. The special interest that attaches to it, is that, while it is a six board chest, and the first chest we have shown of normal size without a frame, it carries carving from motives seen on the oak chest, and carried out with a considerable degree of taste. Thus the front is marked off as if the central portion were a panel. This portion as well as the outside of the entire front is surrounded with a single arch molding made, of course, by carving. The lunettes and reversed lunettes follow the analogy of more elaborate ones seen on chests already described. In the central section these lunettes are repeated in a kind of interlaced design which forms a series of circles from each of which four shuttles are outlined. In the center there is the outline of a sunflower, which connects this piece with Connecticut examples. It came from Connecticut. The inverted V or bootjack end is somewhat relieved in its plainness by an irregular contour.

There are a considerable number of carved pine chests. This one is perhaps more highly regarded than many of the others. The chest affords an amusing instance of rapidly increasing estimation of merit. It was found by a dealer who obtained it for practically nothing and sold it for a little more. Again it changed hands for a very low sum. Quickly, however, its unusual and quaint qualities began to be felt, and the next carved pine chest that appeared was held at so respectable a value as to be compared with the values placed upon carved oak pieces.

No. 37 is a Hadley chest formerly owned by Mr. Brooks Reed of Boston. The carving of the middle panel is differentiated somewhat from the last example.

No. 38 is a miniature decorated chest owned by the Metropolitan Museum. The word decorated in this connection has now been specialized so as to apply to painted decoration, as distinguished from carving or from applied turnings or other ornaments.

In this case the decoration is very effective, but the inability of a photograph to pick out colors satisfactorily does not do the subject justice. The ball feet and the flush drawer belong with the period.

No. 39 is a variation from the Hadley chests previously shown, in that it has two drawers, and, more particularly, is carved with the full name, Elisabeth Warner, across the top rail.   It is owned by Mr. Philip L. Spalding of Boston.   It was found in or near Deerfield about 1916, by Dr. Miner of Greenfield, who also found in the same region the three drawer Hadley chest No. 42.   The condition of both pieces was good.

No. 40 is another two drawer Hadley, the carving of which is somewhat superior, in some respects, to the one drawer pieces.   Or perhaps we should say that its variation from them is a pleasing change.   It will be observed that the short stiles in these chests are very wide.   Probably this was so arranged, since as the stiles were carved, more room was left for the full development of the carving pattern.   The very close keeping to the tulip, however, indicates that the ancient tradition of Holland was still powerful.

The initials, slightly indistinct, are H. A.   The effect of the carving is a little softer than that on some pieces.   It will be seen also that the chamfering of the panels in these Hadley chests is more in the form of a looking-glass frame and is entirely done on the bench, into the very corners, so that the chamfers match as they meet.   This is an interesting mark of change and enables us to date furniture.   The carving, also, on the bottom rail of this piece departs from the conventional, being a series of spade shaped leaves.   Here also the heart on the middle panel is repeated on the bottom drawer.

Size: 44 by $42\frac{3}{4}$ by $18\frac{3}{4}$ inches.

No. 41 brings us to a Hadley chest, if we may so call it, of a more interesting and artistic design, and makes it appropriate to point out certain analogies.   Mr. Erving found his chest in 1893.   The chest before us was found in Hatfield.   Mr. Luke Vincent Lockwood whose large and well known volumes show a good many of these chests, has recently discovered a chest of high character which he believes did not originate in Hadley.   That name is probably a misnomer but answers as well as any other to fix a type.

The remarkable discovery by Mr. Lockwood of a chest on which appears the legend " Mary Allyn's Chistt Cutte and Joyned by Nich. Disbrowe," is perhaps as important as any fact which has come to light for years regarding American furniture, unless we are to except the discovery of three Plymouth court cupboards.   Mr. Lockwood has given the public a scholarly and accurate dissertation in the bulletin of the Metropolitan Museum concerning this chest.   It appears that Disbrowe died in Hartford in 1683.   We have, therefore, an earlier date for the earliest type of this chest than had hitherto been assigned.   The carving upon the Disbrowe chest is sufficiently similar to that on the Eastman

82. A Whitewood Chest with Heavy Block Panels. 1700–10.

83. A Pine Nine-Panel Chest. 1720.

84 & 85. SMALL AND LARGE PINE CHESTS. 1710–20.

chest before us to suggest the probability of community of knowledge between the makers, or possibly the same maker. Each chest has a diamond in the side panels in which the initials are inserted. Four of the half diamonds on the top drawer of the Disbrowe chest appear on the Eastman chest. The continuous scroll carried around the outside stiles, the rail above the top drawer, and thence onto the inside stiles, is obviously the same motive in each case. In this Eastman chest the scroll of the inner stiles, however, connects with the stem of the tulip on the top rail.

Another variation of an important character is the sunflower and the five centered rosettes cut respectively in the upper and lower drawer of the Eastman chest. Of course there are many variations in detail.

Now as to the origin of these pieces, the chest before us, owned by George P. Eastman of Orange, New Jersey, has the following light thrown on it by the owner: His grandfather Lucius Root Eastman, Sr. saw as a boy the chest in the woodshed of *his* grandfather Martin Root. When L. R. Eastman, Sr. grew up he obtained the chest from an aunt to whom it had come meantime. Mr. Eastman, the present owner, informs the writer that John Allis was a resident of Hatfield and that his daughter Elisabeth Allis was married to James Bridgman in 1704. In the inventory of Bridgman's estate there is mentioned a " Wainscott Chest." The Martin Root above mentioned was the grandchild of this couple. Mr. Eastman says that there seems to have been a family connection by marriages between the Allises of Hatfield and the Disbrowes of Hartford. It is believed that the initials E. A. stand for Elisabeth Allis and that it was a dower chest. The sunflower motive on this chest allies it somewhat with the Hartford sunflower chest. It should be remembered that the first road was the river, and that the first land road was built up and down the Connecticut river, and that the connection between the towns on the Connecticut was very close.

Captain John Allis, father of Elisabeth Allis, died in 1689, six years after Disbrowe. It is entirely possible, and perhaps we should say probable, that the chest was made by her brother, who was in business with a Belden who had married the widow of Captain Allis. These two carried on business for many years and the firm name was used for about a century, and the firm has been continued under another name to the present time. Mr. Lockwood states that Mary Allyn married in 1686; that Disbrowe was born quite probably in Walden, Essex County, England, in 1612 or 1613, and that he was the son of a joiner, and that there is a record of him in this country back to 1639. We are greatly indebted to Mr. Lockwood for his thorough search.

Our conclusion as to the whole matter of these two chests is that they antedate the other Hadley chests known, and also are far superior to them in design. We call attention to a later discussion in this book on the carving of these chests, as compared with the box No. 134 which probably antedates both of the chests.

No. 42 is one of two known three drawer Hadley chests. The owner is Mr. Harry Long of Boston and Cohasset. We speak with reservation regarding the number of these chests because the only one we have seen beside this is in the Deerfield Museum. We have, however, had a report concerning another but have not yet seen it. This piece was found near Deerfield, in excellent condition, except that it had lost the handles. A flat wooden bar was run down inside the chest in front, passing through slots in all the drawer bottoms so as to lock them. Thus one key at the top was all that was necessary. Most of the Hadley chests have their stiles beveled, another term for chamfered, on their inside faces, below the body.

The next step to three drawers would naturally have been a chest of drawers in the Hadley style. One or two have been found somewhat resembling the Hadley chest, but perhaps should not be classed under that name. The going out of carving, which occurred very shortly after the coming in of the chests of drawers, may account for this hiatus.

With this chest our review of the Hadley type ends. It has attained more prominence perhaps than it merits, yet it is an interesting example of the influences at work about the year 1700.

No. 43 is a large and extremely rare chest in that it has two rows of panels on the front. These are formed, indeed, of applied pieces on the four true oak panels. All structural parts of this chest are oak including the four back panels, except the lid which is extraordinary in its width and condition, it being formed of pine and $24\frac{1}{4}$ by $53\frac{1}{8}$ inches. The applied decoration on this chest may possibly be lacking in some particulars. It is impossible to ascertain whether there were drops on the outside stiles to match the three on the other stiles or not. Decoration of this sort, when undertaken, was usually more complete, so that the appearance is suggestive of something omitted.

The applied decoration on this chest may possibly be lacking in some and the triangular blocks of the panels, the channel molding and the applied ornaments, and even the thumb nail molding of the lid, are painted black, the panel moldings and the chamfers on the end panels are painted red.

The feet at present are only $3\frac{1}{2}$ inches long and that is probably half of what they were originally. The bottom has been nailed on so as to

86. An Oak Two-Part Chest of Drawers. 1670–80.

87. An Oak Chest of Drawers. 1670–90.

88 & 89. An Oak and a Pine Chest of Drawers. 1680 & 1720.

show on the outside, which of course was not the original construction. The legs are thus shortened an inch.

Size: 52½ by 30½ by 23⅜ inches, excluding the lid overhang.

This piece was found in Connecticut, and has been slightly restored, the original hinges being missing.

No. 44. An oak chest with the original pine lid which is, however, in very bad condition. It has the cleat pin hinge. The date is cut in the long inserted block in the bottom of the center panel. A feature of particular interest in this chest is the application of very slender drops on the panels. They appear incomplete and apparently were formed by cutting off the ball ordinarily seen at the bottom. Compare with the long drops on No. 118 and No. 203. Also compare the finely divided panel work with that on No. 118, No. 126, and No. 203. Here then we have four pieces, a chest, a chest on frame, a Bible box, and a court cupboard, all with the same miniature, long and narrow, horizontal panels, all of which probably bore small bosses, such as still appear on a part of these pieces. The presumption is that all of them were made by the same artificer. The date on No. 203 is close to that on this chest. We think the application of the miniature drops on the panels is not happy, especially as they are not fully carried out. The panel work, however, on the drawer, is attractive. The very large split turning on the leg stiles calls our attention markedly. In another piece, having a turning as large, it is shown lower down, so as more fully to simulate a leg. This chest is all of oak except the lid, drawer bottom and back, which are of yellow pine.

Size: 31 by 29½ by 19 inches, excluding the moldings and the lid of the overhang. The feet are now only 5½ inches long.

No. 45 is a very handsome chest with the side panels arched and an attractive group of four central panels with nail heads. This chest was found in southern New Hampshire where it had been for a very long period. The lid and panels are oak. It strongly resembles English chests and other chests already referred to in this connection. It has, however, been in this country long enough to become acclimated and to receive its citizenship papers. It has a very attractive beaded mold and the unusual paneling of the end is obvious.

We are continuously met by a small class of pieces like this all in oak in chests and court cupboards and sometimes in chests on frames whose origin is not precisely certain. We do not wish to be understood as maintaining the certain American origin of these pieces. We only say they are probably American.

We do not remember to have seen chests elsewhere with applied pairs of short drops between the drawers having also such drops at the ends of the drawers of a different length, as here. There is a very pleasing columnar effect secured by the long drops in conjunction with the arches. The ensemble of the chest is most attractive. It is owned by Mary M. Sampson of Boston.

Size: 48 by 31 by 21 inches.

No. 46 is a board chest, the lid of which has an applied plain bevel molding, which laps down upon the body of the chest. The initials and the elaborate rosettes are very well done, when we consider that the work is on pine. There is also a little flirt of carving on the portion of the end near the bottom, just above the break of the lines that run down to the floor.

Size: $41\frac{1}{2}$ by $26\frac{1}{2}$ by $18\frac{3}{4}$ inches.

No. 47. This chest, with the initials A. B., has the good but rare scroll on the bottom rail. The frame is of quartered oak but the panels appear to be of whitewood. The ends instead of being paneled in the usual fashion are molded horizontally at the rails which are, of course, pinned as usual. A board is then inserted between the rails in the fashion of sheathed paneling. The bottom rail is extraordinarily wide, about ten inches, and is molded to represent a rail with a skirt board. The back is a whitewood board rather than a panel. The lid is of pine.

Size: 42 by 31 by $19\frac{5}{8}$ inches.

No. 48 is a miniature chest of pine with the single arch molding. It is of much better character than the plain board pieces, owing to the heavy mold at the base and the ball feet. The owner is Mr. Arthur W. Wellington of Boston and Weston.

No. 49, owned by the Metropolitan Museum, has curious triangular blocks above the long drops. They somewhat resemble crude capitals. The heavy moldings are all stopped on the front. The distinction has been made, in this use of molding, between the stile legs and the ball-foot legs. It has been thought bad form for the molding to run around the ends of the piece in a stile foot chest. In that case No. 30 would be challenged. It certainly is very rare in the application of its moldings. In the chest before us we have the first highly specialized geometrical paneling on the upper drawer, consisting of V's running in from the ends of the drawer and from the division at the center.

No. 50 is the first ball foot chest of considerable size which we have shown. It has the further peculiarity of moldings scrolled in regular curves. It bears the initials A. D.

Owner: Mr. G. Winthrop Brown of Brookline. The long drops are

90. An Elaborately Paneled Chest of Drawers. 1680–90.

91. BALL-FOOT CHEST OF DRAWERS. 1690–1700.

92. CHEST OF DRAWERS. 1680–1700.

93. An All-Pine Chest of Drawers. 1690–1700.

94. An Oak Ball-Foot Chest of Drawers. 1680–1700.

95. A Two-Part Oak Chest of Drawers. 1680–90.

precisely similar above and below. That is, the turning motive is doubled from the center, like the stretchers of chairs.

The base mold on the ball foot chest is, in the good forms, generally heavy, as here.

No. 51 formerly owned by Mr. Brooks Reed of Boston, is, in spite of its appearance, a chest. The fact that the upper part of it simulates drawers is, of course, an indication that it was made after chests of drawers became well established. We somewhat wonder at this system of ornament, because the earlier plan, as in the chests previously considered, seems in better taste. The drawer element seems to predominate in the mind of the maker and he carries his decoration to the top as he had begun from the bottom. The early fashion, however, of ending the between-drawer molds on the front, obtains here. It will be seen also that the true bottom drawer and the top false drawer are alike and that the second false drawer is molded with sufficient heaviness to give a blocked appearance. The back legs of the chest are in the ancient fashion formed by a continuation of the frame, and are otherwise called stile legs. The front feet are somewhat clumsy but probably indicate an early period.

No. 52 is a chest belonging to Mr. H. W. Erving. It has three panel ends. As appears, it has no rail beneath the drawer. This is an unusual form as is the chest below it. Nevertheless we find it in some of the oldest pieces, notably in the Parmenter court cupboard, No. 195. The feet are somewhat abbreviated.

Size: $45\frac{1}{2}$ by $24\frac{1}{2}$ by $18\frac{1}{4}$ inches.

No. 53 is another chest belonging to Mr. H. W. Erving. It has the usual oak frame, but pine panels, with a raised panel in the end. Whether this is a mark of a later date we do not yet feel certain. In any case the raised panel is rare. We have, however, found it on an oak cradle of the very earliest period. It seems to have been considered an unnecessary thing. Of course it strengthened the panel by making it thicker and improved the appearance of the chest at the same time.

Size: $41\frac{3}{4}$ by $28\frac{1}{4}$ by $18\frac{1}{2}$ inches. The difference between the hight of this and the preceding is seen to be chiefly in the legs, those on this chest being the proper length.

No. 54 is a plainer chest than any we have hitherto featured. All the panels, including the three at the back, are of oak. The lid is of pine and is seemingly original. It is molded on the front only. The stiles in the back were not smoothed at all after riving. This is the first instance we have seen of this kind, though leaving the backs of the back panels rough, as in this case, was common enough. Some question has been raised in relation to the chamfering of the legs. What purpose was conserved by thus cutting them away is not apparent, but the cut is very old and some good judges have thought it original. This chest affords an interesting opportunity to study the decoration around the panels. It will be seen that the top rail-molding, against the panel, fades away as it approaches the inside stile. Thus over the central panel it fades away at both ends. This construction is always a mark of early work.

Size: 47 by 29 by 20½ inches.

No. 55 is an oddly molded oak chest. The owner is Mr. Dwight Blaney of Boston and Weston. All the oak of this chest is quartered including the panels. The drawer is peculiar in that the top and bottom of it are so constructed as to blend with the repeated moldings, and to hide its outline. We do not remember another chest with so much of repetition in the molding. The effect is interesting.

No. 56 belongs to Mr. H. W. Erving. It shows no very great deviation in style from some that have preceded it. Instead, however, of the turned drops flanking the drawer and dividing it in the center, we have sets of triglyphs matching those on the top rail. The effect of so many of these ornaments is to increase the apparent hight of the chest.

The moldings are of Spanish cedar. There are two panels in the ends. The quartering of the panels shows with fine effect. The blocks when placed around the panels, as here, are called center side blocks, as distinguished from corner blocks. They are, of course, always applied.

Size: 45½ by 33 by 20½ inches.

No. 57 is the first example we have given of an oak six-board chest. Its plainness is relieved by the gouge carving at the ends of the molded front. The molding on the joints in front is similar to that of the earliest wall sheathing. The chest was formerly owned by Koopman's, Boston.

No. 58 is the first example to be considered wherein the oak stile feet are cut off slightly below the frame, and continued with ball feet. This construction, while unusual, is not unique. Another feature of interest in this chest is the application of thin blocks surrounded by molding in the center of the panels, as bases on which to impose the turtle backs.

The turtle backs on the upper rail are of odd shapes and we think no better on that account. The diagonal setting of the turtle backs on the drawer should be observed.

Owner: Mr. G. Winthrop Brown, of Brookline.

No. 59 is a small, somewhat late board chest, with carving more in the style of the Sheraton period than anything we have hitherto shown. We presume the carving to be original although it is very unusual on chests. The central decoration is quite similar to that on a corner cup-

96. WALNUT CHEST OF DRAWERS. 1690–1700.

97. LITTLE CHEST OF DRAWERS. 1700–10.

98. An Oak and Walnut Chest of Drawers. 1690–1700.

99. Oak and Pine Chest of Drawers. 1690–1700.

board of unmistakable early character. We do not pretend to the capacity of being able to ascertain in every instance whether carving is recent or ancient. It is probably the most difficult of all questions, when the imitation is well done. Far better men than the writer have been grievously deceived in this matter. Brushes are used to give the grain of the carving an aged effect. One coat after another of paint is applied, then perhaps washed off in part.

Size: 32 by $14\frac{3}{4}$ by $12\frac{3}{8}$ inches.

No. 60 is a chest belonging to Mr. Dwight Blaney. The large applied turnings on the leg stiles are almost identical in style, size and placement with those on No. 44, though the smaller drops are different from that chest. They appear, however, to be more in harmony with the large end drops. This chest is left in an unrestored condition. It is obvious that at one time there were moldings on the drawer.

No. 61 is owned by Mr. H. W. Erving. The channel or shadow molds are strongly emphasized as was the intention, being painted black originally and properly. The end panels are supplied with blocks to give the effect of Greek crosses, whereas the central panel has triangular blocks forming an octagon. The entire front is of strongly featured oak. There are two panel ends.

Size: 43 by 31 by $20\frac{1}{2}$ inches.

No. 62 is a highly decorated chest. The owner is Mrs. Hulings Cowperthwaite Brown, of Boston and Brookline. The chest was inherited from the Waters Estate. The ball feet are somewhat smaller than is usual. The paneling is very odd, especially at the sides. The application of the turtle backs on the top rail seems odd and we are led to wonder whether or not there may not have been others. Perhaps the effect, however, is as good in the form in which the piece stands.

No. 63 is a chest with highly featured oak, and excellent ball feet. This chest was found with fourteen of the sixteen original ornaments in place. The paneling of the drawer is peculiar and gives the appearance of two miniature drawers at the ends. The design of the middle panel should be observed. Usually the small oblong divisions were at the bottom of the middle panel.

It will be noticed that no ornaments whatever are applied on the top rail. This may be owing to the unusual beauty of the oak in that member. The feet are of flattened balls almost in the onion shape, technically so called.

No. 64 is an all pine chest with turnip feet. This is a term roughly applied to most ball feet, but we think it more appropriate when there is a small necking above the ball as here. The feet behind are simple continuations of the boards. The single arch molding we consider arbitrarily as ten years earlier than the double arch molding. All parts of this chest are original.

Size: 35 by 39 by 17½ inches.

No. 65 is an amazing example of reversion to an earlier period. While the date is very plainly marked as 1776, some of the features of this chest would have been appropriate a hundred and fifty years before that date. This remark applies to the architectural arch. The great extent of the imbricated carving is also startling, as is the highly elaborate double rosette at the top of the side stiles. The bracket also belongs to an earlier period. As we recollect this chest it is in walnut. It belongs to Mr. Stanley A. Sweet of New York City.

No. 66 is our first example of a chest with complete painted decoration.

The owner is Mr. H. W. Erving, who purchased the chest when it was entirely covered with a thick coat of brown paint, which was very old. He carefully removed this paint, and the figures as seen here all came out, and have simply been touched up line for line with absolute fidelity. An interesting circumstance has been brought out by the removal of this protective coating of paint. That is the great brilliancy of the original coloring. It has often been supposed that the reds and greens on these old pieces were soft. They were quite the reverse. Our ancestors had so little color in their lives that they were somewhat lavish of it on their furniture. The truth obliges us to state this fact, although it proves that their taste in design was better than their taste in color.

As retraced the painting on this fascinating little chest teaches us several things. The background appears black but is a few shades off, rather green-black.

We have noted in other pieces that the black will change to bottle green. The thistle blossoms and buds and crown are most intense and varied centers of color. They are to be compared with the decorated chest of drawers No. 100, and the bird on the end should be compared with that on No. 71.

The material on these decorated chests or chests of drawers is usually of whitewood, at least on the front. In some instances they are pine on the ends and the lid is of course generally pine. We shall later discuss their connection with Moravian furniture. Their origin is Connecticut, on the Sound, perhaps twenty miles east and west of New Haven. Our present example was a miniature.

Size: 25¼ by 19 by 16¼ inches.

No. 67 is a new feature in chests to be considered. Although it is

100. Decorated Whitewood Chest of Drawers. 1690–1700.

101. Little Pine Chest of Drawers. 1700–20.

102. END OF CHEST No. 99.

oak it is decorated. The inadequacy of photography does not show clearly the design which covers the panels and the drawer front. The chest is from Branford, Connecticut, and is owned by Mr. George Dudley Seymour. The painting is evidently imitative of contemporary English imitations of lacquer work, brought into England from the far East. The end panels are in a thistle down design. The central panel bears the painted date. The chest is now in the Wadsworth Atheneum, Hartford.

Size: 48½ by 32¾ by 20½ inches, including the lid overhang.

No. 68 is a chest belonging to the estate of Mr. George F. Ives. The chest has lost its feet, but is otherwise in good condition. The painting is distinctively different from the designs we have hitherto shown. It exhibits a considerable freedom and no small degree of artistry. It will be seen that the base carries much the same design as the portion immediately under the lid. Apparently to give room for a handsome spray between the drawer panels, the latter were set very far apart.

There is a large tulip on the ends as on No. 102.

Size: 42 by 40 by 20 inches, to which we should add about 4 inches for the original hight.

No. 69 brings us back to another painted oak chest. This piece has lost its drawer. Its great oddity is the ball feet attached to the extended stiles. Another unusual feature is the raised panel at the ends. The chest was found in New England, painted a heavy red. When this was removed quaint tree decoration was found on the side panels, and on the central panel what appear to be painted imitations of bosses. The numerous channel molds are all black and so are the small moldings applied around the front and end panels. The back has one large panel of pine. The front and end panels and the original lid are of pine.

Size: 43 by 30¾ by 18⅞ inches. The length of the leg below the end rail is 6¼ inches including the ball, and the ball is 3 inches to the extended stile.

No. 70 is another oak chest with decorations. In this case they are of the sort called sunburst, and appear on the front panels only. Instead of a molding around the drawer there are a black and a red stripe dividing the drawer into two painted panels. There are two long vertical end panels. The panels are oak, including the single long horizontal panel behind. This chest came from Connecticut, and, like many from that neighborhood, has a bead on the front of the lid, rather than the thumb nail mold on three sides.

Size: 43 by 22 by 20½ inches. The stile feet are now 6 inches long.

No. 71 is another painted whitewood chest which belongs to the state of Connecticut and is in the Stone House, at Guilford. The decoration on the upper panel is very like that on one of the drawers on No. 101. The frame is of oak.

Nos. 72 and 73 are miniature pine pieces. No. 72, on the left, has two little drawers and the single arch molding. The lid is 19 by 13 inches. It is 16¾ inches high.

No. 73, the other chest, with the heavy base mold, ball feet and double arch molding, is a successful effort to secure good style with simple material.

Size: The top is 23 by 13¾ inches. It is 20 inches high. Both pieces are owned by Mr. Chauncey C. Nash of Milton and Cohasset.

No. 74 is a most interesting example, because it continues the tradition of oak for a material and carving for a decoration, but in its construction is a six board chest.

The carving on the drawers is fluting. The three hearts carved over the elaborate lunette, and indeed interfering with them, seem like an afterthought. They probably indicate that the chest was a dowry piece.

All the moldings are carried around the ends, a feature very rare in this method of construction. This chest was bought in Boston, but was probably found in Connecticut, the discoverer not being living to verify that statement. The piece was formerly in the B. A. Behrend collection. The year given as the date is carved on the till.

Owned now by Pennsylvania Museum.

No. 75 is a small decorated piece of pine. It will be observed that, curiously enough, the decorator carried his scrolls across the whole front ignoring the drawer divisions. We find here the much loved and often repeated tulip blossom. On the bottom drawer, however, the designer became more ambitious and sketched two birds which we may fondly hope are doves.

The piece belongs to the southern Connecticut type.

Owner: Mr. Chauncey C. Nash.

No. 76 is owned by Mr. G. Winthrop Brown of Brookline. It is another example of a six board oak chest, carved. It has elaborate lunettes resembling but not identical with those on No. 74. There is also a band of imbricated carving below the top section, and a " pencil and pearl " decoration just above the drawer. There is also immediately under the lid a plain serration which suggests the Plymouth chest. At the ends of the front we have the quite usual gouge carving. Whether this was easier to work than a mold, or for what reason it is so frequent, we do not know.

The drawer of this chest is pulled by reaching under the front, so that it requires no knob. This omission of a rail below the drawer, while a rare feature, is, nevertheless, found on some of the oldest cabinet pieces.

103.   A Flemish-Legged Highboy.   1680–1700.

104. A Painted Highboy. 1700–10.

105. A Five-Legged Highboy. 1690–1710.

106. A BUTTERNUT HIGHBOY. 1690–1710.

Size: 28¾ by 23¾ by 18 inches. While we have not the dimensions of No. 74, that chest also is small.

No. 77 marks the transition to the plain chests of the eighteenth century, but it has not quite reached their perfect simplicity of design. It has more pleasing lines. A single arch molding is also carried out throughout. It is owned by Mr. G. Winthrop Brown.

No. 78 is most unusual in that the ends as well as the front are carved. The carving is simple but effective. We have on the lower panels a starfish design, which is merely a variant of the Gothic wheel window. The other carving, principally in discs or semi-circles, predominates. The serrated motive, doubled so as to form a zigzag ribbon, appears on the top and the bottom rail and the outside stiles, and the single serration under the lid on the ends, whereas the rest of the ends follow in general the decoration of the front. Two other oddities of this chest are its framing. It is mortised entirely through the front stiles, the ends of the tenons frankly appearing. The lid, also, is fixed in position in the rear and breaks with the movable portion in a grooved joint. Thus the chest has no hinge, but when unhasped the front was lifted as usual. The piece was found in southern Connecticut, and most of the material is yellow pine.

Size: 42⅛ by 30¾ by 18 inches. The legs are 6½ inches long. The front of the lid is formed by a band vertically thicker than the rest of the lid, for what purpose does not appear.

No. 79 is a simple chest of interesting construction. It has the scrolled bracket end. A slight effort at decoration has been made. The front is sheathed with boards molded at their matching in the manner of the best early house sheathing. There are also brackets between the frame and the ends. They indicate the survival of an earlier style and add much to the chest. The lid has the most elongated thumb nail molding we have seen. The original lock seems to be in position.

Origin: New England. Size: 49 by 24 by 17 inches. The material is all yellow pine.

No. 80 presents an interesting variation from the ordinary pine chest in its circular central panel, and in side panels carved to correspond. It is to be observed in this and many other interesting instances that the panels were carved in the solid wood, and are therefore only simulated. Thus what began in joined furniture as a structural feature was, when the age of paneling passed away, sometimes retained as we see it here.

Owner: Mr. George Dudley Seymour.

Size: 48½ by 23 by 17 inches, including the lid. The chest was found in the Captain Charles Churchill house, Newington, Connecticut. The original coat of red paint is intact.

No. 81 is a pine chest relieved from plainness by the oddity of the shoes upon which it rests, by the projected base and by the gouge carving at the corners. It also has scratch carving, running around the front, which is scarcely discernible in our picture, on the left side. The owner is Mr. George Dudley Seymour.

No. 82 is a style known to exist in at least three examples. Its marked peculiarity is the heavily blocked central portion of the panel ornamentation. The panels are painted black, as are also the incised (channel) moldings on the rails and stiles. The applied moldings are painted red. A peculiarity is the running of the molding on the outside stiles down through the width of the drawer. The chest here shown was formerly in the collection of Mr. George Dudley Seymour and is now owned by Miss Mary Miles Lewis Peck, of Bristol, Connecticut. It is an heirloom of the Lewis family of Farmington. It was found in Bristol, an offset of the town of Farmington, by Mr. Seymour, about 1895.

Another chest almost precisely like this is in the author's collection and a third was found by Mr. Seymour in 1920. The three chests appear to have been made by the same hand.

The material in every case is of whitewood, the close grain of which was well adapted for decoration, and more highly regarded than pine.

No. 83 is a chest with numerous small panels similar to overmantel decoration. The middle panel is relieved by three flutes. The brackets of this stile, while they survive for an earlier period, frequently appear on early eighteenth century chests of the better class.

The owner is Mr. Edward C. Wheeler, Jr. of Boston.

No. 84 and the larger chest under it, No. 85, are doubtless intended to go together, and were perhaps made for a mother and child. Or perhaps the more valuable articles were kept in the smaller piece. There is one drawer in each chest, the other drawers being simulated. The scroll board at the bottom, variously called the skirt or valance, is a feature which always adds a good deal to furniture, if the style permits it, as here. These pieces are owned by Mr. George Dudley Seymour, and are at present in the Wadsworth Atheneum at Hartford.

The size of No. 84 is $20\frac{1}{2}$ by 17 by $11\frac{1}{2}$ inches, including the lid. The size of No. 85 is $28\frac{1}{2}$ by $24\frac{1}{2}$ by 13 inches, including the lid.

With these chests we conclude the examination of this subject except for the two chests appearing on the last page of this volume. We believe every well known type of American chest is represented, as well as many others that are too rare to be reckoned in any class.

107. A Cross-Stretcher Highboy. 1710-20.

108. HERRING-BONE WALNUT HIGHBOY. 1690–1710.

109. A Herring-Bone Walnut Highboy. 1700–10.

110. HERRING-BONE WALNUT HIGHBOY. 1690–1710.

CHESTS OF DRAWERS

THESE are neither so important, so early nor so good as the chests. In their period also they are not so numerous. This is accounted for by the fact that chests of drawers no sooner began to come in, in the form in which they evolved from chests, than the high chest of drawers was developed. This style, otherwise called the highboy, prevented the further development of the low chest of drawers. It is impossible to say now when the first oak chest was made in America. We can estimate the date within about a score of years. We find them about 1660. The style seems to have followed the oak chest as known among us, for about thirty years. It is a far more convenient article of furniture than is a chest.

No. 86 represents such a chest of drawers owned by Mr. George Dudley Seymour. We feel, however, that the brasses on this chest make the date we have assigned to it at least ten years too early. A peculiarity in the piece is that it is made in two parts and is separable at the center, being kept from slipping out of place by dowels, as well as by the molding, originally.

This separation should be covered by a molding. The piece is shown as it was found in the rough state without the molding. It is said that the piece was brought into Boston from Dedham. It was put in order by Patrick Stevens, then employed by Robbins Bros., of Hartford.

Size: $56\frac{3}{4}$ by $38\frac{3}{4}$ by $20\frac{1}{2}$ inches, including the overhang.

It will be seen that the hight is such as would naturally develop from a chest.

No. 87 was in the Waters collection. The extraordinary amount of ornament upon it is typical of a good number of pieces made as the seventeenth century drew to its close. It will be seen that the first and third drawer are alike in ornament, also the second and fourth, on the end panels. But even here there is a variance in the central panel. It will be noticed that No. 86 had a two-panel end, whereas this has a four-panel end. The drops on this piece are incorrect, and have now been changed.

The molding in the very top element suggests that on a Plymouth chest. The panels in front are all of oak.

Size: 46 by 43¾ by 21¾ inches.

No. 88 is a chest of drawers in which all the panels are oak including the two vertically long back panels, and the end panels. The drawer bottoms are pine, as is also the lid but the backs of the drawers are riven oak. The molding immediately under the lid is a series of close set dentils. They are really not much wider, in the openings between them, than saw cuts. The large moldings on the front are cut off square and do not return. The piece is agreeably small. It was found in eastern Massachusetts in 1922.

Size: 30 by 36 by 20 inches.

No. 89 is a little table chest of drawers, all of pine. The heavy moldings give it character and dignity. The drawers show an interesting increase of depth from the top to the bottom one. This is the first piece we have shown with the overlapping drawer front, a mark of the coming in of eighteenth century work. The drops are not original. All other parts are original.

Size: 15 by 23½ by 10 inches. These dimensions do not include the very broad base which is 19 by 11½ inches.

No. 90 is an oak chest of drawers formerly owned by Mr. Brooks Reed. No one can say that the front is monotonous. The top and the bottom drawers, which are alike, are very boldly blocked. The other two drawers are narrow and also are alike. The stiles are treated by applied moldings, as a series of small panels. The heavy moldings are returned on the front. It would appear that the base should have had a molding.

The end panel is built up with a series of moldings together with a central block on which a boss is affixed, resembling a chest we have already treated.

No. 91 is an oak chest of drawers, the top and bottom members of which resemble those in the chest of drawers just discussed, except that they are somewhat lighter in effect.

The piece was found in Connecticut, and came immediately from the Henry Stearns collection.

One mark of a somewhat later date than the chests hitherto treated is the square stile legs. Previously we have had them larger and in a flat section.

There is an amusing variance between the huge foot and the small stile. We have shown this fashion in one or two earlier examples. The front panels, the large end panel, the single long horizontal back panel, and the lid are of yellow pine. The end panel is heavily blocked in the fashion called bolection molding, and resembles one or two already

III. SMALL DRAWER HIGHBOY. 1690–1710.

112. A Simple Highboy, without Stretchers. 1720.

113. Curly Maple Highboy. 1710–20.

114. A Simple Five-Legged Highboy. 1690–1710.

treated. The moldings are painted red, and the blocks and feet black. The piece has been restored to a considerable degree.

Size: 39¾ by 38 by 19¾ inches.

No. 92 is a chest of drawers the picture of which is furnished by Mr. H. V. Weil of New York City. The end panel is raised and has bolection moldings. The ball feet are attached in the more usual manner directly to the frame. The piece is not a miniature, but, by accident, is shown on a small scale.

No. 93 is an all pine chest of drawers formerly owned by Koopman's, Boston. While it is made of boards instead of being framed it has many of the features of the earlier period. The end terminates at the bottom with a series of scrolled openings reminding one of Gothic arches. The heavy single arch molding is prominent. We would presume that it had lost such part of the feet as would naturally be missing through attrition. We have here the first chest of drawers in which all the drawers are alike. The style of dividing drawer fronts in this fashion is called geometric molding.

No. 94 is an oak chest of drawers owned by Mr. George Dudley Seymour. The center panel on the top drawer contains the initials R.B. The center panel of the drawer below has the initials A.P. The chest ends are two panels separated by the returned ends of an applied molding extending between the two upper and the two lower drawers. The other applied moldings between the drawers do not follow around the end. The ball feet again are attached to extended stiles. The single set of triglyphs seem a trifle lonely. Is it possible that the piece bore others on the stiles?

Size: 45½ by 32 by 20 inches, including the overhang.

No. 95 is a two part chest which has the molding to cover the joints of division. The owner is the estate of J. Milton Coburn, M. D.

The applied ball-turned molding is an odd feature. The decorated moldings on the second and fourth drawers are more conventional but perhaps not as gracefully arranged as we usually find them.

With No. 96 we reach the first object shown in this volume in walnut. The age of walnut in England began somewhat earlier than in America. This is a case where walnut was used with an oak stile, rather than in the turned stile. This attractive little chest has the stiles divided into small panels as was the case with No. 90. The four drawers are all alike. There are two end panels side by side, vertically. The piece has undergone some repairs. The handles are not original.

Size: 38¼ by 33½ by 21 inches.

No. 97 is an attractive little quaint piece, the photograph of which is furnished by Mr. H. V. Weil. The handles of course are of the size usual for a large chest of drawers and therefore display humorously the contrast between the size of the drawers and the handles. The single arch mold, the heavy base mold, and the ball feet establish the date.

No. 98 is another chest of drawers in which the frame is oak, and most other parts walnut. Thus we see the transition between the two woods. The top is half inch walnut. The frame and the end rails are of oak. The end panels are of pine, there being two, one above the other, sunken, with perfectly plain rails and stiles. The drawer fronts are pine covered with an eighth of an inch walnut veneer, and all the moldings are of walnut. The piece has the groove side runs on the drawers, indicating a date not later than 1700. The feet are pieced and are in the small square section of the somewhat late chest of drawers, which followed the analogy otherwise of the oak chests of drawers.

Size: 36 by 33 by 22 inches. The moldings project to give an over all length, top and bottom, of 39 inches.

No. 99 is an oak and pine chest of drawers in the former collection of the author. The width of the stiles is quite noticeable, but there was no evidence of drops ever having been applied. It is impossible, however, in every case, to know whether there should be drops or not. Fifty years or so after such a chest was made some of the drops would naturally try to justify their name. When part of such ornaments were gone, it was common to eliminate all of them, and to refinish the piece. As they were ordinarily applied by glue, there is now no means of knowing except by analogy, whether drops orginally existed.

The most interesting feature of this piece is its excellent ring drop handles and rosette plate and 'scutcheons.

No. 100 exhibits for the first time the full development of the painted decoration. The front of this piece is in whitewood, the ends and lid and drawer interiors are pine. The frame is of oak. The two short drawers at the top are identical in decoration and attractive enough, had not the artist essayed the conceit of a human face, into the lips of which is caught the stem of a spray of blossoms. The three long drawers are each decorated with separate motives. The flower pot design, in the drawer above the bottom drawer, is found, with some variation, on the Pennsylvania German pieces, the inspiration of which very likely came from Moravia. In Moravia we find the same flower pot motive, used on a very great number of pieces. The design on the bottom drawer is that already shown on a chest. We have the thistle blossom surmounted by a crown. At the right is the rose and at the center the fleur-de-lis with

115. Sycamore and Applewood Highboy. 1690–1700.

116. ARCH-AND-STAR CHEST-ON-FRAME. 1670–80.

117.   A Carved Chest-on-frame.   1670–90.

118. Small-Panel Chest-on-frame. 1690–1700.

the crown. These arms of England evidently have nothing to do with Moravia. They are a kind of patriotic expression.

The end panel is boldly done in a very large tulip stem surmounted by a fully opened blossom, under which there depend, one on either side, a large bud. The importance and the interest of the tulip bud and blossom as a motive for hundreds of years can hardly be overestimated. In Holland the national flower was the natural object to delineate on furniture. We have seen the tulip carved on all the so-called Hadley chests and on the sunflower chests. It will appear later in household hardware form, latches, hinges, etc. This piece of furniture has its painting in better condition, and, on the whole, is rather more elaborate, than any other to which our attention has been called. The drawers are made in the early style, with side runs. The feet have been pieced about three inches. The piece is otherwise original.

Relating to whitewood as a material, it is perhaps more attractive when it is called tulip wood. This wood is commonly found in New England, and for fifty years has been a cheap commercial finish wood. The tree grows to a lofty stature, and excites wonder in European botanists who visit us, and find a flowering tree of such size. The wood is semi-hard, of close grain, and none that is apparent. It is therefore a good material for decoration. It is an odd coincidence that the tulip should have been painted so much upon tulip wood.

Reverting to the coloring, the border tendrils are nearly white. The flowers are in shades of yellow, old red, pink, etc. The sprays and foliage are very delicate, and are done by an assured hand. Birds appear facing one another, on the outer leaves of the fleur-de-lis. Their necks are long. Let us call them pheasants. We note a tendency, as we approach 1700, to raised panels in the ends of cabinet pieces, although we find occasionally a raised panel, as in a cradle to be shown, of a date a great deal earlier. Also we notice a tendency to flatten out the curves of the base molds until eventually we get the mere bevel, such as appears in No. 98.

We notice also the substitution of brass drop handles for the wooden knobs, in all classes of furniture except tables.

Size: 42 by 43 by 19 inches.

No. 101 is a little board chest of drawers of the Harry Long collection. These little pieces are sometimes called child's chests of drawers. The end handle perhaps indicates that the piece was set upon a larger one.

No. 102 is the end view of No. 100 and has been discussed.

HIGHBOYS

THE highboy, called in England a tallboy, is merely a chest of drawers set on a frame. Wherever a sense of style works strongly it immediately tends to an extreme, as some of us have noticed in relation to feminine apparel.

No sooner did the feeling of discomfort, at stooping over chests, get well into the blood of the people of 1700, than they began to place their chests upon legs. They then made so many drawers in their chests and the legs so long, that they were obliged to stand on stools to get into the upper drawers. The highboy in some form or other reigned supreme for eighty odd years. It was matched by the lowboy, which is only another name for a dressing table. The chests of drawers had answered for dressing tables to some extent when they were low. The highboy and the lowboy therefore went together to form a proper complement for a chamber. The highboy was longer, higher and deeper even as regards its frame, than was the lowboy. At the present time there are a large number of highboy bases being shown as lowboys. It is only necessary to sit down at one to learn that it is not of a convenient hight as a dressing table. Furthermore, the lowboys, with only one exception that we know, were so built that it was possible for the knees to go under the table, as they could not do in the five or six legged highboy style.

As the feeling for style passed out it was the custom, throughout the nineteenth century, to divide a highboy between two daughters, of whom the one took the top and the other the bottom. It was almost as bad as Solomon's proposed division of the baby. The parts certainly are incongruous and unrelated, and are neither one of them worth more than half of a baby.

Slowly and painfully the effort is now being made to reassemble the separated units. Negotiation, following search, and sometimes litigation following negotiation, goes on, to bring the lost members into place again.

In No. 103 we show a highboy supposed to be of American oak. The base scrolls following the Flemish design seem to be bass wood. Poplar is also sometimes used. There is another highboy of this style in Connecticut, and a third in the collection of Mr. Luke Vincent Lock-

119. SPRAY DECORATED CHEST-ON-FRAME. 1690–1700.

120. TURNED CHEST-ON-FRAME. 1690–1700.

121.   SPOOL-TURNED CHEST-ON-FRAME.   1680–1700.

122. BALL-TURNED CHEST-ON-FRAME. 1690–1700.

wood. We have also recently seen an English importation of such a piece.

The clumsy heavy scrolls of the chest suggest the inspiration of the awkward, nineteenth century, degraded Empire style.

With the exception of the cap board this piece is original.

The age of highboys is indicated in part by the frame on which they stand; in part by their moldings and in part by the woods of which they are constructed.

The five legged pieces are more rare than those with six legs. Those with four legs are still more rare than either. We do not know that there is any special merit or value of one style over another, as far as the number of the legs is concerned.

The long drawer in the frame is the mark of an early type, it being the survival of the chest fashion. The piece before us has a flush drawer. That is to say, the face board of the drawer has no lip or rabbet projecting over, and covering, the joints on the frame.

The name highboy was doubtless a sly joke at the stilted appearance of these pieces of furniture. These pieces began with flat tops and we show no other type. The "bonnet top" came in with the cabriole leg about 1720. For that reason the so-called six-legged highboys are more in request, although they are not as decorative, at least at the top. This lack of design in form was made up largely by the beauty of the walnut or maple veneer so common on this class of furniture. Steps to hold a display of pewter or other ware, were often placed on these flat tops.

It will be observed that the frame or base of the highboy invariably extends considerably beyond the top. A wide and heavy mold was applied at the edge of this base, to afford a framed enclosure to receive the top.

The piece before us probably originated in Connecticut.

Size: $39\frac{1}{8}$ by $21\frac{3}{4}$ inches, on the body of the frame; 37 by $19\frac{7}{8}$ inches on the body of the top. The hight is 48 inches over all. The moldings extend these dimensions $2\frac{1}{4}$ inches in length and $1\frac{1}{4}$ inches in width.

No. 104 is a painted highboy with something the same decoration as appeared on No. 101. In fact the more closely we study this decoration the more we do find points of connection. The bad lighting is such as not to show the tulip end, which is like No. 101. The piece belongs to Mr. James Davidson of New London. We have lacquered highboys though we question if they are American. We do not remember another painted highboy.

No. 105 shows a five-legged highboy belonging to Mr. Chauncey C. Nash. It is in walnut. In this piece we have the first instance of the so-called chased handles, which are intermediate between the drop handle and the willow pattern of the later Chippendale time. It is a popular notion that the decorations on these brasses are tooled by a graver. Those who have studied the subject carefully, state that the ornaments are a part of the casting.

We have in this piece the single long drawer of the early type.

No. 106 represents a butternut highboy, in the single arch pattern. This term "single arch" is simply the description of the half round edge cut on or applied to the frame around the drawers. The backs, the lid, and the interior of the drawers of these pieces, are pine in this case and generally. The pine is sometimes yellow, sometimes white. The legs are frequently of a lighter and cheaper material than the rest of the piece. The size, on the frame is $25\frac{1}{2}$ by $26\frac{1}{2}$ by $20\frac{1}{2}$ inches, excluding the molding. The top is $33\frac{3}{4}$ by $29\frac{1}{2}$ by $19\frac{1}{8}$ inches, excluding the molding. The total hight is about 56 inches, therefore. This piece was found in New Hampshire in 1922.

No. 107 is a cross stretcher highboy, in the former collection of the author. The incipient pair of legs is represented by the acorn drops. The turnings here have a pleasing flare, and are called trumpet turnings, in distinction from the piece last shown where they are called cup or bowl turnings, from a resemblance to an inverted cup, at the top of the main turning.

This highboy and most of those that follow it have a thin lining mold, attached to the curves of the scroll, and projecting with a half round edge, very slightly.

The higher arch of the center between the pointed arches of the side, is to be observed as a type.

No. 108 is a highboy with a border, around every drawer, of herringbone veneer, the central portion of the drawer being filled with walnut burl veneer. The turning is not so delicate as the preceding one. It was bought in Boston.

As distinct from the preceding which has no molding at all, this has a double arch molding. In the frame there is here the single drawer with three identical arches below it.

It was in the author's former collection.

No. 109 is a highboy with similar veneer to that on No. 108. The piece is in very fine condition and has the three top drawers, the central drawer being a little longer than the side drawers. Compare this with the two drawers in the top of No. 108, the three drawers of equal length in No. 107. Also note that in this case the drawers are flush. The dating is probably a little late, since the flush drawer was the earlier.

123. SPRAY DECORATED CHEST-ON-FRAME. 1690–1700.

124. INITIALED OAK CHEST-ON-FRAME. 1680–90.

125. Lunette-Rosette Box. 1670–90.

126. Oak Box with Panels and Drops. 1680–1700.

127. Plain Oak Desk-Box. 1680–90.

128. A Pond Lily Box, Raised Carving. 1670–90.

129. Double Lunette Table Chest. 1660–70.

130. Carved Oak Box. 1660–90.

Size: Over all, 42½ by 62 by 23 inches. Size of upper frame: 37 by 30¾ by 20¼ inches.

No. 110 belongs to Mr. Edward C. Wheeler, Jr. It is one of the most beautifully preserved pieces we have seen, every part being original and the veneer in fine condition. It is in the herringbone pattern. Having a flush drawer it is early. This piece has never been cleaned.

Size: The frame is 38½ by 21½ inches in length and depth. The upper section is 36½ by 20 inches. The total hight is 61 inches. The outside front of the frame mold is 40½ inches, and 22¼ inches from front to back.

No. 111. This is the only highboy we have seen with two small end-to-end drawers over the central arch. The scheme of the drawers should be examined in all these pieces. The conventional type is supposed to have three drawers in the frame — deep drawers on the sides and a shallow drawer in the center.

As to the origin of highboys in this walnut veneer type, we are more likely to find it here than in Pennsylvania. The supposition that Pennsylvania is the home of the walnut highboy should be understood as meaning solid walnut, which of course is found there and in the South. The turnings in this piece are beautiful, the flare of the post being very marked.

The piece is further distinguished from those we have hitherto considered by its torus mold under the cap mold.

No. 112 is a simple highboy which we feel certain is original. It differs from those we have seen by being a little later in date, and in the omission of stretchers. In other words it is simplified. Its button-like feet indicate turnings of the later Queen Anne type. This piece was found by Mrs. E. B. Leete of Guilford, Connecticut.

No. 113 is possibly a country made highboy. It belongs to the estate of George F. Ives. The ring turning on the drops is odd. The curly maple of which it is constructed is a beautiful wood, a little later in its use than walnut, but paralleling the later walnut period, and continuing well on in the century. Of course, the legs have not the boldness of turning which we should desire. We have here also a cross stretcher such as appears in the lowboy.

No. 114. This simple piece is a fascinating example made perhaps by the village cabinet maker. It has the plain long drawer and there are no arches on the frame. The five legs are an effort to adapt the table frame style to the highboy style. We hardly know how to account for the variations in styles unless it was that the makers did not have the conventional patterns available. Then it was that their ingenuity displayed itself in original adaptations which are now sought after.

Owner: Miss Mabel Choate, of New York and Stockbridge.

No. 115 exhibits a highboy belonging to Mr. Horatio H. Armstrong of West Hartford. It is of sycamore and apple wood, an unusual but very agreeable combination, since sycamore is a very beautiful furniture wood. Apple also turns to a hard and smooth surface and takes a polish like ebony. Here the single long drawer below, the flush drawers, and the single arch molding indicate an early date. The arches, as in single drawer pieces for the most part, are alike. The turnings are differentiated considerably from those usually seen.

131. ROPE SCROLLED TRIPLE ROSETTE BOX. 1670–90.

132. HADLEY BOX. 1670–90.

133. PINE AND OAK ROSETTE BOX. 1690–1710.

134. Hadley Box Carved in the Round. 1670–90.

135. Pine Ball Foot Box. 1690–1700.

136. Double Fluted Oak Box. 1660–90.

137a. Miniature Box. 1700. 137b. Foliated Box. 1670–90.

138. Foliated Scroll Oak Box. 1670–90.

139. Carved Tulip Box. 1670–90.

140. Foliated Scroll Oak Box. 1670–90.

SMALL CHESTS–ON–FRAMES

THESE alluring little pieces of furniture excite our interest partly because they are small. Any miniature piece of furniture is like a child of the human species. We seem to love it more. Another element of interest is the greater or less degree of mystery which surrounds these pieces. We refer to the long continued discussion as to their purpose. Again they win upon us owing to their intrinsic merits and beauty. Last of all their rarity of course excites the average collector.

These pieces have been called almost everything from pulpits to washstands. We must deny that they were either of these. Nor do we feel that it is the thing to call them desks-on-frames. They are always, so far as we know, found with flat tops. There are desks-on-frames containing cabinets and surrounded with no mystery. One of the pieces to follow was called a tabernacle table, by the three generations whose word we have for it. These pieces are quite different from the boxes that follow in that those boxes never have drawers as far as we have observed. Some of the chests-on-frames, however, have been found with removable tops, so that, if taken away from their original stands, they are precisely like the boxes discussed in the next chapter. Ordinarily, the frame of these pieces, for they all have frames, passes up through the base and the box, making a unit of the whole piece, so that it may not be taken apart. Like other furniture these chests-on-frames were unquestionably used for more than one purpose. As side tables in the dining room they would have been convenient. One in the author's possession was always called the linen chest. More generally we may presume that they served the purpose of small chests to contain the more valuable belongings. No doubt the great Bible was sometimes placed in such a piece. We sometimes forget that there is no law compelling a distinct and uniform use for a piece of furniture. At the same time they are fascinating, and more ornamental than absolutely necessary. Few of them seem to have existed. We are treading on a treacherous path when we explore the number of any particular style of furniture. Still, their date in most cases was not as early as that of court cupboards, and there is no reason for their extreme rarity except that not so many of them existed originally as of other kinds of furniture. Perhaps thirty more or less are generally known. A half dozen have come to light within quite recent years. They belong to that class of furniture that never remains in the market long and of which not a single example is known to be available now.

The aristocrat among these pieces is the first that we will discuss.

No. 116 belongs to Mrs. J. Insley Blair of Tuxedo Park. The frame is of oak but the lid and the bottom of the frame and drawer are of pine. The American origin of such pieces is much discussed, especially of late. We see pieces from England with similar drawer bottoms. This piece, however, has been in America for a long time. It was found a few years since in York, Maine.

It has several features which distinguish it, and place it in a class by itself so far as our present knowledge goes. One of these features is the vase turning of the leg. It is quite in the style of that found on court cupboards. If we consider this feature in conjunction with the broad stile legs in the rear we are still more impressed by the similarity to court cupboard construction. The ball turned stretcher system is another important feature. Since this piece was discovered a table has come to light with stretchers in the same style, though of smaller size. The cross brace doubled stretcher of course gives much strength, and the feeling of solidity, and adds greatly to the charm of it. The upper part had arches in the side panels and an eight pointed star in the center panel. These arches should be compared with those shown on a chest. The applied ornaments are quite like those on chests and court cupboards. This like all other chests-on-frames has one drawer in the frame. It will be seen that the ornaments are carried around on the end and that there is a diamond shaped applied decoration in the center of the end panel. It is somewhat too large to be called a nail head. This piece is in an unrestored state.

We have previously shown the inaccuracy of designating these pieces as dower chests. It is an equally loose phrase to term them Pilgrim chests. The earliest we know were indeed made in the Pilgrim Century, but are no more likely to be found in Plymouth Colony than in southern New Hampshire.

Size: $26\frac{1}{2}$ by $35\frac{1}{2}$ by $17\frac{3}{4}$ inches.

For the most part these pieces may be thought of as about three feet high, two feet long and a foot and a half deep.

No. 117 is perhaps the next best sort of chest-on-frame with the exception of one owned, and shown, with carving, by Lyon. The piece before us is owned by Mrs. J. Insley Blair. It is a fine specimen, and in its original condition, with the possible exception of the lack of a shelf

141. CARVED BOX. 1660–90.

142. CARVED OAK TWO-PANEL BOX. 1670–90.

143. BOX WITH IMBRICATED CARVING. 1660–80.

144.   FLUTE AND LUNETTE CARVED BOX.   1660–80.

145.   INTERSECTING LUNETTE BOX.   1670–90.

146.   ALL PINE LUNETTE CARVED BOX.   1680–1700.

147. PINE STAR FISH BOX. 1680–1700.

148. FRIESIAN CARVED BOX. ABOUT 1736.

149. PINE CARVED BOX. 1690–1700.

150. Curly Maple Desk Box. 1700–20.

151. All Pine Carved Box. 1700–20.

on the stretchers. We believe that a shelf was common when the stretchers were square. In this case particularly the edges of the stretchers, on the top, especially on the inside, are quite sharp. The discoverer of this piece admits that there was a shelf, but that he regarded it as not original, and hence destroyed it. His judgment is to be taken as to the particular piece removed. However, it may have been a substitute for the original shelf.

Several chests very like this have been found. In fact the resemblance is so close that we presume they are all made by one person. A piece in the possession of the Pennsylvania Museum has an applied molding covering in part the front stretcher and in part the shelf above it. This mold is cut off flush with the outside edge of the post. The carving is intended to be identical with this piece. This piece, however, has one strip of applied ball molding on the outside stiles whereas the Pennsylvania Museum piece had two such strips. The drawers of these pieces are practically identical in their carving. The frames are oak and the lids pine. The turning is of the earliest character.

No. 118 is an unusual chest-on-frame, which has been somewhat restored. The small panel design on the front is like that of the drawer of chest No. 44, as are also the slender long split turnings. Compare also the court cupboard No. 203 for the similarity of the small panel work, and the little split turnings each side of the bottom drawer. These are like those on the chests and are the only ones we have ever seen without the ball at the bottom. They appear meagre on the court cupboard and raise the question whether they were not originally in pairs. The unusual turning here resembles that on No. 121. The brackets and the drops suggest seventeenth century tables. This piece is of oak with the initials S. A. H.

Owner: Mr. Hermann F. Clarke of Boston.

No. 119 is a chest-on-frame owned by the Rhode Island School of Design. The turnings are somewhat light and therefore indicate a little later period than No. 117. The spray decoration also found on the panels is an evidence of change in taste. This decoration is usually in black on a red ground. We believe that the turnings are in maple, at least they belong to the maple period.

No. 120 is a slight variation from the last in that the stretchers are turned and the body is higher in relation to the base. The decorations on the panels do not pick out in the picture.

Owner: Mr. Arthur W. Wellington.

No. 121 has a character somewhat like No. 116 in so far as the back legs are stiles. The simple early period is further carried out in this piece by the use of plain stretchers on the end, the turning being restricted to the front.

On the other hand the false upper drawer is usually found somewhat later. These pieces invariably have one drawer, no more, no less. We have hazarded this categorical statement, and now await the almost inevitable upsetting of its accuracy by some new discovery. The piece before us is of oak with pine lid and panels, but it has been to a considerable extent restored. A cloud rests on the title, as it were.

Size: $27\frac{3}{4}$ by $35\frac{1}{2}$ by 16.

No. 122 is distinguished by ball turnings on every part of the frame. The chest is shown as it was. The drawer has since been restored with moldings. It is of rather heavy and satisfactory construction.

It will be seen that the rail under the drawer is molded more boldly than is usually the case. The end panel has a chamfered border, whereas No. 120 has a raised panel, and the border is not chamfered. These little touches have something to do with the date.

No. 123 is still another decorated piece in good condition and with very attractive turnings. The drawer is very deep. The attachment of the lid by cleat hinges is obvious. The decorations in this case are not confined to the upper panels but are found also on the drawer.

Owner: Mrs. F. G. Patterson of Boston.

No. 124 is one of two pieces of almost precisely the same style, and with leg turnings, between the stretchers and the body, exactly similar. The other piece, which we do not show, has a pine box attached, whereas the piece before us has an oak box. These two pieces, with the carved Dr. Lyon piece, have their boxes attached by heavy nails to the frame, through the bottom of the box. This is a radical distinction from the boxes previously shown in which the corner post goes through the box. That is to say we have here a table frame with a box set upon it, which is in all particulars, even as to size, like the detached boxes which follow. This piece came from eastern central New England. That with the pine box came from the old tavern kept by the Ballard family in Ballardvale, Andover. It was called by the last member of the family who owned it a tabernacle table, the name having come down to her from her ancestors. This is an interesting fact as throwing light on the regard in which such pieces were held, and the possible uses to which they were put. In none of the three pieces mentioned is there any question but that the table and box originally went together. No. 124 when found had had the faces of the turned posts flattened in order to apply boards to form a cupboard.

Both this and the Ballard piece have notched corners or gouge carving.

153. CARVED DESK BOX. 1722.

152. MINIATURE BOX. 1690–1710.

154. SCRATCH CARVED LITTLE CHEST. 1677.

155. A Painted Pine Box. 1700–10.

156. Scratch Carved Box. 1700–20.

157. Scratch Carved Box. 1694.

158. Walnut Desk Box. 1680–1700.

159. Walnut Desk-box with Turned Feet. 1700–20.

160. WALNUT BALL-FOOT SECRETARY. 1690–1700.

In the Ballard piece, however, the ends of the lid are treated in the same manner, whereas in this case the lid has the thumb nail molding and is also of pine. The moldings on these two pieces are identical, and we believe them to have been made by the same cabinet maker. There is a slight difference in the turning of the feet. We may plainly see, between the initials S. A., scratch outlines for a carving design which was never carried out.

Size: $25\frac{3}{4}$ by $32\frac{5}{8}$ by 17 inches. The Ballard piece is a little smaller across the front.

The name tabernacle table perhaps indicated that a Bible was kept in this box. It has been suggested that these pieces were sometimes kept on the rear of pulpit platforms and that Bibles were placed in them when not in use. This suggestion is quite unreasonable. We should be likely to know, at least in some instance, if such a custom had been followed. All these pieces bear marks of taste and skill. The fact, however, that so few of them are initialed, discourages the supposition that they were frequently dower chests. A bride-to-be would undoubtedly resent the supposition that she would need only this little box to bestow her belongings.

BOXES

W E HAVE advisedly used this brief title because there is no reason
to assign boxes generally to a use restricted by the name Bible boxes.
There is still less reason to name them desk boxes, if a desk is to be thought
of as a writing desk. Nor do we feel at liberty to name them miniature
chests, as a class, although many of them are merely that, having a till.

Without exception all the boxes which we have seen are built of boards
not framed. They are generally rabbeted so as to strengthen the construction and allow the front to extend over the end and yet permit the
end to be nailed to the front. Perhaps the majority of them are oak,
but a good many of the later and even interesting specimens are pine.
The bottom is almost always pine and more often than not projects in
the form of a plain bevel. It is nailed in place.

The use of these pieces as receptacles for precious articles is often
negatived by the lack of a lock. Wherever the piece never had a lock
and at the same time had no till or pigeon holes it was more likely to
be a Bible box than otherwise. A considerable number of the large
ancient Bibles, it is found, will fit conveniently in these boxes.

The English boxes are quite likely to be carved on the ends. The
American boxes are generally carved only on the front. The same is
true of applied ornaments. In America they appear as a rule, only in
front. The pieces were light and easily movable. Their hinges were
for the most part cotter pins like those we find on chests. In the case
of slant tops, however, we find, in several instances, good butterfly
hinges.

No. 125 is an attractive and distinctive box belonging to Mr. H. W.
Erving. The material is oak and the box is initialed. Mr. Erving rails
genially at the author's box with the initials B. C. We appeal to a candid
world, are not the initials B. C. more respectable than B. D.?

The rosettes on this piece are attractively carved and suggest the
connection with the sunflower chests of Connecticut. The lunettes are
cut in a heavy channel mold and their bases terminate quite like the
vertical flutes.

The rest of the carving is of the scratch variety. The birds in the
spandrels of the lunettes are particularly amusing.

161. HEAVY PINE DESK. 1680–1700.

162. BALL-FOOT DESK. 1700–10.

163–169. IRON LAMPS. 19th CENTURY.

170. SMALL PINE STRETCHER DESK. 1720–30.

171. Turned Frame Walnut Desk. 1700–20.

172. Walnut Desk. 1700.

173. Pine Desk. 1700.

There is a series of incised turned ornaments on the ends.

No. 126 has the small panels like those shown on the chest-on-frame No. 118. In two instances the little turtle backs are omitted to provide a space for the initials H. S. This box is mostly original except the lid. It was found in Connecticut. The odd little turnings applied, which we have mentioned before, are found here, some one end up, some the other. We refer to the outside members of the three sets of three each.

Size: 28 by 10 by $17\frac{3}{4}$ inches.

No. 127 is a very satisfactory piece because it is so completely original. It is of heavy oak. The hinges are particularly good specimens of the butterfly sort. The slant top and the row of pigeon holes within mark it unmistakably as a desk box.

Size: Over all, 25 by $9\frac{3}{4}$ by 19 inches.

No. 128. Owner: Mr. H. W. Erving. The carving on this box is very peculiar for several reasons. So much of the wood is cut away from the design that we may call the carving raised. Of course there is no distinction between this and other carved designs, like the Hadley, except in the extent of the cutting away. However, the work is quite delicate and in the pond lily pattern and therefore a pleasing and rare departure. The other notable feature about the box is that it is asymmetrical in its carving, the design on the right as we view it being quite different from the other side, and of a very interesting pattern.

Size: $25\frac{1}{2}$ by 9 by $16\frac{3}{4}$ inches.

No. 129. A box unusual in several particulars, one being in the method in which the bottom is attached. It will be seen that the face boards of the box extend to the very bottom and therefore the bottom board is set in like a drawer bottom.

The carving on this piece is a series of lunettes and reversed lunettes, which are elaborated into something like a palmated pattern. It was found as it is, except that there was a hole where the lock should be. The bottom and the lid are pine and the rest is oak. The lid is molded on the front and back. The carving is most unusual and approaches closely to carving in the round, as some of the foliage is shaped on the surface. The box was found in Granby, Connecticut, in 1922. It is said to have been on a farm there since 1660.

Size: $24\frac{1}{2}$ by $7\frac{3}{4}$ by $14\frac{5}{8}$ inches.

No. 130 is a handsome box belonging to Mr. G. Winthrop Brown, with arched flutes and a series of rosettes alternately different, with a ribbon interlaced scroll enclosing them. The curious and quaint effect appears of leaving the last of these rosettes cut off by the outside margin, which indicates that the designer did not plan far enough ahead. It is rather deeper than those boxes which we have discussed hitherto.

No. 131.   A box with a handsomely carved front in a daisy or rosette pattern, surrounded by interlaced double straps or ribbons, which terminate in imbricated scrolls.   The box is of oak, but it is nailed from the front. The bottom and the lid are pine.

It was found in eastern central New England.

Size: 23 by 9½ by 16 not including the overhang.

No. 132 is a shallow Hadley box of which one or two others are known.   It is about a half of the depth of No. 134, but corresponds with the rails on Hadley chests as to its width.   It will be seen that the carving on this box is in the round in part.   We may therefore presume that it antedates most of the Hadley chests.   Otherwise we are to suppose that the great extent of the front of a Hadley chest discouraged the worker from attempting to do it all in the round.   Of course carving of this character is very much better than that found on any Hadley chest.

Owner: Mrs. J. Insley Blair.

Size: 25 by 5 by 14 inches.

No. 133.   Owner: Mr. H. W. Erving.   We have here a box initialed R. N. with a stippled background for the letters.   The simple carving of the two star designs is quite like that found on some of the Pennsylvania barns.   The ends of this box are of oak and the front and back and lid, and of course the bottom, are pine.   Red and black paint is applied in the cut-away sections of the rosettes.

Size: 23½ by 8½ by 18 inches.

No. 134.   This is the only Hadley box that has so far come to our attention with a depth sufficient to allow a full element of the tulip and leaf design seen on Hadley chests.   The carving like that in No. 132 is in part in the round.   It is only necessary to compare this with the face of a Hadley chest to see that the latter is merely roughly scratched without artistry.   This box has all its side pieces of oak and the top and bottom of yellow pine.   The lid is worked into a slightly raised central panel. The condition is absolutely original.   The box was found overlooking the Connecticut river in the town of Lyme, New Hampshire, which was settled from Old Lyme in Connecticut.   The box was therefore probably carried up the river from that place, although we would not seem to force such a conclusion.   If it was made in Old Lyme then the extent of the work on these Hadley pieces was greater than has hitherto been supposed. Of course it may have been taken from Hartford to Old Lyme originally or it may have been purchased as the settlers moved north.

At any rate its general type is very early, quaint and satisfactory and intriguing.   It suggests the first efforts at this type of carving.

174. WALNUT CROSS STRETCHER DESK. 1690–1700.

175–178. BELLOWS. 18th AND 19th C.

179. PINE CROSS STRETCHER DESK. 1690–1700.

180–183. PIPE BOXES AND SAND GLASS. 18th C.

184. Turned Stretcher Desk. 1710–20.

185–190. Tinder Box and Sparkers. 18th Century.

191. WALNUT TURNED STRETCHER DESK. 1720–30.

192–194. WROUGHT ANDIRONS. 18th CENTURY.

Size: Over all, the lid: 26 by $17\frac{1}{2}$ inches. The frame is $23\frac{5}{8}$ by $8\frac{3}{4}$ by $17\frac{1}{4}$ inches, including the thickness of the lid.

No. 135 is a box formerly in the B. A. Behrend Collection, and doubtless intended for a desk. The excellent butterfly hinges are visible. The large ball feet are unusual on so small a piece.

No. 136 is a deep box received by the author as a lecture fee. There was missing a small portion of the front of the oak lid. The piece is otherwise original, and has some odd features. One of these consists in an applied molding above the base which we believe is not shown in the case of more than one or two other boxes in this book. The carving consists of two rows of flutes and extends around the ends. This unusual feature leads us to challenge its American origin, but the author's kind friends are accommodating enough to say that it is American.

Size: $23\frac{1}{2}$ by $11\frac{1}{4}$ by 19 inches.

No. 137 a. is a very quaint miniature box belonging to Mr. Hollis French of Boston. The design is called Friesian. There is beautifully serrated or notched carving on the base and the lid. The same thing appears as an almost constant motive in Norman cathedral architecture. Probably the name toy box would apply to this piece. It may have been used for jewels and placed in a larger " strong box." Many perfectly simple boxes of this size are found which do not merit treatment.

No. 137 b. is a deep box belonging to Mr. Hollis French. The carving is the double foliated scroll so much found on chests and court cupboards. The widely spaced gouge carving at the corners is noticeable.

No. 138 is a box with foliated scrolls running horizontally instead of vertically as in the previous box. Here also we have the initials A. H. The owner is Mr. B. A. Behrend. The foliage here resembles the acanthus.

No. 139. A beautifully carved box in which the tulip element occurs again. The attraction of the carving consists not so much in any accurate delineation of the tulip as in the grace of line. The carved details surrounding and depending from the 'scutcheon are also an interesting feature indicating that the carver did what is frequently not done. He had regard to the arrangement subsequently to be made for locking the box. Most of these boxes seem to have lacked that attention, so that we see key holes freely inserted in the midst of the carving in a somewhat awkward and defacing manner.

Size: 27 by 10 by 15 inches.

No. 140. Owner: Mr. George Dudley Seymour. The carving here may be presumed to represent the tulip. In fact, it is a rather better setting forth of that favorite flower than we usually find. We notice the usual stippled background and gouge carved corners.

No. 141. Owner: Mr. Dwight Blaney. The carving is very happily designed and executed. The box is deeper for its length than is usual.

No. 142. Owner: Mr. George Dudley Seymour. This is the second example we have shown in which the front panels are not alike. One panel bears the initial W. The pattern represents the tulip less conventionalized than usual. The piece is in the Wadsworth Atheneum, Hartford. It originated in Guilford.

No. 143 is a large and interesting box. The carving of two bands of imbrications is combined with heavy moldings and several bands of scratched serrations. The top and the bottom are pine. The box contains the original till of pine. All the other parts are oak. The lid is molded on the front and gouge carved on the end, a style which is carried out on the ends of the front also. The box is large, being $26\frac{1}{4}$ by $9\frac{1}{2}$ by $17\frac{3}{4}$ inches, not including the overhang. The original hasp is in place.

No. 144. Owner: Mr. H. W. Erving. The band of vertical flute carving above is interrupted to afford room for a 'scutcheon. This shows thoughtfulness. Scratched carved lunettes, a row of three, finish the front. They are filled with rays which may be variously designated. A flower fills the spandrels. The same carving is repeated on the end, which is most unusual.

Size: $21\frac{1}{4}$ by $8\frac{1}{2}$ by $14\frac{1}{2}$ inches.

No. 145. Owner: Mr. H. W. Erving. Here the top line of carving is unusual. The intersecting lunettes, each done with four parallel lines, is of course a very obvious motive. The top carving is repeated immediately below the lunettes, and there is a line of imbricated carving at the bottom, or at least it was probably so intended.

Size: $27\frac{3}{4}$ by 11 by 17 inches.

No. 146 is a somewhat attractive box although it is pine in every part. It has a coat of old paint which, as it is somewhat flaked off, will be cleaned entirely. The spandrels are carved with fan like designs.

Size: $24\frac{1}{2}$ by $8\frac{1}{2}$ by $15\frac{1}{4}$ inches, without the molding.

No. 147. Owner: Mr. George Dudley Seymour. The carving is of a most unusual and interesting design, though it is not fully explicable. The lunettes and half lunettes are bordered with small triangles like the Norman notched carving. At the center there is a kind of spiral wheel which again is centered with a small starfish design. There is also a row of starfish running across the center of the front. All these elements are raised. What term we should apply to the battle axe shaped designs which fill the spandrels we do not know. The piece is in pine. It will be seen that it lacks the base molding.

195. Parmenter Court Cupboard. 1640–50.

196. Carved Oak Court Cupboard. 1640–60.

No. 148. Owner: Mr. George Dudley Seymour. A small box of whitewood, pine and soft maple. It is from Norwich, Connecticut, where it was owned by the Fanning family. The front ends and lid are profusely enriched with carving as done in the northeast province of Holland and thence called Friesian. According to family tradition it was made by David Fanning of Norwichtown, when he was nine years old, which would give the box the date of 1736, as his birth was in 1727. Fanning died at Groton, Connecticut, in 1817. He was a soldier in the French and Indian War and a man of some local prominence.

Size: 20⅜ by 6⅜ by 10⅜ inches. The lid is 21 by 10½ inches.

No. 149. Owner: Mr. George Dudley Seymour. A carved and stippled pine box related in its type of carving to Friesian designs. The position of the spiraled wheel at the bottom is somewhat mystifying.

No. 150. The only good curly box we have seen in a form so small. It is a desk, pure and simple, with its original plain hinges. The ball feet add to its attractiveness, as does the heavy mold which is applied around the base and covers the base, which is nailed on, coming flush to the edges of the box. The original scrolled brass 'scutcheon is in place. The interior in the rear contains two plain cubbies with single arched molding.

The size of the box over all is 17⅝ by 12⅞ by 10 inches. The size of the body is 15⅝ by 12 by 8 inches.

No. 151 is another all carved pine box with a lattice work front. It contains no till.

Size: 21 by 8⅞ by 11 inches not including the overhang. It has pin hinges, a cleated lid the front and back of which carries a molding.

No. 152. This little box owned by Mr. George Dudley Seymour, has its entire surface covered with carving in the Friesian manner. The body of the box is worked from a single piece of wood, apparently whitewood. The cover, also a single piece, has thinned edges sliding in grooves. On the cover are the initials A. C., while the initials N. J. are incised on the end of the cover.

Size: 4½ by 2½ by 1½ inches. We assume that this piece is native since whitewood is the material. The box was found in Cheshire, Connecticut, about 1900.

The author possesses a miniature wall box with a slanting lid, all of whose parts are carved in the same manner.

No. 153. This carved desk box is a very interesting example of the survivals in style. The wheel carving on the upper section is purely Gothic in motive. The other carving on this part is obvious. On the lid, however, we have a crude scratch carving and the name, "Lydia

Culver 1722." The little drawer in the bottom is very unusual for a small desk. The material is birch or maple.

Size: 14 by 19 by 7¾ inches.

No. 154 is a box of oak. The outlines are filled with chalk in order that the date and the initials may show more plainly. The carving is crude and possibly unfinished. The spiral wheels, particularly, are merely scratched. The base is either not original or is quite rare in being cut flush with the box. The lid is pine with a long bevel on the front and ends.

Size: On the body, 22¼ by 9 by 17½ inches.

No. 155. A simple pine box owned by Mr. George Dudley Seymour. It was bought in Hartford. The bottom molding is a restoration. The painting, not restored, shows a vine enfolding large flower-forms. The piece is now in the Wadsworth Atheneum, Hartford.

No. 156. A simple box with scratch carving filled in with white. A decorative border which is carved is not so filled and does not appear plainly. The box is owned by the Connecticut Historical Society.

Size: 10½ by 5½ by 7 inches.

No. 157 is a painted pine box from the collection of Mr. B. A. Behrend. It is slightly carved with the initials E. A., and at the center a diamond is marked out in scratch carving with the date. Simple moldings appear under the lid and above the base.

No. 158. A walnut desk box with a cabinet, and mirror inserted on the under side of the lid. This dainty little piece, the moldings of which are especially well done, was found in New York in 1923, in bad condition, so that there are considerable restorations. The sunken top is filled in, as it was found, with old leather. The end moldings are outlined to follow the contour of the sloping lid, and gain much grace thereby. The box is molded in the back with applied pieces precisely as on the front, except that the corners of the two panels outlined are blocked. Thin applied blocks form the centers of all these panels. The hinges are especially attractive. They appear when the box is opened. Around the mirror there is an outline of two strips of inlay, the outer one of holly, the inner one of whalebone.

Size: 9½ by 3⅝ inches in front, and 5⅜ inches in the rear. The depth is 6¾ inches.

No. 159. An all walnut desk box with feet of the same material. There is a cabinet within. We presume in this case that the slant of the front was not really used for writing as it is rather narrow. It turns forward instead of backward.

Size: 19½ by 14½ by 11½ inches.

197.   Prince-Howes Plymouth Cupboard.   1660–70.

198. PLYMOUTH COURT CUPBOARD.   1660–70.

SECRETARIES AND DESKS

OF COURSE the secretary was an outgrowth of the desk. It is merely a desk with a cabinet or cupboard placed on top of it. This is proved by the fact that some of the earliest examples had detachable tops, whereas later on the piece was made as a unit.

In the seventeenth century for the most part people got on with small desk boxes. Good desks of this period are very rare. They may have been inspired by French examples, whence comes the word bureau, with a meaning among us of an office or department of state. The word escritoire, often used in a great variety of spelling, most of which eliminated the first letter, strongly suggests the French influence. It was not until the walnut period that elaborate desks began to appear in numbers.

Desks today are valued largely according to the elaborateness of their cabinets. In the earliest period the cabinets were quite simple. The failure to find desks with oak frames, at least in any number, indicates the tardy arrival of desks in the seventeenth century.

No. 160. A walnut secretary made with the top detachable. A curious feature of this piece is that the top juts back about an inch and a half beyond the back of the base. We have found this feature in some mahogany secretaries. It is an arrangement designed to accommodate the dado, which, in the form of panels surrounded rooms in the first period of paneling in America. Thus the desk proper abutted against the dado, and the top also abutted directly against the plaster wall, above the dado.

Attention should be given to the shapes of the panel tops in the doors. This form appears in the earliest panels in New England furniture. In Pennsylvania the form continued well into the eighteenth century, much later than in New England.

The hinges which appear here to be butts are really H hinges nailed into the edge of the doors, and closing up like modern butts. This is not a very unusual method.

The square pulls for resting the slant front when it is thrown open are marks of the earliest type. A little later it is seen that these pulls are in the form of a board on edge. Curiously enough the lid here is yellow pine though it seems original and the piece is otherwise of walnut.

Size: $33\frac{1}{2}$ inches across the front, $67\frac{1}{2}$ inches high, $20\frac{1}{2}$ inches deep.

No. 161. This heavy desk, set on a frame, is a rare and important piece, belonging to the Rhode Island School of Design. It has that delightful effect of softened corners and steady wear which appeals to the heart of the collector. The molded stretchers here are early and the heavy effect of the frame indicates an early date. The desk is small. It has its original and excellent butterfly hinges.

No. 162. Owner: Horatio H. Armstrong, West Hartford, Connecticut.

This handsome desk shows quite clearly a desirable cabinet of the period. The cabinet in the secretary No. 160 is about the same in pattern. The difference in the style of feet of the two pieces should be noticed. In Mr. Armstrong's piece there is a sort of shoe below the ball. This style is a little later than the other.

Nos. 163–169. A series of tin and iron lamps belonging to Mr. Anthony T. Kelly of Springfield, Massachusetts. We have found it necessary in order to show all the examples we wish to illustrate, without producing a too ponderous volume, to insert some small pieces of hardware below the furniture, and we have thought it more convenient to treat them as they are reached.

The lamp on the left is of the simplest sort to carry about; the next is a reflector; the third has a small extinguisher which may be folded down over it; the fourth is a quaint lamp which evidently is evolved by adding the bowl of a lamp to a candle stick. The fifth lamp, with its double wick, is of the fluid type just preceding kerosene, as is also the sixth example, only that is set against a wall sconce. The last example is a very interesting multi-sided wall sconce with glass to protect the candle. We consider this a very attractive design, especially as it is convenient even for present use.

In showing lamps and all other classes of hardware we do not confine ourselves to the Pilgrim Century. We eschew glass and for the most part show only such lighting fixtures as were made of tin and iron up to the time that kerosene came into use.

No. 170. A pine stretcher desk with a maple frame. The opening in the molded book rest was probably left for the staple which is now lost. We have here the lip on the drawer which indicates the eighteenth century style. There are excellent original butterfly hinges.

Size: Over all, $29\frac{1}{4}$ by $38\frac{1}{2}$ by $22\frac{3}{4}$ inches.

No. 171. A frame desk of walnut, of a desirable type. The turnings are very meritorious, and their large size indicates an early date. The lip on the drawer and even the drawer pulls, however, indicate that

199. SERRATED PLYMOUTH CUPBOARD. 1660–70.

200. SUNFLOWER AND TULIP COURT CUPBOARD. 1690–1700.

201. SUNFLOWER AND TULIP COURT CUPBOARD. 1670–78.

202.   Sunflower and Tulip Court Cupboard.   1660–70.

the base is a survival of a somewhat earlier style. The piece was in the former collection of the author. It is one of the best examples known, although the interior is very simple.

Owner: Mr. Harry Long.

No. 172, a walnut veneer desk resembling No. 162, except that it is a little earlier in the feet and in the molding. In the former collection of the author.

No. 173. A small pine desk on a frame with the early stretchers. When found this piece had hinges on the back of the lid. But as there were holes for pulls, the arrangement was reversed, to the original position.

Owner: Mr. B. A. Behrend.

No. 174. In this desk we reach, for the first time, a somewhat elaborate turning. The cross stretcher pieces of this character seem to form a connecting link between seventeenth century furniture and the six legged highboy turnings. This desk has fine original butterfly hinges. It has been to some small extent restored. We question whether or not the arched molding is correct. It should be compared with Mr. Wheeler's desk No. 179. It seems somewhat incongruous to run a mold of this kind except all around. A finial probably rested at the intersection of the scrolled cross stretcher.

Size: 38 by 32¾ by 21 inches, these measurements being over all. These turnings should be compared with the large square oak refectory table.

Nos. 175–178. We give here four forms of bellows. No. 175 shows a flat surface; No. 176 shows a rounded surface with stenciling: No. 177 has ornamental turnings; No. 178 is the plainest and simplest form. These bellows like most others have brass snouts. They were a very necessary household article.

No. 179. Owner: Mr. Edward C. Wheeler, Jr. A delightful small desk turned in the same type as No. 174 and probably by the same maker. It was found not very far from Boston, and is the only desk known to the writer in pine in this style. It has its early original butterfly hinges.

A desk with cross stretchers is convenient for the feet of one sitting at it. It also matches the style of the cross stretcher lowboy.

Size: The frame is 29¾ by 19¼ inches. The length is 31¾ inches. It is 33½ inches high, and 19¾ inches from front to back.

Nos. 180–183. The objects here depicted are owned by Mr. Arthur W. Wellington. The outside pieces are pipe boxes, the first having its back carved like a fan and pierced with the familiar and favorite heart shaped opening, which is repeated on the front of the box. The second object in the row is a little hanging box initialed and dated and also having a heart motive. The sand glass is of an early type. These glasses when very early are usually made in two parts and are connected by wax. It was thus possible in the manufacture to regulate the opening more precisely for the number of minutes required to pass the sand from the upper to the lower compartment. The phrase hour glass is hardly descriptive, for the time was more likely to be fifteen minutes or less. These glasses are found very convenient even today.

Pipe boxes were apparently used as early as the seventeenth century. In fact, they were needed as soon as the habit of smoking came in, in Queen Elizabeth's time. These boxes were used for the insertion of the long brittle clay church warden pipes. The drawer below was for the tobacco. The boxes were hung high on the wall to be out of the reach of children.

No. 184. A desk on an all turned frame and having chased brass handles, the hinges being of the butterfly pattern.

Owner: Mr. Chauncey C. Nash.

The obvious arrangement of a table frame for a box here appears. The style existed along with the other style in which the posts ran through the desk proper.

Size: 29 by $23\frac{3}{4}$ by $18\frac{1}{2}$ inches.

Nos. 185–190. These are fire making implements owned by Mr. H. W. Erving. The first is the more common tinder box, the steel for which lies in front of it. The steel was struck upon the flint and the spark was caught on a piece of tow, these articles being kept within the box, and the candle was set in the lid so that it might serve as a kind of pilot candle to light up all the others in the dwelling.

The next two objects are waistcoat pocket sparkers. These exist in a very great variety, one collection numbering over a hundred. The knife sparker is an odd variant. The last object is a wheel sparker. Some sort of fire maker was an important household article until the day of sulphur matches. It is remarkable how generally the old fire making tools were thrown away. They were no small nuisance in practical life, and our fathers seemed to have been glad to be rid of them.

No. 191. A walnut turned stretcher desk formerly owned by Mr. I. Sack, of Boston. Of course the handles do not belong with it. A desk constructed in this manner with drawers and turned table frame base, and drawers in the desk box itself, obviously required a high stool or high desk chair. A few such seats are found and will be shown later. Even with such a seat one could not sit as comfortably as one could wish.

203. SPLAYED CONCORD COURT CUPBOARD.   1670–90.

204. Stanton-Clinton Court Cupboard. 1660-80.

Therefore, the usual fashion for the later desks provided a knee hole. We are uncertain whether the medial stretcher was designed to give foot room or was an object of economy or grace, but it achieved all these objects.

Nos. 192–194. Three pairs of wrought iron andirons. The left hand pair is one of the commonest designs found, having a kind of gooseneck and a pointed square head. It should not be confused with the proper gooseneck and head andiron. The second pair is rare in that the posts are twisted. The third pair also is rather usual. Of course the object of the rings, or the turned-over tops, was for convenience in moving the irons. We do not know a time when andirons were not used. They bring back the early sentiments connected with the fireplace, and are still found in most homes.

COURT CUPBOARDS

T HE court cupboard is the most stately and important piece of furniture that has come down to us from the early settlers. Its possession was always a mark of dignity, wealth or family. People aspired to own a court cupboard as a token of assured position in society. Thus we see in Plymouth, a poor colony, that Governor Prince had such a cupboard. We find them more frequently, however, in Boston, Salem and the richer cities of the Puritans.

Most of all we find court cupboards on the Connecticut river, especially from Hartford south, and along the Sound.

A collector in these days who can secure a court cupboard feels that he also has achieved no small success. These objects are very much sought for, and hence, if one exists, hitherto hidden from the light, it is quite likely to become known in a short time.

The number now in museums is very small, more especially as we confine ourselves to American examples. The large majority of these cupboards is in private collections. There can be no doubt, however, that within a score of years a large number of them will gravitate to museums, where they will afford to the casual student a new conception of the furniture of our fathers.

An amusing and rather trite phrase in connection with Pilgrim furniture is " crude design." Every paragrapher and reviewer and novelist seems to feel himself aligned with those who know when he uses the word crude or some such adjective in relation to old furniture. For some years we have made notes, as a matter of curious interest, on the allusions by novelists to antique furniture. It would almost seem that writing people would wish to avoid marring their tales with wholly misleading statements. Perhaps they think they create an atmosphere. Certainly one cannot look for nice distinctions in their references to the subject.

We think it would not be difficult to show that in the period between 1670 and 1700 Americans built better homes, from the standpoint of taste in design, had better furniture, were better clad, and spoke better English than has been the case at any time since. An English traveler, going up to the North Shore, used in description of the homes he visited

205. DURHAM OAK AND WALNUT PRESS CUPBOARD.   1690–1700.

206. OAK PRESS CUPBOARD. 1680–90.

phrases so extravagantly commendatory that we dare not even quote them. A dwelling containing as much good furniture as the inventory of Governor Eaton of New Haven Colony shows, does not exist in America today, except in the case of a few collectors perhaps, who should not count in such a comparison, because Governor Eaton's home was designed merely to be the residence of a gentleman.

Anyone who looks at the Parmenter court cupboard can hardly call it simple. Anyone who examines a slate top table of 1690 must admit, if he has studied the subject at all, that for daintiness and elaboration it has never been matched since. The fact is that while we find simple furniture, in the homes of the poor, in the seventeenth century, we also find everywhere, even among the poor, marks of excellent taste, and a feeling for design.

Were a citizen of that day to "revisit the glimpses of the moon" and enter a conventional modern home of some pretentions he would be aghast at the medley and confusion that would greet his eyes. It is not at all uncommon to see a piece of furniture which combines the motives of three or even four centuries and so warps and twists and degrades them all, and mixes them with unconnected motives of a shapeless and mongrel character that the result reminds one of a musical medley, with the music left out. A professor in entomology was waited upon by some of his smart students who had concocted a bug, by using the wings of one insect, the legs of another, the body of a third, the head of a fourth, the antennæ of a fifth, and so on. They inquired what kind of a bug this was. The professor replied: "That, gentlemen, is a humbug." The phrase would aptly describe the desks and the chairs of those who with an overweaning and wholly unjustified presumption in favor of the present mechanical and tasteless age, write of the past as crude. The age of the Renaissance, the age of Shakespeare and Milton, the age of those who inherited and preserved the cathedrals, was strong, but whatever else it was it was seldom crude. The furniture was neither shoddy nor flimsy nor inharmonious.

The court cupboard is the outstanding example to prove these statements. The old inventories which unhappily ceased too soon, indicate that probably many hundreds of such cupboards existed. Perhaps less than sixty, of presumably American origin are known to remain.

All of these cupboards, belonging strictly in the seventeenth century, are of oak, as regards their frames. The great pillars are of some wood adapted for turning like maple. The drawer fronts and the panels may be of oak or yellow pine. The same is true of the main shelf, the top shelf and, in the open cupboards, of the bottom shelf. The various applied moldings and ornaments may be the same wood as the pillars or they may be of red cedar, walnut or pine, but rarely of the last.

We distinguish three sorts of court cupboards according to design, and perhaps we should include a fourth. One design like No. 200 has its shelf cupboard, which names the piece, splayed, or in the semi-octagon shape. A second variety is like No. 195, with a straight but recessed cupboard.

A third sort has a straight front without pillars like No. 219. All of these styles except the last are found either open below or closed in by panel work and a door or doors.

No. 195 was taken to Sudbury apparently when it was founded, from Boston Bay. The Parmenter Tavern was erected in 1683, in South Sudbury, long before the Wayside Inn was built. Joshua Parmenter, who carefully preserved this cupboard, was born in Framingham in 1824, and died in 1903. The writer secured the cupboard from his widow, who survives him, and their children. Joshua Parmenter remembered the occasion when the feet of this cupboard were cut off by his uncle, about 1835. He inherited the cupboard from that uncle and when the Parmenter Tavern was destroyed he took the cupboard to South Natick where the writer found it. Against the remonstrances of his friends who wondered at his preserving such a queer old thing Mr. Parmenter carefully cherished the piece. His widow and children have the same respect for it, and their regard is enhanced by their respect for him. By a clause in its bill of sale it must bear its brass plate stating its origin, and cannot pass out of the family in which it now is except to a public museum.

Mr. Luke Vincent Lockwood, with whose friendship the author has been honored, regards the piece very highly, from the standpoint of antiquity and merit of design. It combines several decorative features. It has that very rare feature in American cupboards, a band of inlay, running around the panels of the doors and on the stile below them and also on the stile above the drawers. The carving on the top member is in the arch or fluted pattern, and this pattern is repeated on the base. The central moldings are doubled foliations. All these moldings, as in the very earliest styles, are carried around the ends. The applied decorations, in addition to the inlay, are in the form of nail heads like triglyphs, in pairs, on the fronts, and sides of the posts. This cupboard belongs to the open style, which we regard as the earlier. The two sets of pillars are practically identical. The drawers are very heavy and are characterized by their lack of a rail below them, so that they never required pulls, but were withdrawn by catching the fingers underneath, on the

207. SPLAYED ANDOVER COURT CUPBOARD. DATED 1684.

208. SPLAYED OAK COURT CUPBOARD. 1670–90.

209. SPLAYED OAK PRESS CUPBOARD. 1670-90.

210. OAK PRESS CUPBOARD. 1670–90.

slight extension of the front, below the bottom. This feature has previously been mentioned in connection with certain chests, and may also be found on the cupboard No. 208.

All the shelves, the back, the inside shelf and the division between the two cupboards are of pine as well as the very heavy drawer bottoms and backs. All the other structural parts are oak except the posts, which are maple.

This cupboard follows the early design of allowing the stile behind to form the leg and of turning the front post. It has the unusual feature of the two drawers side by side and a drop between. This was in such a condition as to raise the question whether it were not a fifth leg. The restoration, however, is believed to be correct.

The carving of a tree with branches in the door panels is so surrounded by applied moldings lapping slightly onto the carving as to give the effect, in the shape of the molding, to a corridor down which one appears to be looking.

The old red paint remains on parts of the end panels and, strangely enough, the back. We do not know of another cupboard with so many intriguing features, or an appearance so generally attractive.

Size: 52 inches long, $53\frac{1}{4}$ inches high, 23 inches wide over all.

No. 196 is a press cupboard in the Metropolitan Museum. The brackets have been challenged, we do not know on what ground, nor do we now recall by whom. The pillars are extremely plain and are not very large in diameter. The doors below are attached on the outside of the stiles and are not recessed, a thing which we can hardly understand. The piece, however, is very elaborately carved. The scratch carving on the end panels suggests that on the Virginian cupboard to follow and that on one of the first chests treated. This cupboard has the structural architectural arches. They resemble very closely those shown in the chest No. 1. We believe the cupboard to be early. Other features of the carving which we have already referred to under other pieces do not require discussion. We do not feel qualified to say whether this cupboard is English or American but it is counted American by some of our best judges.

No. 197. This cupboard is one of six known in this style only one of which, that in the Metropolitan Museum, was generally known two years ago. One of these is in New Jersey, one in Boston, one in New York, one in Bridgewater, which completes the list. Of the six one is in such a condition as to be positively valueless. We show the New Jersey specimen and the Metropolitan Museum specimen besides No. 197. We apply the name Plymouth to these cupboards because the example now before us and the New Jersey example are traced directly to that place. The example in New York came from Plymouth Colony. That in Bridgewater was also derived from Plymouth. We have not yet traced the origin of the other two, but we are confident that as the eight or more chests known of this style are traceable in part to Plymouth, that this style had its home there and not elsewhere.

The author has examined four of these pieces, some of them with great care. The drawer bottoms, backs and fronts are pine. This pine does not seem to us as hard as yellow pine, yet we must presume it can be nothing else, for it certainly is not white pine. In all cases it is riven. The drawer fronts are completely covered by the molding, and the painting of the center of the panel, formed by the molding. There is some divergence in the back panels of the various specimens, as they are sometimes oak, sometimes pine and sometimes, as in the Tracy cupboard they are pine in one section and oak in another. There is also a divergence in the material of the panels of the upper part. There is the usual variation in the turning of the great pillars, though in all cases the pillars were very large. The fronts of the cupboard section also vary for the sake of that individuality which we have mentioned as a feature of the Pilgrim furniture.

Thomas Prence (Prince) came to America in the Fortune. By 1634 he became governor of Plymouth. He married Patience, daughter of Elder William Brewster. In 1635, having lost her, he married Mary Collier of Duxbury. He was allowed to live at Eastham, otherwise known as Nauset on the forearm of the Cape until 1665 when in 1657, he was elected Governor for the third time. But in 1665 the permission for a governor to live away from Plymouth was cancelled, and he was granted "a seat" a mile north of Plymouth at *Plain Dealing*. This was the Lothrop farm occupied in 1832 by Isaac L. Hedge. Governor Prince was continually re-elected from 1657 to his death in 1673. His fourth and last wife was Mary, widow of Thomas Howes, an original settler of Dennis, then part of Yarmouth.

Governor Prince's will of March 13, 1673 has been published. It contains the following items:

"My will is that Mary, my beloved wife shall have such household goods of Any kind as were hers, before wee married, Returned to her againe."

"Item I give onto my said loveing wife my best bed and the furniture thereunto appertaining, and the Court Cubberd that stands in the new parlour with the Cloth and Cushen that is on it."

Thus after the governor had specified that his widow should have such

211. SPLAYED OAK COURT CUPBOARD. 1660-90.

212. Press Cupboard Base. 1670–1700.

213. Pine Desk. 1700–10.

214. Spool-turned Court Cupboard. 1690-1700.

215. DECORATED WHITEWOOD PRESS CUPBOARD. 1690–1710.

household goods as she brought him, he adds the bed and cupboard. The inference is clear that these articles were not a part of her dowry. This is important since it is the tradition in the Howes family that Thomas Howes brought the cupboard from England. The mention of the " new parlour " evidently refers to an extension of the governor's house, made between 1665 and 1673. His fourth marriage occurred not long before August 1st, 1668. The cupboard may therefore be assigned to the period, 1665–1670. The widow returned with her legacy to Dennis, for that had been her home, and her grown son by Thomas Howes lived there. Her inventory dated December 23, 1695, mentions " an old chest and a cupboard at Prence Howes's."

Various additional minute details of evidence were published in *Antiques* October, 1922. The Prence Howes last above referred to was Mary's grandson. There is a fascinating record of inter-marriages and relationships. He died in 1753.

The Howes family retained this cupboard, which was about a hundred years old on Lisbon earthquake day, and about a hundred years after that Joshua C. and Polly Howes restored the cupboard in some degree, and attached a legend to the inside of the doors. The author purchased the cupboard from a lady of the Howes family who had inherited it. No other member of the family seemed to be in a position to hold it. In this particular case all the eight panels of the back, the interior divisions and shelves, and the upper outside panels, are of yellow pine in addition to the pine parts already mentioned as common to all this type. The pillars shown in detail in the chapter on turnings are, it is noted, reversible, being alike at both ends. We have not noticed another instance of this sort.

The piece when found had all its upper ornaments but one. The applied drops on the lower section had been lost. It is probable that a large single drop existed on the feet but we have hesitated to restore it. It will be found on another piece shown of this type.

The characteristic feature of the Plymouth cupboards is the serrated molding, which appears on this piece in seven lines on the front, reckoning from the top to the bottom. The wood is cut away to form these saw teeth, quite similar to Norman cathedral work. All these pieces that we know also have heavy modillions on the canopy. There is also a " pencil and pearl " ornament repeated on various sections. The carving also in part extends around the ends. The large oak molding is attached by wooden pins. The top is separable from the base.

Another feature of the Plymouth serrated pieces, both chests and cupboards, is the pair of short drawers, the upper set on the base, or in case of an open cupboard, the only pair. In the chests whether there are two ranks of drawers or only one, the drawers are all only half length on the front. We do not remember seeing this feature elsewhere except in the Parmenter court cupboard.

Photographs of this piece in detail, before its restoration, front, back and ends, are in the possession of the author.

Size: 51 inches across the front, 56 inches high, 22⅝ inches deep, over all.

No. 198. The serrated Plymouth cupboard in the Metropolitan Museum. The high importance of this piece is enhanced by its central panel in the form of an arch which some have claimed was a certain English stamp. If anything was made in America these cupboards were. This piece has been restored at the bottom and more or less otherwise. It is most interesting in being open below, most of the others of the type being built below as chests of drawers.

No. 199. This cupboard, so near like No. 197, has come to light through the publication of pictures of No. 197. A member of the Tracy family writes that Stephen Tracy came in the Ann in 1622. Patience Brewster, daughter of Elder Brewster, is said to have been aboard. It was she who married Thomas Prence, mentioned under No. 197. Their daughter married Stephen Tracy's son John. His descendants moved to Hartland, Vermont, and took the cupboard we are now considering, with them. It was brought back by a direct descendant of John in 1878.

Of course the tradition is that it came in the Ann. This is impossible, owing to the style and the construction. The strong presumption is that John Alden or Kenelm Winslow built these cupboards and chests. Plymouth town was very small. It was so reduced between 1660 and 1670 that there were fears that it would be entirely depopulated through removal to more fertile lands. We know of no other master carpenters or woodworkers except the two we have just mentioned, and the smallness of the town would seem to call for no more. Further, one of these cupboards has been inherited in an Alden family.

No. 199 has undergone slight repairs. The turnings on the feet are important and original as are nearly all if not all of the other ornaments.

Owner: Howard C. Tracy of Plainfield, New Jersey.

No. 200. Introduces another class of court cupboards with chests to correspond. They are called the Connecticut sunflower pieces, but in every case we believe they also have side panels of tulips. Up to the discovery of the Plymouth serrated cupboard these were the only outstanding class of highly important cupboards of American origin, found in sufficient number to afford a good basis of comparison. It is both difficult and dangerous to say how many of a certain class exist, but we

216.   Virginia Bulbous Court Cupboard.   1640–60.

217. Essex Institute Press Cupboard. 1670–90.

218. Court Cabinet. 1670-90.

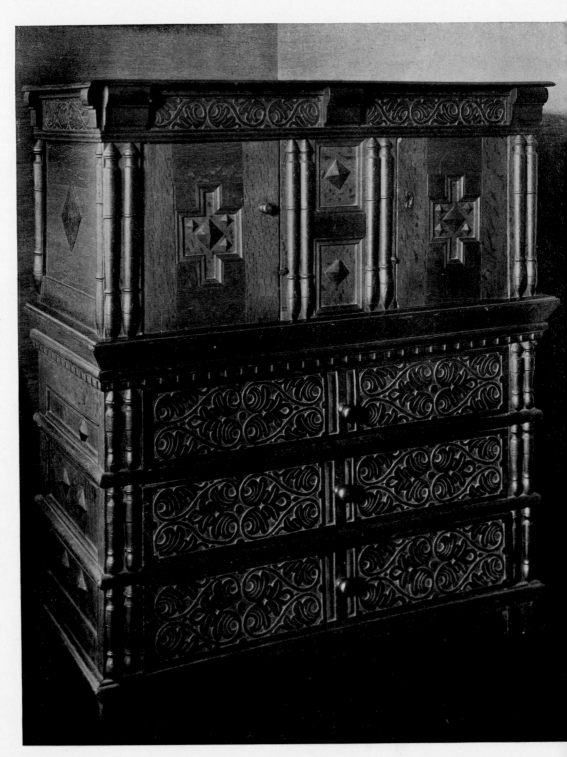

219. STRAIGHT FRONT PRESS CUPBOARD. 1670–90.

will hazard the phrase, eight or ten more or less. This particular piece differs rather widely from most of the others known. It has the rare feature of the splayed shelf cupboard. The turnings of the pillars are sharply different from the conventional type found on No. 201. The rosettes on the drawer, on the upper door and on the architrave, otherwise called the canopy, or the cap, or the hood, or the cornice, are also a variant from the usual style. The piece also is somewhat higher in proportion to its width than others we have seen. An important feature, which we consider points to a somewhat later date, is the narrowing of the face of the long stiles which form the legs, and their division into panels. This should be compared with the wider stiles on others of the type, on which stiles applied drops appear, matching those on the inner stiles.

We should mention that for the most part the shelves and cap boards of the sunflower cupboards are in oak, together with their panels.

Owner: Mr. Winthrop Edwards Dwight. The cupboard is an heirloom in the Wheeler family and was derived from Fairfield County. Whether or not it was made at Hartford, as we suppose most of this type to have been, we cannot say. Possibly its variation from type would indicate that it was done by a maker south of Hartford.

No. 201. A cupboard in the sunflower or aster and tulip pattern, of the conventional type. When the author was looking in Clinton, Connecticut, for the cupboard in the Stanton house there, he mistook his directions for Clinton, Massachusetts, and as a consequence came upon this cupboard in the Lancaster Library, Clinton having been set off from Lancaster. The Rev. Jos. Rowlandson married a Mary White. He was the first minister of Lancaster, 1654–74. He died in Wethersfield, Connecticut, 1678. His heirs sold the cupboard in 1825 to the Rev. B. R. Woodbridge of Norwich. He died at South Hadley, in 1648, leaving the cupboard to his nephew, Mr. J. W. Dunlop of that town, who sold it to the library. It is a fascinating bit of information that the library bought the cupboard because it was a piece of furniture belonging to the first minister of the town, and not from any supposed importance of the furniture itself. The fact that Mr. Rowlandson died at Wethersfield accounts for his possession of the cupboard, Wethersfield being only four miles from Hartford. The piece when found was painted red. Nothing has ever been done to it except to wash off the paint. Its condition is more perfect than that of any other piece of its age that the author has seen. It is a pleasure to present so ancient an article of furniture in a condition so fine, and on which no hand has been raised by way of restoration. It is this piece, therefore, that should supply our data for style. There is a little variation in the bases of these periods. It appears in the carving of the tulip and the "asters." All specimens we have noted have a heart-shaped fret work applied above the drops. The lines of molding and methods of construction vary very little. Another feature to be noticed is the slanted dentils below the main shelf and below the cap shelf. Of course these are merely strips of molding cut up and spaced. The central one is in triangular form below the main shelf. Another feature is the series of applied blocks, on the cornice, with four tulips whose stems meet. These blocks are seven in number. All those pieces that we know, at least, have cupboards below, and all but one that come to our mind have straight fronts on the recessed portion behind the pillars. There are also two doors, and the panel is in the center, on this section. This particular piece is the only one we have seen with its original drop depending from the center of the hood. It is not an acorn but is an attractive large turning. The shape of the door panels does not vary as much as some other features. All the pieces have turtle backs and all except No. 200, we think, have them on the drawer, the upper doors, the hood and all the end panels.

The piece before us enables us to supply a more precise date than we have hitherto been able to do, since the owner died in 1678.

It is supposed that these cupboards and chests of a similar style originated in Hartford. The peculiar and strongly marked individuality of the turning on the large pillars, quite similar in most of the cupboards, separates them from No. 200.

No. 202. A sunflower cupboard owned by Yale University. It does not differ markedly from No. 201. It has, however, been somewhat restored. It is very much to be desired that the three court cupboards owned by Yale University should be in a public room where students of furniture could feel at liberty to examine them at leisure. At present it is only by infringing upon the privacy of the president's office that they may be approached.

No. 203. A court cupboard of unusual character, discovered in Concord, New Hampshire, and probably taken there from Connecticut whence came the three other pieces with the finely divided panel work of an identical character. If these were from England we should look for them on Massachusetts Bay.

Owner: Mr. Philip L. Spalding of Boston.

An interesting question sometimes arises in relation to the pillars of these cupboards. They have sometimes been found with the small end uppermost. Were we to follow the analogy of architectural pillars that placing would be correct. Some English cupboards have capitals obviously copied from the Greek. In such instances no question arises. In the

220. TORUS MOLD PRESS CUPBOARD. 1680–1700.

221. CARVED CUPBOARD. 1650–70.

222. ARCHED PANEL CUPBOARD. 1660–80.

223. INLAID CUPBOARD. 1680–1700.

224. WHITEWOOD CUPBOARD. 1690–1700.

225.   PINE PRESS CUPBOARD, APPLIED MOLDINGS.   1690–1710.

226.   SUN SCONCES.   227.   OVAL SCONCES.

228. SHELL CUPBOARD. 1720–30.

purely American cupboards that we know it is a vase or urn and not an architectural pillar that we have to do with. In the piece before us, for instance, there is no question that the lower pair of pillars is correctly placed. In fact, they were set where they are, when the piece was built, and could not be removed without taking the frame to pieces. We therefore conclude that the upper pair of pillars is correctly placed.

The shelves of this piece are oak. The splay of the cupboard with the double arch on the beveled portion, together with some other points of construction have raised the question of an English origin. We think the piece to be American. The stile legs have been cut off for the addition of casters, an incongruity that we feel should be corrected.

As an instance of the change in our attitude toward such furniture we may mention that not many years ago it was offered at a price such as one would now pay for moving it, but that it was declined!

We have wondered whether the square of the turning above the upper pillar should not bear an applied ornament. It would seem to be called for by the construction. We have also wondered whether or not these ornaments did not exist, originally, on the three squares in vertical line on the corner, in pairs. Also, whether or not ornaments of a similar character should not appear on the outside ends of the posts.

This very handsome specimen is to be compared with the base belonging to Mr. Wellington, No. 212, in respect to its recessed lower cupboard, an interesting and attractive feature but very rare.

By an inadvertence the precise date which appears on the upper cupboard door was omitted from the legend.

No. 204.   The restored Stanton-Clinton court cupboard. In this piece we have another example of which sufficient numbers exist to form a class, a half dozen at least being known. In our first edition this cupboard was shown in a somewhat grotesque restoration. All the superabundant ornaments have now been removed and the piece has been left severely plain. The restoration is certainly conservative. This cupboard is on public view in the Stanton Collection which is in the Historical Society edifice of Clinton, Connecticut.

The pillars of this class of cupboards are rather unhappy, as it seems to us, in the style of their turning. This appears more clearly in the picture of No. 220. In other respects the decoration of the cupboard is attractive and dignified. It is difficult in the picture before us to pick out the arch and drop on the splayed sides. These features are seen in a similar but reduced form on the door between these sides. The great torus molding covered with a double band of foliated scrolls, running also around the ends, is the drawer of the cupboard, and opens on the miter at the corner, similar to that on the cupboard No. 205. This probably marks a second stage of construction.

The molding about the hood, also carried around the ends, is similar to that below, though somewhat more condensed.

No. 205. A cupboard marking, somewhat, a decline in the highest standards, and therefore a later date. It came immediately into the author's collection from the family in which it had been inherited in Durham, Connecticut. They had made some repairs to render it practical for modern use. One of these was the substitution of modern butts on the lower door, an error which has since been remedied, by restoring the dowel hinges of wood, like those in the upper doors. The drawer interior and the lower panels in the rear have also been renewed. For the most part the piece is original and its appearance is not altered at all except in the incorrect modern drawer pulls.

The heavy molding on the drawer level is of oak. The drawer opens on the miter. All the applied moldings, the bosses, the drops, the triglyphs, the pillars and the feet are walnut.

Size: outside all, front, $44\frac{1}{2}$ inches; hight 59 inches; depth, 22 inches. The front and end dimensions of the frame, below, are 42 by $20\frac{3}{4}$ inches.

No. 206. A press cupboard owned by Mr. James N. H. Campbell.

The reader will note the word " press " in the title of this piece. If we attempt to be quite specific we name a court cupboard that is closed below with drawers or a cupboard, a press cupboard, whereas those pieces that are open below are strictly denominated " court " cupboards. This distinction is more or less arbitrary, and we make no pretense of claiming that it is the only proper method of distinguishing the style. In fact, we find Governor Prince using in his will the term court cupboard for the cupboard filled with drawers below. We are merely attempting to establish an intelligible distinctive nomenclature. This cupboard has pillars which, though lacking a taper, are an improvement on those in No. 220. The effect of the cruciform sets of applied decorations is good, and quite unusual.

No. 207. A splayed cupboard all of oak, which has not hitherto, we believe, been illustrated.

Owner: Mr. Franklin T. Wood, Rutland, Massachusetts. The cupboard was inherited by him from an aunt in North Andover. It had previously been found in an exposed and weathered condition. The restorations, however, appear to have been slight. In fact we question whether they have been carried quite far enough. We presume that there were drops on the square above the upper pillars both on the front and on the ends. This example is very rare and certainly unique among

229. Pine Shell Cupboard. 1752.

230. CARVED PANEL PINE CUPBOARD. 1710–30.

231. CARVED PINE CUPBOARD. 1730–60.

232. SCROLLED PINE CUPBOARD. 1740–80.

those we show, in that while it is open below it has a drawer beneath the lower shelf. The knobs on both drawers are late and incorrect.

It is the all oak construction of this piece and of other all oak chests or cupboards, with arches, that has raised the question of their possible English origin. We can only say that this specimen has many analogies with American cupboards and that it is presumably native. At any rate it has been here longer than any of us. Indeed, all these pieces have outlasted so many generations of men as to make our criticisms seem trivial. It will be noted that there are two sets of initials which may represent successive generations of owners, or they may be the initials of a husband and wife.

We have in the upper drawer of this piece finely divided panels resembling those on Mr. Spalding's cupboard. Possibly there should be minute turtle backs applied at the cross members of the molding. The plainness of the lower drawer may be challenged. We have not made an examination to learn whether or not it was originally paneled like the upper drawer, but a complete structural scheme would seem to require such paneling. We wish to call especial attention to the similarity between the drops at the end of the main shelf on this piece, on No. 203, and on the court cupboard table, No. 681. There is also a marked similarity between the pillars on that table and those on the two court cupboards here referred to. We can trace this Andover cupboard and the court cupboard table to the same neighborhood. It is entirely possible that these pieces were made to go together. At any rate, their similarity of construction suggests the same origin.

No. 208. Owner: Mr. James N. H. Campbell. This cupboard has the same beveled dentil or sectional molding as is found on the Connecticut sunflower cupboards. The pillars above are simple but in excellent taste. Here it is a question whether or not they have been reversed. This piece was restored a good while ago by the father of the owner. For a simple cupboard it is one of the most satisfactory that we have seen.

No. 209. Owner: Mr. George Dudley Seymour. We have here on the hood the corbels, often called modillions, which are properly so named only when horizontal and which we have noted on other cupboards. In this case, however, the arrangement is somewhat different. The panel ornaments, on the beveled sides of the cupboard, instead of being in the form of an arch or double arch are here in geometric panel work. We are of opinion that the pillars here would be better if reversed.

The other features of this cupboard call for no special comment. It will be observed that on most of the cupboards there is a good deal of channel molding, and this is no exception.

Size: The main shelf is 45 by 20¼ inches. Over all, the piece is 54½ inches high; the upper section is 21½ inches high. The depth of the lower section is 19½ inches.

No. 210. This is a good example of a press cupboard. We suppose that where the lower section is all done in drawers that a piece may be ten years later than a piece with doors below. Of course, the time named is purely arbitrary. We have here a very condensed center arch and a straight front cupboard section. In this case we think the pillars should be reversed to correspond with the pillars so similar to these in No. 203.

The repetition of the triglyphs and vertical lines, there being the amazing number of twenty-seven on the lower section, gives the piece an appearance of unusual hight.

The use of drawers, rather than an open space in the lower section, indicates the movement toward utility rather than ornament. It may also mark a growth in the number of a family's possessions.

Owner: Mr. Dwight Blaney.

The original object of these cupboards was to hold the plate, and to display it. A cloth running along the top of the cupboard and depending at the ends in the fashion of mantel ornament of a generation since, was used. On this cloth were placed cushions and on these again the plate was displayed, very much as now-a-days a set of jewelry in a shop window is shown.

The cupboards were the sideboard and safe of their time. They were placed in the parlor which was also the dining room. It was later that the parlor was shut up and a special dining room was provided. The court cupboard was the principal piece of cabinet furniture, and that one from which guests obtained their idea of the family wealth and dignity. Governor Prince's bequeathing of his bed and cupboard to his wife marked out the choice pieces of furniture in that generation. Of the stately and important, but not publicly seen bed, we shall speak later. The cupboard was in the eyes of all guests.

No. 211. Owner: Mrs. Hulings Cowperthwaite Brown. The double set of pillars in this open cupboard are matched in our knowledge only by those in the Parmenter cupboard in respect to the fact that they are identical above and below.

We have the arch motive in two separate sections, instead of in one panel on the bevel of the cupboard. The drawers here in their moldings closely resemble the Plymouth cupboards, but their fronts are oak. The applied ornaments on each side of the drawers are reversible.

A feature of no small interest is the scolloping, improperly engrailing, of the lowest member on the front. This also should be compared with the other examples in this work.

233. HEAVY PINE CORNER DRESSER. 1730–60.

234–236. GOOSE, BALL AND CROOKED NECK ANDIRONS.

237.   SCROLLED OPEN CUPBOARD.   1750–80.

238. NEW ENGLAND DRESSER. 1740–80.

239. BUILT-IN CORNER CUPBOARD. 1745.

240–242. CROOK BALL, FLAT SCROLL, AND PIGTAIL ANDIRONS.

No. 212. Owner: Mr. Arthur W. Wellington. A very attractive base for a press cupboard, the top member of which is unfortunately lacking. The initialing is arranged for by a small block in the paneling of the drawer below. The broad blocking of the recessed drawer reminds one of the fronts of some of the heavy chests of drawers, and the acute angled ornamental molding there and in the top drawer carry out the analogy. The turning of the pillars is extremely bold and interesting. It is really a bulbous turning that we do not remember to have seen on any supposedly American cupboard except No. 216. The ball feet on this piece are applied in the same manner as those on a chest or a chest of drawers.

On the shelf the evidences are plain of the attachment of the missing portion. The piece never had wooden knobs but always the brass drop handles. The arrangement of pulling the bottom drawer is very quaint.

No. 213. This little pine desk is placed here out of order as there was no previous opening. It is evidently a country made example following the line of the six legged highboy, but failing to retain the full conformation which gives the legs of those pieces so much character. Nevertheless the piece with its drawers resembling that of a lowboy, is of much interest, and great rarity.

It came from the Pierce family.

No. 214. Owner: Mrs. J. I. Blair.

This cupboard was for a considerable time in the rooms of the Historical Society in New Haven. There are many features of interest about it, one being the use of " modillions " at the elevation of the drawer. The posts, in a kind of ring and ball turning, or what some might call a spool turning, are of small diameter. The panel on the door very closely resembles that on No. 223, as do also the splayed side panels. The " modillions " on that piece also are located with the same arrangement, so that we judge the maker of one of these pieces knew the other.

Size: width 43¾ inches, hight 57¾ inches, depth 21 inches.

No. 215. This is one of four whitewood or pine press cupboards made after the analogy of the court cupboard. Such is the interest in furniture of this period, that, at any exhibition of court cupboards, the public gather around these quaint lighter specimens much more than about an oak cupboard.

A diagonal view of this piece is presented in No. 224 in order to show the scroll of the board end which forms the feet. In this piece it will be seen that the base mold is carried around the end. All the moldings are applied so that we have no true panels. This is the case with all cupboards so far found of this character. We believe one of these cupboards is in the Metropolitan Museum, another in the possession of the author, and another in New Hampshire. This piece is very much more elegant, if we may use the phrase, than the author's specimen. We have here a decoration of new moons. The painting is, altogether, when one compares it with other painted pieces of the period, attractive. An amusing feature is the application of the drops and 'scutcheons above the drawer in locations where their use can only be that of ornaments.

Owner: Mrs. G. C. Bryant, Ansonia, Connecticut.

No. 216. Oak furniture undoubtedly existed in Virginia in considerable quantities because the state was settled in the age of oak. Two circumstances operated to cause the disappearance of this furniture. The persons who owned it were mostly members of the landed aristocracy, who kept in close touch with English fashions. When new styles came into use in England they were imported. The other circumstance is that the wealthy and free-hearted Virginians always had the poor with them in the persons of their negroes. To them were donated old pieces of furniture as well as old clothing. The blacks usually reasoned, like their white brethren, that furniture that was given away was of small importance. It therefore went the way of all the earth. The remarkable piece before us is the only oak cupboard we have ever been able to hear of south of the Potomac. It is said to have been found in a barn loft about fifteen miles from the site of old Jamestown in 1922, and that it was sold to a dealer for ten dollars. In parts it has suffered very much from weathering, and was thoroughly gray when recovered. It appears to have its original top of yellow pine, since it is pinned down by very large square oak pegs. We have been particular to learn by examination that there are no other holes in the top. The piece as found lacked the drawer and the left hand door, as we view it. It is the only piece of this general character to be found in America with great bulbous turned posts, which are fully six inches in diameter. Here, as in other examples with large posts, in the other cupboards we know the enlarged portion is never turned as a unit with the entire post but is set in by dowels. Here the great bulb alone is separated from the rest of the piece. The blocks on the top rail were also missing and it required a great deal of study and involved some failures, before we could finally arrive at the correct restoration. The carving of the door in the tulip pattern and in the round was taken, however, as a model and reduced but so as to obtain a piece somewhat more square in shape, as is necessary. The present blocks have now been changed to intaglio carving, as they would otherwise project too much. The conventional foliated scroll appears and is carried around the ends. Interesting carving also covers the faces of the corner posts. The intaglio carving

243. FAIRBANKS HOUSE DRESSER. 1720–50.

244. FRONT OF LIVERY CUPBOARD. 1630–50.

245. SCROLLED CORNER CUPBOARD. 1740–80.

246. PENNSYLVANIA GERMAN CUPBOARDS. 1730–70.

247. SCROLLED DRESSER. 1740–80.

of the center panel is very interesting. We have previously noted the simple and easy and inferior carving on the end panels. The door carving, and the middle panel, are in the earlier style of the art, which lead us to believe that this work was done under the influence of the Elizabethan period, and hence we have assigned the date. The scrolled skirt is here an important decorative feature. The balls of the feet in front have lost something, it is difficult to say how much, because we cannot precisely define their contour. If we say two inches we shall probably not be far amiss.

Size: 48 inches across the frame in front, 48½ inches high, 19 inches deep.

No. 217. The cupboard of the Essex Institute has been shown previously in Lockwood, and perhaps in other works. We have broken over our rule in this piece and in Nos. 219, 221, 222 and 223, in showing pieces that were published previously. We do this to make a very complete showing of these cupboards. But because they have been shown before Nos. 221–223 are now set forth in reduced form, for comparison only. No. 217 is an interesting and handsome specimen. We have had before practically the same detail of large pillar and of double arch on the bevel of the cupboard. The channel mold on the square above the pillars, however, is something different.

There is a curious scratch carved molding just above the top drawer. It appears to be almost like rude lettering. It is possible that it is reminiscent of the Norman serrations seen on the Plymouth cupboards.

This cupboard is on public exhibition at the Essex Institute, Salem.

No. 218, from a photograph made for the author, but unhappily very dark, shows a court cabinet or a cupboard with doors. We give it the name cabinet to distinguish it from a court cupboard, because within its doors it has a series of drawers. The phrase " cabinet " has been commonly and loosely used of court cupboards. Cabinets are far more rare than cupboards. Three or four other examples are perhaps known. This piece has the characteristics in its brackets, " modillions " or corbels, names loosely used to indicate the same thing, and in its upper door moldings, and in the cross division of lower panel doors of the Plymouth cupboards. But there the similarity ends. We have here the ball feet, in the flattened or onion pattern, which are seen on some of the good chests. The heavy moldings and shelf between the sections has much the appearance of the two part chests. The piece has been slightly restored. It is understood to have been found not a very great way from Albany. Perhaps we are right in assuming that it originated in New England and that it was removed to New York state when the owners changed their location. Of course it is entirely possible that a New York state cabinet maker got his design from New England or from old England.

Owner: Mr. J. F. Bernard of Albany, New York.

No. 219. This cupboard also was shown in Lyon. He left in his estate another cupboard varying but slightly from this example.

The owner of the piece shown is Yale University. The cupboard is of oak except the drawer bottoms of pine. The parts are made separable as usual. It is interesting to note the statement of Lyon that this cupboard was bought from Durham, Connecticut, the source of No. 205. The origin of the cupboard that Dr. Lyon left in his estate was Madison, Connecticut. The coast region in that vicinity was rich in pieces of the kind, which is also apparently the home of the torus-molded cupboards, two of which we show. The special interest of this cupboard, aside from its handsome decoration, is that it has a straight front and that the cupboard section is not recessed. It is thus of a different type from any others that we know. It is affiliated with the court cabinet already shown in that respect. The very heavy between-drawer-moldings, all carried around the ends, and the nail heads on the front and ends, are striking features. The raised diagonal square at the center of the top end panel is also a peculiar feature. Is it the basis for some other decoration to be attached?

The series of dentils under the central, principal, shelf appears also under the cap board of No. 205, the other Durham example. This is, of course, a far more important piece than that, and earlier. It has lost several inches from the feet.

An outstanding impression at first glance is the peculiar and extraordinarily heavy molding at the base of the upper part and the same mold, repeated in smaller section, at the base of the lower part. At first thought one would say that this molding was reversed. It is found, however, in its correct form here. We do not see it often enough to become accustomed to it, and we are not sure that it adds grace. However, it is very distinctive and interesting.

Size: $51\frac{1}{2}$ inches across the front, 57 inches high, $23\frac{1}{4}$ inches deep.

No. 220. This is almost a repetition of No. 204. In fact the similarity is so great as to force the conclusion that the pieces had an identical origin. The torus molded drawers are identical. A slight difference appears in the cornice or hood mold, it being divided in the specimen before us into two parts with triglyphs between, corresponding with the triglyphs at the ends.

The drops on the stiles of the lower section indicate that something is not quite right, as they are not set true. Probably they became detached

248. ARCHED PANEL SCROLLED CUPBOARD. 1720–50.

249. CANOPIED CUPBOARD. 1730–60.

250. WALNUT GLASS DOOR CUPBOARD. 1730–60.

251. CARVED AND ARCH PANEL WARDROBE. 1720–30.

and were carelessly returned. Their appearance at present is too lean and meagre, so that it may be they existed in pairs originally.

Owner: Brooklyn Public Museum.

No. 221 is a straight front cupboard belonging to the Metropolitan Museum in which we believe some critics recognize foreign elements. It is a handsome piece but if it is not American, perhaps we had better not discuss it. In this we may be wrong but we have not been able to go into the matter.

No. 222 is also in the Metropolitan Museum, from the Bolles Collection. The interesting feature about it, is that we have here the same torus mold on the drawer as is shown in No. 220, only that here it is perfectly plain. The open base is supported by pillars that duplicate those in design above them and are of practically the same size. The pendant from the keystone of the arch, on the door, and on the splayed sides, is practically the same in design as those seen on other cupboards. We may consider it probable that this piece originated in southern Connecticut.

No. 223. An inlaid cupboard, has previously been illustrated, but this example is so interesting in many particulars that we venture to show it again, although in a reduced form. The inlay is on the heavily blocked central panel, and on the drawer, in the form of diagonal checkers. The general type seems to be a little later than most oak cupboards, a conclusion strengthened by the smaller section of the corner stiles. The arrangement of the blocked panel was perhaps copied in the whitewood chest No. 82, a later example.

Owner: The Rev. Edward C. Starr, Cornwall, Connecticut, to whom we are indebted for the courtesy of the photograph.

No. 224 has already been mentoined in connection with the other view of it.

No. 225, a court cupboard in yellow pine. It seems straining a point to name a simple piece of this nature a court cupboard. Nevertheless the owner doubtless made it in this form in order that he might claim the name. We may call it the poor man's court cupboard. While not as good a piece as No. 224 it has some features of great interest. It is not decorated, but had a plain red paint upon it. It shows its fine old butterfly hinges on two levels. The "panel doors" below project from the front in the manner of one oak cupboard shown. The applied moldings, forming the false panels, are all original. One of the posts was missing and also the drawer, but its location and size were marked by the remaining run or rider which shows in the photograph. There is an overhang at the ends corresponding to the hooded section in front. This overhang has also the narrow shelf in front of the recessed cupboard, and has the favorite gouge carvings. There is a pine shelf inside each cupboard at about half the distance from the base to the top.

Size: the section of the post on the square portion is $1\frac{1}{2}$ inches. The cupboard frame is 35 inches across the front. The hight is 51 inches and the depth 17 inches. The size of the cap board is $43\frac{1}{2}$ by $20\frac{1}{4}$ inches. The cap board is molded at the top, in front, to match the applied moldings.

Origin: The piece is said to have come from southern New Hampshire where another one exists with painted decorations and a splayed cupboard.

We here conclude our view of court cupboards, which we have tried to make sufficiently ample, in the examples and the data, to prove satisfactory for a cursory student.

Nos. 226–227. Shows two pairs of sconces from the estate of George F. Ives. The pair at the left is of a design frequently seen in tin, with grooves stamped to represent rays. The design at the right showing a set of three candles in front of an oval reflector, is quite distinguished. It would appear, however, that the reflector is inadequate for the position of the candles.

252. Scrolled Pennsylvania Cupboard. 1730–70.

253. ROBINSON HOUSE CUPBOARD WALL. 1737.

254. PANEL WORK FROM CONNECTICUT. 1720–50.

255. Paneled Cabinet. 1680–1700.

256. Pine Cupboard. 1700–30.

257. DINING ROOM OF QUINCY HOMESTEAD. 1740–50.

258. OVER MANTEL CUPBOARD. WILLIAMS HOUSE. 1717.

PINE CUPBOARDS

THE interest in pine cupboards may be said to exceed the interest in any other class of furniture of their period. It is difficult to distinguish between the classes of cupboards because they blend into one another so gradually. We have already discussed several pine court cupboards. For the greater part the class we now take up is made of white or soft pine as distinguished from the earlier yellow pine. We are including in this class of pine cupboards the walnut cupboards of substantially the same period and design. We are also including the built-in side or corner cupboards, and the wall cupboards, which, for the sake of clearness, we could also name suspended cupboards. Hanging cupboards is an expression which we have found used of wardrobes, the "hanging" in that connection referring to the hanging of clothing. If a hard pine cupboard happens to be found in any of this classification we shall discuss it here.

No. 228. The altogether best built-in cupboard we have ever seen was in the Jaffrey House in Portsmouth, New Hampshire. It was purchased by the Boston Fine Arts Museum. It is of great hight so that there was room for an elaborate and extended capital consisting of carved foliage upon which the upper member of the cornice proper is imposed. Cornices of rooms of the period were properly and often built in the same design as the cupboard cornice. Perhaps the builder thought of it the other way about, and ran his cornice around the room, afterwards accommodating his cupboard to it.

The demidome cupboard of this class is either of wood, and carved as here, or of shaped lathe and plaster. A comparison should be made between the plastered demidome and the half-barrel plaster domes of doorheads.

The Jaffrey cupboard has the best carving in its dome of any that we have noticed. The foliations about the rosette at the center of the spring of the arch are freer and better than we usually find. The same is true of the somewhat elaborate semi-circle with which the arch ends on the face of the cupboard.

The ribs of the arch are usually supposed to represent a shell. In this case they seem to be more strictly architectural, suggesting groined arches.

The date of this cupboard is very early. It shows pilasters on its face whereas nearly all other domed cupboards have their elaborate pillars or pilasters hid behind the wainscot which the author cannot think to be otherwise than an architectural blunder, caused by the confusion of the introduction of cupboards about the same time as the wainscot. The pilasters here have the stopped flutes, and there is an enrichment by carving near the top of the flutes. The molding of the cornice is enriched by a " pencil and pearl " member and above that by a wider band of serrations.

The door of the cupboard is very good, the two panels being handsomely scrolled in an unusual pattern at the top. There is a slide immediately below the main cupboard, and then a drawer, and below all there is the usual small cupboard in the base. There is the further differentiation of a drawer in the very bottom. Hence, in the number of its details, its enrichment, and its peculiarities, it is easily first.

No. 229. This is a somewhat simpler shell top cupboard in the side wall of the Webb House, Wethersfield, which is open to the public, it having passed from the author's hands to those of a patriotic society. The cupboard stands on one side of the fireplace. On the other side the paneling is identical, but the door opens to a passageway to the back parlor. The custom of placing cupboards in the side wall rather than in a corner is not unusual, hence it is not proper to use the term " corner " cupboards in general of these pieces. We have yet to learn of a cupboard with a shell top and in pine that was not built in. Of course the plaster domes were always built in.

It will be seen here that the cornice of the side wall does not match with the cornice work over the cupboard. This arises from the fact that the cornice was the outgrowth of the beam construction as we find it in our colonial houses. It will be seen that the cross panels of this cupboard, called after St. Andrew, are common in Connecticut, sometimes in a scrolled or more elaborate form. The doors below in this cupboard have the H hinges. The fine pillars are entirely hidden by the wainscot. The detail of the shell, the initial point of the carving on which is a corbeled turning, with a sunburst above, is interesting. On the panel work, without, the keystone is carved like a wild rose.

Regarding the date of these cupboards, that of the Jaffrey House previously described is the earliest that we have been able to trace, of a design so good. If we say that these cupboards ranged from 1720 to 1760 we shall be very close to the truth. None has ever been seen, to our knowledge, in dwellings of the Revolutionary period. By that time cupboards were being built in mahogany, especially in Pennsylvania.

259.   PARLOR OF SPARHAWK HOUSE, KITTERY.   1740–50.

260.   CARVED EMBROIDERY YARN HOLDER.   1680–1700.

261. COCKED HAT CUPBOARD.

262. SUSPENDED CUPBOARD.

263. HEART HANGER CUPBOARD.

264. CORNER CUPBOARD.

265. MARSH HOUSE CUPBOARD. 1730.

266. LITTLE DRESSER. 1720–50.

267. SPINNING ATTIC. 1760.

268. 17th CENTURY PARLOR.

269. Pennsylvania Wardrobe. 1730-60.

But in New England detached corner cupboards of a fine type are almost nonexistent, and we cannot think that they were found, except possibly sporadically.

No. 230. An unusual feature of this cupboard is the carving from the solid of the irregularly shaped panels, which form the sides of the opening. At the top the same contour of the scroll is carried out, but without the carving. Mr. Lockwood shows another cupboard almost like this except that the small square panels in his specimen are carved. This it will be observed was a side cupboard.

Owner: Mr. Edward C. Wheeler, Jr.

No. 231. A beautiful and very unusual corner cupboard. Owner: Mr. Sherwood Rollins of Boston.

An interesting feature of this pine cupboard is the two urns which are cut, intaglio, on the cornice, each side of the central medallion or sunburst. The sunburst in this form is otherwise denominated a patera. The happy conceit was used a great deal at a later period in painted or inlaid decoration in Sheraton furniture. We find it here carved. The row of smaller pateræ, on each side of the cupboard opening, is the chief decorative feature.

No. 232. A pine cupboard with a scrolled opening at the sides and top. The door is a restoration. Cupboards of this sort are now being called pewter cupboards, although we do not suppose them to have been in use until about the time china was introduced, and we believe that, owing to their small size, they were designed chiefly for the exhibition of china. Perhaps the very long open dressers, to be shown, were more generally used for pewter. Those large dressers, being usually a part of the structure of the kitchen, would naturally be used for the polished pewter. Whereas, the smaller cupboards, being portable, and often found painted, might be found in dining rooms. There is no class of furniture more sought at the present time than are the narrow pine cupboards.

Size: The width across the front is 37½ inches. The hight is 77½ inches.

No. 233. This heavy corner dresser or open corner cupboard, is owned by the Pennsylvania Museum, and was in the author's former collection. It acquires its charm largely from the very small circumstance, as would appear on first thought, that the boards of which it is constructed, instead of being ¾ to ⅞ of an inch, are a flush inch in thickness. This slight difference gives a solidity and permanence of feeling hardly believable. It has its original HL hinges, and the two panel door. The moldings are simple and are applied under the main shelf and down the angles and corners. It is quite difficult to date a piece of this kind, since its vogue extended through a considerable number of years. Its boldly scrolled end boards and its curved shelves add to its beauty.

Nos. 234–236. We have on the left a pair of true goose neck and-irons with the head worked on the iron. The center pair is merely of straight balls and not uncommon. The right hand pair is crooked neck with balls, varying but slightly from a pair already shown.

No. 237. This is a scrolled open cupboard, whose odd features are the scrolled shapes of the feet and the scrolled back. Here also, as is most unusual, the main shelf extends over a scrolled section.

No. 238. A New England dresser with the usual cornice, in the plain form, and the usual scrolled boards at the sides. The end board is in one piece from the floor to the cornice, as distinguished from the Pennsylvania type, which is made in two parts. In the author's former collection.

No. 239. A corner dresser with cupboard below, in the Benning Wentworth House at Newcastle, New Hampshire. The corner post of the house is availed of to form a finial for the cupboard, which is recessed on each side of the post, into the wall. A most interesting and tasteful arrangement.

Nos. 240–242. The middle pair of andirons has its tops hammered thin, like a pie crust dough, and rolled over. The right hand pair has its tops turned down to a flat surface, on which is hammered an extension in the form of a simple colonial scroll of the " pig-tail " sort.

No. 243. The Fairbanks House is perhaps the oldest frame dwelling in our country. Certainly it has that appearance. The picture of the kitchen shown has a dresser with handsomely scrolled end boards, built against the wall sheathing. The dwelling, which is supposed to date 1636, is of course much older than the dresser. Nevertheless, the style of the scroll, with its fine beaded edge, indicates a very early type.

No. 244. Mr. George Francis Dow has furnished us this photograph, which we believe to be the front of a livery cupboard, in oak. It was found in the Capen House at Topsfield. We do not know of any other ancient American example. The turnings closely resemble those in our oldest chairs, especially one Brewster chair. It may be that the turnings on such cupboards suggested this spindle work on the oldest turned chairs. It is supposed by Mr. Dow, that the cupboard on which this front was used hung on the wall. There is in the Capen House a hutch, which was found in an old farm house, some three miles away. The specimen resembles the English type, the only one we know to

270. Decorated Kas. 1690–1710.

271. WALNUT KAS. 1730–60.

272–276. WOODEN SPOONS AND BOWL.

277. Suspended Cupboard.

278. Suspended Cupboard.

279. Cross-paneled Cupboard.

280. Spoon Rack.

281. SMALL CUPBOARD.

282. PINE CRADLE.

283. CORNER CUPBOARD.

have been found in this country. The door differs from the livery cupboard front, and the result might be called either a hutch or a cupboard.

A point of much interest is the fact that the back legs are made shorter than those in front. In some instances back legs decayed more than the legs in front. In this case it is believed that the legs were originally made shorter in the rear, to rest upon the ancient sill, which in the oldest houses projected into the room, as now in the Capen House.

No. 245. A corner cupboard, with a scrolled opening, from the George F. Ives Collection. The hinges here shown are one of the earliest types, without pins. We do not know whether they were originally on the cupboard.

No. 246. There is shown here the proper arrangement for a short cupboard and wall cupboard. They should be placed one above the other, so that a person may not stumble upon the lower one or hit his head against the upper one. If either of these two cupboards is missing the effect is unfinished. Their origin is Pennsylvania. The lower cupboard had drab paint upon it. When this was removed, bright star decoration, in black, was found on the raised paneled door, and on the drawer. It was necessary to retouch these stars. The cupboard at the top finishes in an interesting scroll. The cupboard above has the mortised hinges, and a similar star on the raised panel. Here an odd feature of country construction is that the molded corner of the cupboard extends through to its base, so that the base mold on the front and on the end is stopped before reaching the corner.

No. 247. A scrolled dresser of the type generally seen in Pennsylvania. The method of attaching the hinge is plainly shown. We have not here the plain modern butt, as the parts of the hinge enter the wood on each side by a mortise and are held in place by a rivet. The quarter round molding in the panels of these doors is the proper type. A more elaborate molding in this location is later. The slots on the lower free shelf, for spoons, are cut through to the front rather than being blind slots, as usual. One should take note of the scrolled top board, such as appears often in Pennsylvania pieces, and seldom in New England examples. The photograph is furnished by the Shreve, Crump & Low Co. of Boston.

No. 248. A cupboard of much interest in spite of the fact that the fluted columns were not provided with space to run to the top. They are left in the air and should, of course, have been confined to the base if they were to be used at all. Notwithstanding this defect the doors are interesting with their small twin panels in the arched form. One should notice that the top of the panel runs in horizontally on each side before the arch begins. This is a stylistic matter of much consequence. The American carpenter tends to arches, and if you ask him to prepare a base for a wall sign he will almost invariably arch the top, but will omit this special feature which really gives character.

As appears, the scroll is molded on the edge, and in the center, on top, there is a spiral wheel or a shell carved.

Owner: Mr. Edward C. Wheeler, Jr.

No. 249. A most unusual and attractive form of a small dresser with a scrolled hood or canopy. The shape of the scroll on the board is that of an elongated C. The scroll also reminds us of the arm of a settle. The material is pine. The piece 'was found in Rhode Island.

Owner: Mr. Edward C. Wheeler, Jr.

No. 250. The finest movable cupboards we find are in walnut. This cupboard with doors, in that material, probably came from Pennsylvania. The doors are designed to be viewed as closed, being each, in their design, the half of a semi-circular arch. The paneling done on the pilasters is simple but effective, as is also the corbel of the keystone.

No. 251. A very rare piece in pine. In fact, it is the only attractive wardrobe in that material that we have seen. The interesting central panel of the door is cut from the solid. The narrow pair of panels above is attractive. The wardrobe is owned by Mr. Edward C. Wheeler, Jr.

No. 252. A fine example of a Pennsylvania dresser with the so-called rat tail hinges on the pairs of doors. There are also the conventional large sized long knobs found in that region. This piece is beautifully scrolled at the top and sides. The cleats placed at the intersection of the two parts, to form slots on the main shelf for the reception of the scroll boards, are plainly visible and are characteristic. The hinges are probably contemporary with hinges we have already shown on similar pieces, but without this form of a brace.

The lower free shelf has a wide molded edge. The bars to prevent the falling forward of objects displayed are also here shown for the first time, in this work.

The owner is Mr. Arthur W. Wellington.

No. 253. When we discuss built-in cupboards we are on that borderline where architecture mingles with furniture design. There has been of late a revival of the idea of built-in furniture, and we confess that it is very attractive to us. The instance before us is that of a dwelling in Wethersfield, one of the oldest now standing in that town, and showing a side wall cupboard back of the arch. The arrangement by which the keystone is blended with the cornice, and by which the cornice is broken to form this keystone, and also the capitals of the narrow pilasters, on

284. NEW ENGLAND TWO-PART DRESSER. 1730–50.

285. Pipe Box. 286. Pipe Box.

287–289. Pipe and Wall Boxes.

each side of the fireplace, is a very good example of the best style of paneling, which came in about the period of the cabriole leg.

No. 254. A remarkably fine example of southern New England panel work. It is in the Metropolitan Museum. We have here several characteristic features. They are the early scrolled top arched panels, the pilasters with an intaglio star or rosette on the capital, and the St. Andrew's cross in the lower panels. There is also about the fireplace molding and about the great panel above it a heavy bolection molding. This molding is the best date mark we know on early American houses. We have seen it in the decade between 1750 and 60. It is usually seen in the earliest American panel work, and before the date named. The earliest moldings of this sort are the largest.

No. 255. A cabinet, perhaps in Spanish cedar. We have in this piece an interesting instance of the difficulty of naming the species of wood. It has an appearance closely resembling walnut, but not as close and hard. It also resembles bay wood. The interior was completely filled with small drawers with light round ring handles. Some of these drawers are lost. A minor portion of the bosses and moldings have been restored. Comparison shows that the panels here are quite like those on the Plymouth chests and cupboards. We do not know the origin of this piece, but it was found in a private house in Boston in 1923. That it was designed to be set upon another piece of furniture is obvious from the shape of the base, and from the ancient handles on the ends. The hinges are handsomely scrolled and are shown later in detail.

Size: Over all, 32 by 23 by $11\frac{1}{2}$ inches.

No. 256. A yellow pine wall cupboard or table cupboard. This piece is of considerable interest, owing to the wide bevel of its raised panels and to the fact that it has a panel of wood below and of glass above in each of its doors. There is a shelf behind the central rails of the doors. We have observed with much interest the manner in which the public "take to" set-in, small, pieces of furniture, which have no very notable features. This cupboard has always excited much admiration, or perhaps we ought to say affection.

Size: Over all, $27\frac{1}{4}$ by $24\frac{1}{2}$ by $10\frac{1}{2}$ inches.

No. 257. The Quincy Homestead, in the town of the same name, is sometimes erroneously called the Dorothy Q. House. The earliest part of this house, very ancient indeed, has been added to, on more than one occasion. The section shown here dates from the earlier part of the 18th century. The picture is particularly satisfying in that it partially reveals the fine pilaster and spandrel of the shell top cupboard, hidden away behind the panel work. If we were to hazard a guess it would be that the panel work was put in place very shortly after the cupboard. Yet, the cupboard should not be thus hidden, and the assemblage of the two elements shows a confusion in design. This cupboard has a narrow drawer. Instead of the usual door below, the large door, now at least, takes the place of it. We should not omit to say that the earliest recessed cupboards are sometimes found without a door, and, if so built, are regarded with the greater interest.

No. 258. A detail showing a recessed cupboard over a fireplace in the Williams House in South Easton. The opportunity to form the cupboard arises from the backward rake of the chimney face above the fireplace. The example is one of the earliest that we know. In the same house there was a diamond-pane leaded window, which has now been removed to the Taunton Museum.

There are other corner cupboards in this house, built without doors above.

The fashion of recessing cupboards in what would otherwise be waste spaces in the walls is excellent. It also appeals to our sense of the romantic and the mysterious. We feel in a house with such receptacles as if we were reading an old time tale of mystery, love and war.

No. 259. This is a distinct surprise to those who first view it. There are here two cupboards set one on either side of the fireplace in the parlor of the Sparhawk House at Kittery. The cupboards are identical, with demidome shell-tops. The line from the front to the main wall runs back in a diagonal or splay. While we cannot feel that the projection of a fireplace into a room is the most satisfactory treatment, we are willing to admit that, if it is to be so projected, its treatment by cupboards of this sort almost redeems it.

No. 260. The objects here shown are the upper and lower sections of a hanging rack to hold skeins of embroidery yarn. Numerous cords at spaced intervals passed in pairs from the bottom to the top element and were gathered above in a quaint iron hook by which the piece hung from the ceiling. By lifting the upper section skeins of silk or wool could be laid in order, their ends projecting and cut open, so as to form needles full. The object was to prevent the blowing about of the yarn simply by the weight of the upper part laid against the lower. The wood is Connecticut hickory, otherwise often called white walnut. It was long before we could learn the use of this piece. The carving, which suggests the sunflower, and other elements of abstruse origin, provides a quaint little article of much interest. The length of the sections is $17\frac{1}{2}$ inches and their width $3\frac{1}{4}$ inches.

No. 261. A little wall or table cupboard with drawers. The tri-

290–292. THREE TYPES OF PIPE BOXES.

293. TAPE LOOM.

294. CORNER FIRE PLACE.

295. CARVED TRIANGULAR CHAIR. 17th CENTURY.

296. ROBINSON WAINSCOT CHAIR. 1630–50.

297. Rector Pierson Wainscot Chair. 1640–60.

angular top section was designed for a cocked hat, and has a rounded rest of wood for the hat. Probably the lower drawers were used for a gentleman's neck linen and his stocks. The piece dates in the earlier half of the eighteenth century. It was in the author's former collection. There is in the Stone House, Guilford, a similar piece; the author has another; and he has seen a triangular table box with the cover opening upward.

No. 262. A set of open shelves with scrolled edges and top, to be attached to a wall. In the author's former collection. The shelves are convexed, and the whole affair is small. It dates probably in the eighteenth century. The sides are rabbeted.

No. 263. A suspended cupboard with hanger cut out in the favorite heart pattern. The design of the raised panel indicates the eighteenth century, probably about the middle. It is from the George F. Ives Collection.

No. 264. A little, primitive, corner cupboard, much weathered. It is probable that the design of the small shelf on the extended scrolled portion below is of Pennsylvanian or Jersey origin.

Size: 12 by 36 inches.

No. 265. This cupboard, with a plastered demidome, was taken from the Marsh House, Wethersfield, from which we get the date. The cupboard was set up in the dining room of the Webb House in the same town. The door with its heavy muntins and its small, quaintly shaped, arched top sash is very good. The shelves within are shaped. The material, of course, is white pine.

No. 266. A little scrolled dresser. The perfect sweep by which the side scroll blends with the top scroll is an unusually good feature. The piece is in yellow and white pine with maple cornice mold.

The recessing of the upper cupboard adds to the attraction of the piece. It was found near Boston.

Size: 73½ by 38¼ by 16½ inches.

No. 267. Is the spinning attic of the Wentworth Gardner House in Portsmouth. It contained a butterfly table and in the distance a garter loom.

No. 268. Is the parlor of the Iron Works House, Saugus, as restored, and showing a huge rug, Brewster and Carver chairs, a wag-on-the-wall clock. The chair at the left foreground is supposed to be of continental origin, and the style perhaps came into western Europe from Constantinople. This is the sort of a chair which Walpole wrote about when he asked a clerical friend to pick one up for him. We do not show this chair in detail because we have never seen one which we believe originated in America.

No. 269. A Pennsylvanian wardrobe. This piece is of much more pleasing construction than a kas. The good cornice with its dentils and the numerous well formed panels, and the quaint central pointed foot, with the bracket feet at the side, contribute to form a piece of much attraction. We now get into a period that demands Chippendale hardware, but the hinges are the quaint Pennsylvanian type. This piece is in walnut, and was found by Mr. C. C. Littlefield of Newfields, New Hampshire. The construction is similar to that of a kas, fastened together by wedges and slots.

No. 270. Mr. L. G. Myers of New York City is the owner of this finely decorated kas. The word is applied to pieces found near the Hudson, and of this general character. So far as we have noted they all have immense ball feet and large cornices. They are usually in walnut, and have as here drawers in the frame or base. They are not made with a true frame but are put together in sections with wedges, and the top is then fitted on to complete the work. The elaborate decoration here reaches its climax. The painting on the two doors is intended to be identical. The three stiles are also identical. The decorated ends did not come out well in the photograph, but they were by no means slighted by the painter. It will be seen that the heavy moldings run around the ends. Altogether we have here a striking example of Knickerbocker work.

No. 271 is a kas on which the drawer handles have now been replaced. It is a somewhat simpler form of No. 270. The material is plain walnut, and the cornice is huge. The plain kas of this sort seems not to be popular amongst collectors. Yet certainly it possesses a good deal of individuality. We believe that as a rule very large pieces are less sought for. This remark, however, would not apply to beds, or to trestle tables.

Nos. 272–276. These interesting spoons, one with scrolled handle, and the slightly oval shallow plate or bowl with scalloped edge, belong to Mr. Albert C. Bates of Hartford. It is not always possible to know whether a bowl is made by an Indian or by the settler who learned the art from him. Of course if the bowl is turned the origin is settled as coming from the American pioneers.

No. 277 is a wall cupboard owned by Mr. J. Stodgell Stokes of Philadelphia. Its appeal is very strong. The cubby above the door is a fascinating affair with its quaintly scrolled border. The arch above, a part of the heavy molding, is an addition to the merit of the piece.

The door attached with the mortised and riveted hinges has in addition to the beveled and raised panel, still another raised surface upon it, with scrolled corners. The side panels on the splay are winning in design.

Altogether the piece is one to cause us to remember the tenth commandment.

No. 278. A long and narrow cupboard to be placed on a shelf or attached to the wall. Its hight, its three drawers increasing in width, and its paneled door with three butterfly hinges, are all elements of interest. The material is pine and whitewood, and the drawers have a lip. It belongs in the earlier half of the eighteenth century.

Size: The hight is 48 inches and the width is 20 inches, and the projection from the wall is 12 inches. These measurements include the moldings.

No. 279. A remarkably good specimen of a cupboard, from its general style and from its rare features. The owner is Lucy Atwater Royce of Hartford. The piece came from a sea captain in Madison, who is eighty-five years old. He stated it belonged to his grandfather. The piece unhappily has lost its cornice. The two doors with what in furniture we call the Connecticut cross, and their raised triangular panels, are, of course, the outstanding features. We would call this a cupboard and not a dresser, since it has a door above. The date would fall within the earlier half of the eighteenth century.

No. 280. A spoon and knife rack shown in larger proportions than the cupboard. The wood is pine, each shelf being strongly molded. Instead of a drawer below there is a quaint little lid hinged like that of a till of a chest. The general effect is very pleasing.

Size: $13\frac{1}{2}$ by $23\frac{1}{4}$ by $5\frac{1}{4}$ inches.

No. 281. Is a small cupboard of walnut, unrestored. The original hinges of the buckhorn pattern are themselves important. The piece stood in a corner so that it is paneled on one end only.

The chief feature of interest is the blocked paneling. Above the ordinary raised beveled panel there is carved to a depth of $\frac{3}{16}$ of an inch a scroll of pleasing contour. The author found the piece in 1923 in eastern Pennsylvania. A little restoration would render this cupboard very handsome.

Size: $25\frac{1}{2}$ by $28\frac{1}{2}$ by $14\frac{3}{4}$ inches.

No. 282. Is a framed cradle with pine sides and ends. The posts follow the analogy of the earlier cradles, since they are finished with turned finials. The date is probably late seventeenth or early eighteenth century. In the former collection of the author.

No. 283. Represents two Pennsylvanian corner cupboards arranged as they should be, one above another, to set off and complement each the lack of the other. The lower piece is in pine and the upper piece in whitewood. The hinges below are especially good. Those above hide their shape in mortises. The general arrangement of the doors, drawers and paneling forms a satisfactory ensemble. The bracket feet of the lower section and the scrolls on the upper section supply a proper finish to the design.

Size: Lower cupboard, 32 by 40¾ by 20¾ inches. Upper cupboard, 35 by 26 by 24 inches.

No. 284 is a two part New England dresser, and is the only New England dresser built in two sections, that we have seen. It is all of soft pine. There are shallow grooves cut on the main shelf into which the end boards of the upper section are made to slide. In addition to this peculiarity the dresser has what we have noticed in perhaps a half dozen New England pieces, a scrolled board on the cornice.

In this work we are not generally using the technical term entablature which of course, properly means more than a cornice. In popular speech the tops of these cupboards are generally spoken of as cornices, a term including the frieze and the cornice proper.

This dresser has all the elements that we look for in a complete piece, including the doors at the sides with their original H hinges, and made with the early panels; also the three drawers between the doors.

The main shelf or dresser proper extends for its full width over the end so as to preclude the possibility of a one piece vertical end board. The origin is Hillsboro County, New Hampshire.

Size: 65 inches across the front; 89 inches high, and 17½ inches from front to back, in the lower section. The cornice is original with the exception of an end return, as the piece stood in a corner where it could not have that return. There is also a slide which required restoration. The feature of a slide in a dresser, together with the other features we have enumerated, is rare if not unique.

298. Governor Leete Chair. 1640–60.

299. A Seventeenth Century Room.

300. THE MOST PERFECT "BREWSTER." 1640–60.

301. THE "MILES STANDISH BREWSTER." 1630-60.

PIPE AND WALL BOXES

W E HAVE hitherto shown some pipe boxes under Nos. 180–183, and are now grouping a few more.

No. 285. A pipe box owned by the Metropolitan Museum. The shape of the scrolled head on this box is precisely like that of the battle axe shaped design on Mr. Seymour's Bible box No. 147. The box on the right belongs to Mr. H. W. Erving and is of unique shape. It appropriately has with it a pair of pipe tongs, of which we have seen three other examples almost identical.

Nos. 286–289. On the left, a pipe box containing the pipes of the shape originally used, and showing the necessity for the deep pocket. The central piece is a simple box with a lid, for what use we are not certain. In lack of a better name such pieces are usually called spice boxes, as is the one on the right.

Nos. 290–292 are three types of pipe boxes, the first having a boldly scalloped edge all about. The material is curly maple but someone has ruined the surface by a heavy obscuring coat. It is a very striking piece.

Nos. 290 and 291 are each odd in their way. The former shows a touch of carving at the hanging handle, and the latter has the odd feature of two drawers. Both pieces are in pine.

No. 293 is a tape loom, commonly braced in place for use against or between chairs. Its special interest here is in connection with chair No. 296.

No. 294 is a corner fireplace in the York Jail, Maine, an edifice now used as the local museum. This fireplace has the unusual device in America of a raised hearth. It was not so easy to take care of and probably not so economical. It is, however, attractive. Corner fireplaces always have a charm exceeding those in the side of a room, and by their use in eight rooms the corners of all of which should touch a chimney, a single chimney stack would be sufficient for a whole house.

CHAIRS

IT HAS been thought that the chair developed from a stool, and the German word for chair so similar to our word stool, would seem to bear out the supposition. However, the use of a throne, which was a chair, goes back to an antiquity so early that we can not claim a lack of knowledge of design, for chair backs, on the part of the earliest cabinet makers.

It is generally conceded that the earliest known chair was a wainscot. That is to say, it was of solid or paneled oak in the back and probably in the sides, since for protection against the cold, and for beauty and dignity, the finest early chairs were enclosed on three sides. There is in the Metropolitan Museum such a chair, but perhaps it is not claimed that the origin is American.

No. 295. This chair, around which some controversy has waged, since it is of the triangular type, and hence naturally to be regarded as foreign, nevertheless has arms and a stretcher of cherry said to be American. If it is American it was made at least a hundred years after its period. It is owned by Mr. Paul A. de Silva of Boston, and is or was on exhibition in the old State House there. It bears a label stating that it was brought from Lyons, France, in 1685.

There is on the front rail what we might call a channel mold were it not filled with carved beads. The back post also is carved as well as the main top rail. The shape of the arms corresponds quite precisely with the earliest American wainscot chair arms.

The design is more interesting than that of the usual three cornered and turned "Walpole" chair. It is not without marks of much grace. We are not ready to make any statement in regard to its origin. We can only congratulate the owner upon the possession of a piece so excellent.

No. 296. A chair which came to great prominence in connection with its sale in Guilford at public auction.

It belonged to Thomas Robinson who removed from Hartford to Guilford in the year 1639. A little book printed for the Robinson Family Association and entitled "The Robinsons and their Kin Folk," contains a sketch of this chair, and some description of Thomas Robinson.

We should be glad to be able to connect this Robinson with the Pilgrim Robinson, but we have not sufficient data for doing so. It will be remembered that the original John Robinson, pastor of the Pilgrims in Leyden, remained behind in the old world to pay his debts. He was a

302. A BREWSTER-TRANSITION CHAIR. 1660–90.

303. The Cotton Mather High Chair. 1640–60.

saint if there ever was one. The reason he stayed is the reason that has hastened the departure for this country of various other immigrants.

We believe his sons came to America.

The chair shows in its turnings the earliest known American type, and we consider it entirely probable that a joint stool to be shown later was made by the same turner. As bought the chair had sections of barrel staves laid in the bottom as a seat. With the exception of the half inch oak which has now been nailed in for a seat the chair is in its original condition, at least back to the time when some ingenious housewife induced her spouse to cut a tape loom in the plain solid panel which forms the back. That this work was not original is apparent from its crudity. The saw cuts are irregular. The holes through which the warp ran are as usual burned smooth. The sharply returning scroll on the under side of the arm should be observed as a characteristic.

Every part of this chair is in oak. The simplicity of the top together with the color and texture of the oak and the construction in general have settled the question that the piece is American.

One may note in regard to the American wainscot chairs that the back legs are in the form of court cupboard back legs, being stiles which are the extensions of the panel frame.

Some six or eight American wainscot chairs have come to light. Carved chairs exist here and there, which have been described in publications as American. We remain unconvinced.

No. 297. The Rector Pierson chair, belonging to Yale University, and in the president's room. It will be noticed that in this example the scroll on the under side of the arm is more fully developed and carried out under the seat frame, not only in front but on the sides. It will also be noticed that the construction of the back is quite like that of chests. Indeed, so great is the similarity that a piece of oak wainscot, which has been found, might either have been the back of a settee or the front of a chest. In the example before us the molding of the stiles is precisely like that seen on chests. The extreme simplicity of this chair in comparison with English examples is to be noted.

No. 298. The Governor Leete wainscot chair. It is in the Stone House, Guilford.

Like other wainscot chairs shown, and like another one in the author's possession with a scrolled top, these chairs mortised the rail between the back posts, not capping the posts. This is the earliest style, as we shall see a little later. It is also a better construction, far less liable to breakage.

The word " wainscot " is in general use confined to oak panel work. The word is a fascinating study in etymology. The wain, the common

English word for a large wagon in the haze of the years reminds us of Constable's pictures. The *schot* (English shot) means partition. Wagon partitions, or panels, were found to be best and strongest when made of oak, and in process of time the best oak for paneling was therefore named wainscot. Elderly Americans can well remember when the sides of wagons were paneled, in Pennsylvania and in New England. The work was done in long curves on boat shaped sides. The purpose was to prevent the tendency of the load to shift forward and backward on hills, and the fashion was maintained even in the Concord wagon. The famous Conestoga wagon which is the finest symbol of the emigration, from the coast states to the west of the Alleghanies, resembles nothing so much as a boat on wheels. It is possible that the term " prairie schooner " used with a later and inferior type of wagon, is derived from the tradition of the Conestoga wagon.

The term " wainscot " as applied to chairs means, therefore, an oak chair with panel work, and so of course with a solid back and sometimes with solid work under the arms, and the seat. This sort of chair was made mostly in those days when the head of the household was the only person having a chair. The chair was, of course, a seat of authority from time immemorial. In fact, the domain of a bishop is named a see, after a chair, through the French *siege*. Going farther back, *cathedra*, the Greek for chair, became the sign of a bishop's authority, so much so, in fact, that the edifice built over it gets its name cathedral from the chair. The analogy between the dignity attached to a throne and that attached to a stately chair is a fascinating one. The patriarch, that is to say, of a family or of a church, possessed a stately seat. It was handed down, among laymen, to his eldest son. When the son sat in that chair his word was law. The connection here is close and interesting with the infallibility predicated of the Bishop of Rome when seated in his cathedra, surrounded in conclave by his advisers, and giving out a dictum.

The chair, therefore, especially in its heavier, older and finer forms with the arm or " elbow," and appropriated by the head of the family, was always a mark of a certain dignity and authority. This fact is curiously set forth by the possession of a fine chair by most of the Pilgrim and Puritan religious teachers. The best known instance is the chair of Elder Brewster, which has attained a like fame with that of Governor Carver, he of the civil authority. Peter Bulkeley, the first minister of Concord, had a very beautiful and stately chair of the carved cane period, with Flemish curves, and later shown. We may suppose that this was by all odds the most important chair in the town. Other clergymen also had

304. "BREWSTER" CHAIR, ORIGINAL BALLS. 1640–60.

305. Carver Initialed Chair. 1640–60.

306. Great Carver Chair. 1640–60.

307. BREWSTER CHAIR. 1640–60.

308. PILGRIM CHAIR. 1650–70.

309–311. CHILDREN'S CHAIRS. 18th CENTURY.

their fine chairs. They were a part of the clerical dignity, a kind of appurtenance of office.

We have instances, as in the case of the Robinson chair, of joint stools made to match the chair. It is fair to infer that the joint stools went with the chairs and were used by the other members of the family. The wife might inherit the bed, or even the court cupboard, but the son and heir was honored by the acquisition of his father's chair. It went to him as the robe of Elijah passed to his disciple and successor.

In process of time the wife, who was much honored, might be favored with a smaller and lower chair without arms, which was called the " lady " chair. It is a curious custom in parts of Connecticut, to this day, to call side chairs, that is, chairs without arms, " lady " chairs.

The wainscot chair in its perfection, even in America, had a scrolled or crested top, as in the Governor Leete chair and in a chair owned by the author and derived from Long Island.

No. 299. Exhibits a room with stately chairs and a huge fireplace, in the Saugus Iron Works House, and shows how much was made of the chair in those days.

No. 300. The Tufts-Brewster chair. This specimen was discovered by the author in the dwelling of Mr. John Tufts, at that time living in Sherborn, Massachusetts. Mr. Tufts was an aged man and had no immediate heirs. He stated that the chair had been in his family for eight generations of record. The posts are at least two and a half inches in diameter, and every portion of it as here shown is original. It is wonderfully put together. Mr. Tufts stated that every spindle was in place as he knew it when a boy. Comparing it with the chair in Pilgrim Hall, Plymouth, from which the name Brewster is derived, we see that this is a more massive and more stately chair than Elder Brewster's. It has not, however, a second row of spindles at the sides corresponding with the bottom row in front. In that respect the Elder Brewster chair was originally more fully carried out. The condition of the Elder Brewster chair is deplorable, it having lost its feet, its back rung and its top rail. It is an amusing circumstance that a manufacturer, a score or more years ago, copied the Elder Brewster chair, and was ignorant of the loss of these two members. The loss is clearly shown by a hole in the post on one side, and the stub of the rail in the post on the other side. The author was hurriedly summoned, and had a midnight ride across a part of the state of Massachusetts to see a marvelous Brewster chair. When he arrived he found one of the reproductions above mentioned, which had been washed off and aged, and was offered at a bargain, if taken that night, at eight hundred dollars!

The name " Brewster " we are arbitrarily confining, in our descriptions, to turned chairs having rows of spindles in the back, usually a row under the arms, and one or more rows below the seat.   There are not enough chairs, however, to form a Brewster class, and the application of the term to slat back, and other chairs, in order to give them dignity and desirability is either a trick or a mark of lack of knowledge.   The Tufts chair had balls on the front posts as had every specimen we have ever examined of Brewster, Carver, and Pilgrim slat backs.   This ball was the first member of the chair to be attacked.   It is generally found either partly whittled away, or it is sawed off, as in the Tufts chair.   The author restored these balls, to the regret of the present owner, Mrs. J. Insley Blair.

Size: Total hight 43½ inches.   The front width of the seat is 23 inches. The depth is 16 inches.   It has probably lost not more than a half an inch at the bottom.

The seat of wood is to be observed.   Such seats are about a half an inch thick, and were set in rabbets on the turnings which formed the seat frame, and they are an earlier type than the seat of rush.   Seats of wood were invariably used with cushions of leather or a richer material.   Thus a foot stool was necessary.   If, however, the chair was used at table it was presumed that the occupant would place his feet upon the table stretcher, a thing so much to the scandal of our books on etiquette.   The tables of the earliest day were higher than our own tables, and of course the chairs were correspondingly higher.   The use of the foot stool was further encouraged by the coldness of the floor.   It was partly to avoid chilblains that stools were used.

No. 301.   A " Miles Standish " Brewster.   The person who discovered this chair obtained information with it which led him to state that it had belonged to Miles Standish.   Various data in the hands of the owner, Mrs. F. H. Lincoln of Hingham, probably bear us out in the belief that the chair actually did belong to Miles Standish.

The best proof, however, of the great age of the chair, is found in its massive character.   Its posts in places reach a present diameter of 2 $\frac{11}{16}$ inches.   The fact that the chair was much cut down, and lacks the bottom section, suggests the amusing relation between the somewhat stunted stature of Miles Standish and his need of a low chair.   The restoration has been badly done.   The spindles under the arms are not original.   The very interesting back finials, however, are original, and we think all the rest of the chair, except the incongruous pieces to which the casters are attached and the balls on the front posts.

One should compare the flattened spindles here with those on No. 300.

312. WELL TURNED CARVER CHAIR. 1650–60.

313. VERY HEAVY PILGRIM "LADY" CHAIR. 1640–60.

314. SLANT BACK CARVER CHAIR. 1640–60.

315. Turned Arm Chair.   316. Light Carver.

317. Pair Pilgrim Side Slat Backs. 1670–1700.

These flattened spindles are found on some other chairs, and we may presume that they are so made in the interest of comfort.

Amongst the ancient worthies we may therefore enumerate as having come down to us, the chairs of Edward Winslow, Governor Carver, Elder Brewster, Miles Standish, Cotton Mather, and Peter Bulkeley, all of the first generation of the settlers, with the possible exception of the last.

No. 302. A Transition turned chair in the George F. Ives Collection. We have here a scheme of spindles in the back like the Brewster chair except that they are reduced to three in number. We have also spindles under the arms, not, however, running into the seat as in the rarest earliest examples. There are, however, no spindles below the seat, and the posts are not so massive as in the previous examples. The student should also notice that the very earliest chairs have no turnings on the posts below the seat, as in Nos. 303, 305, 312, 314. We have quoted, we think, a convincing number of examples. The first turnings on the front posts below the ball were an ornamental turning between the ball and the seat, as in No. 301. We then get a second ornamental turning below the seat as in No. 300. The process goes on increasing until as here we have turnings on the front posts so that the only plain portions are those that receive the rungs. We also notice here a slight falling off in the styles of the finials. The movement toward a somewhat lighter chair was natural and from this period on is very marked. Another chair like this is known.

No. 303. The Cotton Mather high chair. This remarkably quaint example has, it will be noted on comparison, a finial closely resembling No. 300, whereas the top rail is different. It is fair to name this chair a Brewster, as it has spindles under the arms and also down the front. The lack of a double row of spindles in the back is easily admissible in a high chair owing to its greatly reduced proportions.

Owner: Worcester Antiquarian Society. This chair is one of perhaps twenty objects shown in this book that have been illustrated in works of other authors.

No. 304. A Brewster chair. It is rare in having its original balls on the front posts and its beautifully turned finials. At the same time it has not so many sets of spindles under the seat as examples already shown. It is, however, very handsome and in very fine condition, the only restoration being a slight piecing of the feet, but below the lower rungs.

A style mark of the turned arm chairs is that they invariably have at least two sets of rungs on the front and on both sides, and only one behind and that near the bottom. Any lack of these members is a certain indication that the chairs have been sawed off or otherwise tampered with. We have one or two late instances of two spindles behind in the base but we can think of none anywhere near the Pilgrim period.

This chair was bought in Boston in 1923, in black paint and with a leather seat as shown, which, of course, is not original, it having had a rush seat. All balls and finials and spindles are original.

Size: Largest diameter of post $2\frac{7}{16}$ inches. Total hight $45\frac{1}{2}$ inches. Outside front width $23\frac{1}{2}$ inches. Outside back width, $17\frac{3}{8}$ inches.

No. 305. A Carver chair bearing the initials B. H. This chair has its original balls in front and very rare and handsome finials. It is original except a piecing of the legs, well below the bottom rungs, and we think the front bottom rung. A peculiarity is the " short waisted " back. This massive chair in the author's collection was also in his former collection. Most of the more important pieces in the former collection have now been added to the present collection.

The woods of Pilgrim turned chairs deserve particular attention. The very earliest are generally of ash. This material is not good for turnings as it tends to chip and break away. Indeed, it is on account of this easy splitting as well of course as its toughness that it was used for bows.

In the effort to ascertain why a wood so unsuitable was used we are led into some interesting by-paths. It used to be presumed that the Brewster and Carver chairs of Plymouth were brought over in the Mayflower. Had that been the case we should perhaps be surprised at finding them in ash, unless possibly they came from Holland, where turned chairs were known. A simple explanation appears, however, in the very defect we have mentioned, the easy splitting quality. The first lading sent back from the new world was that of barrel staves of ash. The cooper, John Alden, came for the express purpose of preparing them. In securing such staves it was the work of a moment to split out roughly in an octagonal form posts for turned chairs. The settlers were not at that time seeking for elegance but rather to supply their immediate needs. We share the belief that the turned chairs of this type were not in any case imported, so far at least as they have remained with us. Oak chairs are common in England even where they are turned. We do not remember an instance of an all oak turned chair of the Pilgrim Century, though we have here and there seen oak rungs and sometimes found oak parts in the later turned chairs such as the Windsors.

Nos. 300 and 301 and 312 are in ash. No. 320 is also of ash, and some of the rungs have so far lost their glutinous connective tissues as to be separate stringy fibres.

The chair before us is in maple, a very satisfactory and beautiful wood for turnings. It retains a close, smooth surface. But woe be to him

318. GREAT SLAT BACK CHAIR. 1680–1700.

319. "Brewster" 1620–40.

320. High Post Carver.

321. Light Carver.

322. Light Carver.

323. Heavy Pilgrim Slat Back. 1640–60.

324. Pilgrim Chair. 1640–60.   325. Carver Chair. 1650–70.

326–327. Wrought Kettle Tripod and Trivet.

who undertakes to stain it, as the effects remain merely on the surface and do not strike in, as in ash and oak and such open grain woods. It is for this reason that the natural maple, a very pale yellow, far lighter than "golden oak," is so much liked and in such good taste, in refinishing these old chairs. In fact, it is not a refinishing, unless a coat of wax may be so termed.

The use of maple came in shortly after ash, and we find chairs of this type and of the slat back Pilgrim period and most later chairs in maple.

Size: Total hight, 47 inches. Outside width, front, $24\frac{1}{2}$ inches; back, $18\frac{1}{2}$ inches. The spindles have a diameter of $1\frac{1}{4}$ inches. The depth from the front to the back at right angles is 16 inches.

The very sharp spread of these chair seats from front to back is noticeable. There is here a difference of six inches in the width, and from five to six inches is common.

No. 306. This great Carver chair has a back superior to any other that we have seen, in its massiveness, and the character of its turnings. The likeness of the finial to the Cotton Mather and the Tufts chairs is close. We assign the same date to the Carver, the Brewster and the Pilgrim slat back chairs. In fact, if there is any difference in date, it is to be found more definitely suggested by the decrease in the size of the posts as the date advances. Other things being equal a Pilgrim chair has an importance in proportion to the size of these posts. A few years since a Carver was a Carver in the eyes of collectors. Now, however, the massive sort is chiefly desired. This statement has in some cases nettled dealers in antiques. We would like their good will, but the facts about the chairs must be stated.

The example before us is in maple. It is original throughout. The fatness of the spindles is amusingly quaint, and their style of turning is of the best early sort. It is even found in a Spanish bed. Possibly the Spanish Netherlands may be connected with our turning styles.

In giving the sizes of the posts of chairs this work follows the rule of naming the largest diameter found on a chair. This method is quite likely to mislead, unless the reader notes the following: Various chairs are curiously made by a taper of the back post, so that the diameter of the post near the floor is considerably less than immediately below the finials. It is also very noticeable that the turnings are never round now, as they have shrunk in one diameter more than in the other. Also we should observe that it is seldom that we find any two posts of a chair agreeing in size, as they were obviously turned by the eye and never with calipers. In the chair before us there is a sad and obtrusive falling off in the front posts from the size of the back posts. Further, these front posts seem to have been turned while so green that they are now in an oval form. It is fair throughout this work to take off from one-eighth to a quarter of an inch from the diameters given of the posts to get at the average diameter of all the posts throughout their length.

A feature of some of these chairs is a very slight rounding in of the posts at the bottom on the back. This rounding in is so slight, however, and so frequently fails to be found, that we can hardly call it a typical feature.

The great chair before us was bought in Boston in 1923.

Size: $45\frac{1}{4}$ inches high; 24 inches and $18\frac{1}{2}$ inches in the outside width, front and back, at the seat, with a depth of $16\frac{1}{2}$ inches.

The largest diameter of the post is $2\frac{3}{4}$ inches.

No. 307. A Brewster chair. This specimen was found with the feet cut off, a loss which included the lower set of rungs. The wood is maple.

The back is especially good and is all original as are all the other parts of the chair except as above stated. It was bought in Boston in 1922.

Size: $43\frac{1}{2}$ inches high, $26\frac{1}{2}$ inches wide in front, $16\frac{1}{2}$ inches behind. The largest diameter of the post is $2\frac{3}{8}$ inches. A peculiar difference in the turning is here observed in the front post above the seat. One observes an extreme distance of ten inches difference in the width of the outside measurements on the front and back. It is such elements as these that give a chair its individuality.

No. 308. This is the first example which we have had of a Pilgrim slat back chair. Doubtless the very earliest of these had only two " backs," which was later increased to three, and finally to four in the rarer examples. One also sees a slat very much wider than is usually found. The similarity between the turnings of this chair and that of No. 358 lead to the conclusion that they were made to go together. The chair was bought in New Bedford in 1922, in a bad condition as regards the feet, a number of inches being missing including the lower rungs. A part of one of the slats is also renewed. The chair, however, is so appealing and so unusual and so quaint that it merits our careful attention. It is of maple.

Nos. 309–311. These three child's chairs are shown here for convenience. It is not probable that any of them run back into the seventeenth century though that date is always possible in such a quaint little example as that on the left. This chair has the rare and interesting slanted arm spindle, and it also possesses its front balls intact.

No. 312. This fine Carver with unusual and excellent turnings, and somewhat massive in form, is in ash. It shows on the left post a flattening caused by being drawn along the floor, probably by children in play. The same feature appears quite generally in children's chairs, though it is

328. Carver Side Chair. 1650–60.

329. Double Ended Fork and Shovel.

330. HEAVY SIDE CARVER. 1660–70.

331–333. SPOONS AND A BIRD TRAMMEL.

334. Baby Carver Chair. 1680–90.

335–340. Trivet and Lighting Fixtures.

341. Odd Carver Variant. 1660–80.

342–344. Heart and Other Andirons.

somewhat mysterious in a great chair like this. The splitting away of slivers from the post on the left at the top bears out our statement that ash was a very unsuitable material for turnings. The same but more serious loss is found on the finial on that side.

There appears here the splint seat. It is contended in Connecticut that a seat in this form is as old as the rush seat, but we can hardly accept that contention. The rushes were ready to the hand of the settlers, and from the counties in England, like the Low Countries, whence a good many of our settlers came, the rushes were available and their use understood. The splint seat is not so durable nor so easy as the rush. Further, it was more likely to wear out the master's unmentionables and cause extra work for the housewife. The use of the rush seat is undoubtedly early.

We would point out the absurdity of claiming for an old chair that it has its original seat, as is frequently done. It may have its fourth or even seventh seat, and yet the seat may appear to be very old. Though a good rush seat may last the chair for possibly a hundred years, it is not at all probable that they had an average life of more than fifty years. Certainly, it is wholly impossible to state that any seat is original. By this statement, so manifestly reasonable, we should like to nail this discussion once for all.

Size: $43\frac{1}{2}$ inches high. The feet are slightly pieced, but well below the rungs. The largest diameter of a post is $1\frac{9}{16}$ inches.

No. 313. A very heavy Pilgrim slat back "lady" chair. It was bought in southern New Hampshire in 1921. It is the most massive of the side chairs that have come to our attention, hence leading us to believe it of very early date. The fact that it has its two sets of rungs also leads to the conclusion that it has not lost very much in its hight. The front rungs have the peculiarity that they are in a square section, like the stretchers of early tables. The total hight is 38 inches. The seat is $22\frac{1}{2}$ by 15 inches, and is now but 13 inches high, and probably never exceeded 14 inches. The ladies of our generation can bear us out in stating that a low chair is more convenient for sewing. We believe the chair to be maple.

No. 314. A Carver chair of unusual design and much merit.
Owner: Mr. George Dudley Seymour. Location: The Wadsworth Atheneum, Hartford. The fact that there are no turnings below the seat establishes the early character of the chair, which is further borne out by its size. By the word turning, in this connection, ornamental turning is always understood.

The finials on this piece are unusual and interesting; the front balls are original and we believe all the other parts.

A particular feature to which attention should be drawn is the fact that though this chair slants back, the rungs are parallel with the floor, which is a proof that the chair was built on a slant, to secure greater comfort. Nor is this an unique instance of the kind, though the emphasis here is somewhat more marked. A chair with a rush seat and a slightly slanting back is as comfortable as any modern chair. We make this statement because the general impression prevails, even on the part of writers on this subject, that antique furniture was uncomfortable.

No. 315. A good example of a light Carver chair, having a richly and handsomely turned arm rail. The very goodness of this turning is a suggestion of its slightly later date than the heavy examples.

No. 316. A light Carver chair with a seat of wood which is formed like a panel with thinned edges, set into slots cut to receive them in the seat rail. This is not unique.

The maker evidently got his proportions a little astray, when he spaced his spindles, and ran his back posts so far above the top rail.

No. 317. A pair of Pilgrim side chairs with slat backs. There is nothing extraordinary nor extremely unusual about these chairs except that they are heavier than the chair so common about 1750. They probably belong, therefore, in the Pilgrim Century.

No. 318. A great slat back chair.

Owner: Mr. Dwight Blaney.

There are several distinctive features here of much interest. The chair is the first example of an intermediate stretcher between the arm rail and the seat. This stretcher, wherever found, is rather handsomely turned, and its principal use is to stiffen the chair.

The arm rails are in a flat section, as were also those of No. 305. Four slats are a feature we have not had hitherto. These slats, especially that at the top, are winged. There is more elaborate turning than usual in the front rungs. The chair is stately and large, but the turnings, which foreshadow the New England slat back, so called, indicate a date succeeding that of the usual Pilgrim slat back. The finials here are very boldly and handsomely turned and are to be compared with those on No. 324.

No. 319. In this chair we have another and attractive variant of the Brewster chair. The turnings of the long back rails are so unusual that the question arises whether the chair is American. The wood, however, is ash, though sold as oak. While ash construction does not compel our belief in an American origin, it favors that belief. The chair is also remarkable in that many of the reduced ends or dowels of the rungs extend through the posts and are finished as small rounded knobs. There is shown a more elaborate chair with this peculiarity in *Lockwood*. The

345. Pair of Carver Side Chairs. 1660–80.

346–350. Fireplace Utensils.

351. Pilgrim Slat Back.

352. Wing Rail Banister.

353. Pilgrim Slat Back.

354. Transition Chair.

355. Spindle High Chair. 356. Banister High Chair.

357. SMALL MUSHROOM CHAIR. 1700.

long spindles in our chair, under the seat, suggest the Cotton Mather chair, No. 303. The long back spindles are $1\frac{5}{8}$ inches in diameter. The largest diameter of a post is $2\frac{9}{16}$ inches. There is an interesting peculiarity in the seat which engages in a slot in the back and front rung of the seat frame, and has no side supports. The chair has lost the tips of its finials and an inch or so at the bottom. It always had a marked rake backwards. An interesting proof of the necessity of a cushion is the rounded ridge of the front rung rising above the seat; so that to use it without a cushion would be torture. This is the only chair which has attained to the dignity of an academic degree, being marked with the initials A.M.!

No. 320. A high Carver chair.

Origin: Western Massachusetts.

Every part of this chair is original with the exception of one rung. The seaman's phrase " shiver my timbers " is very appropriate here, as the construction of loose grained ash, in the rungs, has allowed them to come to pieces, almost like bundles of small sticks. The other parts of the chair, being maple, have been very well preserved, the condition, particularly of the original balls and finials, being the best that we have seen. The latter are extremely unusual and interesting.

Size: $48\frac{1}{2}$ inches high, the highest Carver measurement we have met. The front is 25 inches across and the back $19\frac{1}{4}$ inches, both being outside measurements. The depth is also extreme, being 19 inches, as against the usual depth of about 16 inches. The largest diameter of a post is $2\frac{7}{16}$ inches.

No. 321. A light and unusual Carver in respect to its finials. It is all original with the exception of the balls in front.

No. 322. A light Carver, the finials of which, as in the last example, show a somewhat later date. Every part is original.

No. 323. A heavy Pilgrim three back chair. We have here the wooden seat set in like those on two or three previous examples. Of course, the feet are not right, and we believe that something is lost behind on the finials. We would not, however, by any means, minimize the importance of this very large and early chair. It is fair to state that not everyone agrees with the writer in relation to the finials.

Owner: Mr. John C. Spring of Boston.

No. 324. A heavy and very satisfactory example of the three back Pilgrim chair. It is in the old red paint as found. It was bought in Boston in 1922. The finials are fine and all parts are original. It will be observed that the scale on which objects in this book are shown is regulated in part by the exigencies of arrangement, and has no necessary reference to the importance of the objects.

Size: $43\frac{1}{2}$ inches high. The diameter of the posts is $2\frac{1}{2}$ inches. We shall, after this example, not trouble to give all dimensions, since those already given are sufficient to afford abundant data for comparison.

No. 325.   A Carver chair of medium weight.   It was bought on the South Shore in 1922.   It was found in black paint, as now, with the exception of the restoration of the balls in front.

Nos. 326–327.   A wrought iron kettle in a tripod, and a trivet.   Ordinarily kettles are cast, especially in New England.   In Pennsylvania it is not rare to find them wrought.   The setting of a kettle in a kind of tripod with ears is an arrangement which naturally suggests itself on a wrought piece.   Otherwise the legs would be riveted to the kettle.

The trivet has a top in pierced work.   It was purchased on the North Shore, but we do not know the country of its origin.

Both pieces belong to Mr. H. W. Erving.

No. 328.   This interesting example of a side chair in the Carver style derives additional merit from the excellence of its finials.   We think that if the reader will compare this chair carefully with No. 306 he will be convinced as we are that this is a " lady " chair made to accompany No. 306.   This conclusion is arrived at through the finials and especially through the top rail.   While this rail is somewhat simpler than that on No. 306 it has elements precisely like it, and it was the regular practice to simplify somewhat the turnings on the side chairs.   With the exception of piecing at the bottom this chair is original.   It is the solitary instance that we know of a single set of rungs.   The set-in places are so low that they could not possibly have a duplicate set below them, and that conclusion is borne out by the location of the rear rung, which is always near the bottom.   We believe that in restoring this chair we have added too much to the length of the leg and that we should have left it about fifteen inches high in the seat.   Thus, the rungs would appear to be nearer the floor, as in many " lady " chairs.

No. 329.   A curious little handle of twisted iron having a perforated miniature shovel at one end and a fork at the other end.   We can sympathize with, and probably suspect the motive of the maker who is always misplacing either the shovel or the fork.   A hand once grasping this handle would have both implements of culinary warfare " at hand."   This piece is an amusing example of Pennsylvanian ingenuity.   It was intended as a flapjack shovel and meat fork, and is only a few inches in length. It is at an ancient inn south of Bethlehem.

No. 330.   A heavy and unusual Carver side chair.   One would at first suppose that something was gone from the finial, but we have no doubt that in some instances the side chairs were made with plain balls at the

358. Heavy Mushroom Chair. 1680–90.

359. Mushroom Chair.   360. Mushroom Chair.

361–363. Toaster, Crusher and Wooden Hinges.

364. GREAT MUSHROOM CHAIR. 1700.

365. Mushroom Chair.   366. Mushroom Chair.

367-368. Mr. B. A. Behrend's Home Room.

back. This example is as high as an arm chair. It has the unusual feature of a ball turning on the top rail.

In side chairs, we do not, of course, look for a ball on the front post. Yet the post projects above the seat sufficiently to give a good space for the boring of the seat rungs.

Formerly in the collection of Mr. B. A. Behrend.

Nos. 331–333. We have a long handled spoon which was supposed to be made for the gentleman who ate with the devil. It is forty-one inches in length. The one shown here attains the respectable length of twenty-three inches, and bears a monogram. The other spoon is of a sort often found in Pennsylvania with a prettily hammered handle ending in a closed scroll hook and having a brass bowl. They were doubtless intended for stirring the pot.

No. 334. A baby Carver chair. It has probably lost simple finials. It was purchased in Hartford.

Size: 24½ inches high; seat 7½ inches high. It shows beautifully the wear on the front resulting from being dragged about a sanded floor.

Nos. 335–340. The heart shaped waffle iron was found in Charleston, South Carolina. Its interesting handles have a hook on one side and a link on another. The lighting fixtures will be treated later.

No. 341. This odd variant of a Carver has its spindles entering the seat rail. Of course the balls at the bottom are out of place. The seat is " paneled."

Owner: The George F. Ives Collection.

Nos. 342–344. The first number is a pair of andirons belonging to Mr. E. W. Sargent, of Providence, Rhode Island. They show one more of the numerous adaptations of the heart motive to wrought iron, and are most interesting. No. 343 shows another unusual pair of andirons with a shoe or flat base instead of two legs. The post runs up with a slight taper into a ball. No. 344 is another odd pair with the same sort of base, but in a flat section and rolled over at the top.

Nos. 345–346. A pair of Carver side chairs with their small original ball finials. These chairs from their moderate hight, and small size, indicate that they were made for ladies. They have lost a little at the bottom.

Origin: Eastern Massachusetts.

Owner: Mr. Chauncey C. Nash.

Nos. 347–350. Utensils for the fireplace, and a Betty, or fat, lamp.

Owner: Mr. Francis D. Brinton, Oermead Farm, West Chester, Pennsylvania.

The little toaster is a charming example. Pieces like this were used in England very much, and in the Colonies also.

No. 348 is a rare and perhaps unique piece. Instead of the kettle there should be on it a very long handled spider. Thus the trivet, which was set over the flame, provided a rest for the handle at two different elevations. We regard this piece very highly for its quaintness and we have learned that Mr. Brinton clings to it.

No. 349 is a little charcoal stove. We have seen a considerable number of these, having their posts turned down and flattened to afford a rest for a cooking vessel. The handle is of wood. The grill top hinges and is lifted by the central thumb piece.

No. 351. A Pilgrim slat back with good finials. In the former collection of the author.

No. 352. A wing rail banister back.

Owner: Mr. L. G. Myers.

The fine bulb-like turning is here to be commended. In a banister back chair we really have spindles which are split, something like the applied split spindles with which chests, chests of drawers, and court cupboards were decorated. The object of splitting the spindle was undoubtedly to secure comfort. We have already had examples of what we may call flat turnings in which the flattening is done on both sides. The banister back was really an inspiration on the part of the person who brought it into use. It is, however, somewhat later than a heavy turned chair. The first examples are probably after 1680. Such chairs continued to be made for about fifty years.

No. 353. A Pilgrim slat back. Here for the first time we get the beginning of a turning resembling the New England slat back, of 1700 and later. The arm rails are flat turnings, that is, turnings from which sections are cut away on two sides.

Date: 1670–1690.

No. 354. A Transition turned chair. The spindles are flattened but they are not banisters. The arms are also flattened turnings. Some parts of this chair are not original.

Date: 1680–1700.

No. 355. We arrive here at an odd example of a turned high chair. The balls on the feet are in part missing. It is the first example in which balls would be legitimate on the feet, bearing out the turnings of the front posts.

Date: 1700–1720.

Owner: The George F. Ives Collection.

No. 356. A flat and molded banister is a feature of the back. The

369–370. MUSHROOM CHAIRS.

371. COURTING CHAIR.

372. X STRETCHER CHAIR.

373. Large Mushroom.

374–377. Types of Lanterns.

378. "CROMWELLIAN" CHAIR.   379. "CROMWELLIAN" CHAIR.

380-383. FOUR BROILERS. 18th CENTURY.

384. Leather Back.

385. Carved Leather Back.

386–388. Toaster and Trivets.

scrolled upper rail has a pierced heart. There is an intermediate spindle between the arm and the seat.

Date: 1700–1720.

Owner: Mr. George Dudley Seymour.

The term describing the molding of the banisters is "reeded." The cresting or top rail is in part missing. It probably had what is called the crown motive, which, usually, is found superimposed over the heart. The material is maple, and the chair was never painted or restored. It has lost something from the feet. It was given to Elizabeth Davidson of Milford by her father. She married Abner Perry in 1795, and the chair has been held by their descendants until the owner bought it in 1921.

No. 357. This is the first example we have shown of the chair which has its front post mushroomed. Such chairs are usually called simply mushroom chairs. The turning of this broad hand rest was always done from the solid post, in one piece with the rest of the post. The chair in date is the same as the banister back, and some of these chairs appear in that form and others in the slat back as here. This chair is interestingly small, and it is possible that it was made for a lady. If so, it is the first instance in this book in which an arm chair could be assigned to feminine use. The piece is somewhat speckled as shown here, owing to the partial wearing away of a coat of light paint.

Owner: Mrs. W. B. Long of Boston.

No. 358. This chair is nearly identical with one shown in *Lyon*. We may presume that one was copied from the other, as the slight difference may suggest a second maker. The interesting scroll of the slats is to be observed. The mushrooms here are of the onion shape rather than flat, in the somewhat later styles. The slant of the arm rail is frequently found in mushroom chairs. The piece is of much importance and interest. We have discovered the third chair which was originally a precise counterpart of this one, before it was mutilated.

Owner: Mrs. J. Insley Blair.

Size: $43\frac{1}{2}$ inches high, 23 inches wide, 16 inches deep. Seat, $15\frac{3}{4}$ inches high.

No. 359. A mushroom chair with a featured, figured or scrolled top and bottom rail, and a well turned arm rail.

Date: 1700–1710.

No. 360. A mushroom chair with slanting arm rail and slat back. Comparing the finial of this chair with the one last described it appears that that finial belongs to the eighteenth century, and this finial belongs to the latter part of the seventeenth century and is better.

Date: 1680–1700.

Nos. 361–363.   At the bottom we have a remarkable pair of oak hinges, in which the strap of the hinge was in the form of a great cleat running across a door, and the hinge portion proper was formed by an oak pin run through a shovel-like piece, which in turn terminated in a dowel, that ran through the jamb post, and was fastened on the opposite side by a pin.   These remarkable hinges were presented to the author by Mr. Chetwood Smith of Worcester, who also loaned, for securing a picture, the quaint toaster at the top on the left.   The cutter, on a post attached to a base board, molded, was used to break up the large pieces of loaf sugar, into smaller sections, which could then be pulverized with the toddy stick.

No. 364.   A giant mushroom chair.   Whether this chair was constructed for the fat man of his county we cannot now say.   The hugeness of its dimensions would force some such conclusion.   The mushrooms are about four and a half inches in their larger diameter, and the posts have shrunk in such a manner as to show the mushrooms in an oval form.   The top slat is $5\frac{3}{4}$ inches wide, each slat below diminishing a quarter of an inch. The width over all to the outside of the mushrooms is $32\frac{3}{4}$ inches.   The back posts are $46\frac{1}{2}$ inches, and the front posts $30\frac{1}{2}$ inches high.   The outside of the seat is 30 inches in front and 24 inches in the back, and its depth is 22 inches.

All parts of this chair are original.

No. 365.   A mushroom four slat back chair, with sloping arm rails, and the first example we have had of the so-called sausage turned front stretchers.

No. 366.   A mushroom chair with handsomely and boldly scrolled slats.   It will be seen that though the mushrooms themselves required a large stick of lumber to turn the legs, the diameter of the main portion of the leg was small, in order to give lightness to the chair, following the trend of taste with the beginning of the eighteenth century.   The dates of this and the previous chair are around 1700.

Nos. 367–368.   A picture of the home room of Mr. B. A. Behrend, in Brookline.   In the foreground there is a butterfly table, a subject to be discussed later, and in the background will be seen a miniature stick leg chair, like a stool, more properly like a milking stool with a back, since there are but three legs.   The other articles here shown are elsewhere discussed.

Nos. 369–370.   The little chair is peculiar in having mushrooms, the only example of a baby chair of that sort that we have seen.

The large chair deserves a considerable degree of attention, since it seems to be a cross between a Pilgrim slat back, a Brewster chair, and a

389. CARVED LEATHER BACK.   1680–1700.

390-391. Pennsylvania and New England High Chairs.

392-393. Rush Stool and Baby Corner Chair.

394. HEART AND CROWN CHAIR. 1690–1720.

395. GIFT LADLE OF IRON AND COPPER.

396–397.   Original Rocker and High Desk Chair.

398–399.   Rush Stool and Joined Stool.

mushroom chair, having many of the important elements of all these three designs. The shape of the mushrooms is similar to that in an important turned chair owned by the architect Mr. Joseph Chandler, and now or formerly on exhibition at the Boston Fine Arts Museum. This mushroom post would seem to indicate the transition between the Pilgrim chair and the mushroom post. This chair was found in Middleboro. It lacked about two inches of its original height. It is shown here as found, but the feet have now been spliced. We must date the chair in the latter part of the seventeenth century.

No. 371. We may call this a courting chair, owing to its having backs on two sides. It is a corner chair, really, with backs meeting at right angles.

Owner: Mr. Arthur W. Wellington.

Date: 1700–1710.

No. 372. A corner chair. The peculiarity of this piece is that it has an X stretcher.

Owner: Mr. L. G. Myers.

Date: 1700–1720.

No. 373. A large chair of the mushroom type. Aside from the giant mushroom previously shown this is one of the most striking examples. One sees, however, a falling off in the style of the finials, they being rather slight and lacking dignity in comparison with earlier examples.

Nos. 374–377. A series of lanterns belonging to Mr. Rudolph P. Pauly. The lantern on the left, called after Paul Revere, could certainly not have been seen across a river. The second piece is a bottomless affair to place over a candle to prevent the wind from blowing it out. It is pierced with oddly shaped holes. The other two lanterns are of a good early type. It is hardly worth while attempting to date such pieces as they are used in this form for a hundred and fifty years.

No. 378. Simple chairs, with ball turnings, and with square stretchers, on the side and back, and with low backs for upholstery, have acquired the name Cromwellian. It has been a favorite theory of historical critics that during the Puritan period in England there was a lull in artistic expression. The destruction of many beautiful features in cathedrals fosters this view. It is probable also that the minds of men were so much engaged in the civil conflict that they had little time for artistic expression. We know that the Protector had some very beautiful furniture. However that may be, this chair dates about 1650–1670.

No. 379. Another Cromwellian chair, somewhat simpler. These chairs are covered with various materials. It would be a great mistake to presume that leather, the simplest and most satisfactory and most durable material, was by any means generally used. Silks, brocades, and petit point were often employed. Of course, the covering on the chairs here shown, especially that on the right, is late and bad.

Nos. 380–383. These four broilers show various good types. The first is perfectly plain in its bars, the second has its bars serpentined and the last has serpentine bars between straight bars. The third was a very beautiful piece of iron work, but many of the features have been destroyed by rust. It is apparent that there was a double scroll reaching from each of the four arms of the circle. The hook handle is spiraled. It is the property of Miss S. B. Eastman of Harvard.

These broilers could be revolved in order to secure even cooking.

No. 384. A class of chairs which we may call leather-backs is very satisfactory, because while their general outlines are in good style, there is a simplicity and homelikeness about them which appeals. Here the leather, instead of going crosswise in the back, as in the Cromwellian chairs, runs lengthwise, and the chair is a modification of the banister back, or the more elaborate cane back, both of which styles have the same general outline.

The construction of chairs in these three types is not to be commended. There is a rather quick curve on the outside of the back posts at the level of the seat. This curve becomes really an angle on the inside, sometimes even on the outside. It is often so sharp that it destroys the strength of the back. Many chairs of this period are broken at this point. That is no doubt the reason why they are now found in such small numbers. The abandonment of double lines of stretchers for a single set is also an element of weakness, and most of the chairs that have been preserved are shaky. Of course, the thought of the builder was to procure greater comfort by slanting the back.

These chairs in the simple styles are characterized by vase, ball or ring turning, or a combination of these elements, with portions of the legs and the back left square. The finials are like turban heads and represent a decline. The front stretcher, in the plainer sort, is usually a large and rather prominent turning.

Date: 1670–1690.

The wood is maple.

No. 385. A carved leather-back. In this chair we have a pleasing arrangement by which a curved rabbet or depression is cut away in the top and bottom rail deep enough to receive the leather, and to leave the leather back, when finished, flush with the rail. This seems a more tasteful and finished arrangement than that shown in No. 384 where the top and bottom rails are frankly used like the stretchers of a picture

400–401. NEW ENGLAND SLAT-BACK. 1700–1720.

402. POTATO BOILER.

403. EARLY GRIDDLE.

404–405. New England Slat-back. 1700–1720.

406. Roller Chair.

407. Dutch Carved Back.

408-409. NEW ENGLAND SLAT-BACKS. 1690-1710.

410-414. BROILER, GRILL, TOASTERS, ETC.

415–416. SERPENTINE SLAT ROCKERS. 1710–40.

417. REVERSED BABY CARVER.

418. CHILD'S WING CHAIR.

frame. We have here also a scrolled stretcher below, corresponding with its main outlines to the top rail.

Date: 1680–1700.

Nos. 386–388. A toaster here shown is a Pennsylvanian type with many twisted members. It must have been used for a huge slice of bread. Instead of the usual base and swivel arrangement it rests on prolonged leg-like members as seen. The trivets were interesting little pieces used to place over the coals for the quick heating of a small vessel.

No. 389. A leather-back chair with an attractively carved top rail. It is a curious fact that carving on chairs of this type sometimes called in England after Charles II, is done much better, in most cases, than the carving on cabinet furniture. The chair carving is often in the round, at least in relief on various levels. Another characteristic of this type is the high stretcher below. The evident design was to give room to draw the feet back.

The wood of these chairs, as found in America, is perhaps oftener maple than anything else. We do find, however, not a few fruit wood chairs. This term is used generally to include the pear and apple and possibly sometimes cherry, though the latter is generally named when used. Pearwood is admirably adapted for good carving. We do not see oak used in American carved chairs. We are now approaching the walnut period. Some of the fine examples are in that wood, but it is rare, and is not so suitable. In England we often find beech used.

In relation to maple in English pieces there is some misapprehension. Maple is not a rare wood in England. One may be surprised on referring to a certain American dictionary to find under a definition, a quotation from a dramatist, referring to a maple dresser. The author was English and the period was that of these chairs.

When leather and sometimes finer materials were used the arrangement of the brass headed tacks was often in an ornamental pattern, or at least was in double rows as here.

In the quest for old furniture it is highly important to notice whether the feet are missing. In the last two examples they are shown as they should appear. Even here something has been worn off, as feet originally, in this style, finished in a turning and sometimes in a little shoe below that. It is considered if chairs are worn no more than these are that their importance as antiques is not interfered with. If, however, the wear is below the largest part of the bulb, the chair is much less desirable. The loss of finials is a still more serious matter, and the loss of both finials and feet renders the chair practically valueless.

It is not considered good style to upholster seats, so that the tops show a marked curve. They are best when rather flat, as in the two examples now being noted. The backs were usually not padded, and never should be heavily padded. Sometimes the leather was doubled in the back.

No. 390. A Pennsylvania high chair. The arch of the slats is not fully carried out. This is our first example of the Pennsylvania chair, a large class, now much sought.

Date: 1720–1750.

Owner: Mr. Chauncey C. Nash.

No. 391. An amusingly sharp rake in the legs of this chair gives it a quaint appearance. Of course, the purpose was to acquire stability. Various other names that indicate this rake are flaring base, splayed base, slant base, straddle, etc.

No. 392. This stool should not be called a joint stool because it is merely doweled together. Such stools, with the rush seat, are rare. With No. 393, a round back baby chair, it belongs to the George F. Ives Collection.

Date: 1700–1730.

No. 394. A low back heart-and-crown chair. The motive in the back is well known. This, however, is the only instance in which we have seen it in a low back chair. The ball turned intermediate bracing rung, or stretcher, between the arm and the seat adds much to the effect. We have here for the first time the rolled arm, a phrase used in describing the contour of the arm in front of the post.

In the former collection of the author.

No. 395. A dainty gift ladle. Among the fine craftsmen in iron in Pennsylvania it was often the custom for a beau to give his sweetheart a daintily wrought utensil in which the heart motive appeared. Such utensils were often hung in the fireplace, more as ceremonial gifts than for ordinary use. Nevertheless we may suppose that on important occasions they were used. This piece is the daintiest bit of its kind that we have seen. The little bowl is of hammered copper. It is only $2\frac{7}{8}$ inches in diameter. On the back, the handle is divided by welding into a cross shape on the bowl so as to secure strength, and it is riveted in three places. The whole affair is about $15\frac{1}{2}$ inches long, and weighs but a few ounces. It was found near Easton in 1923.

No. 396. The chair here shown is supposed to be an original rocker. This inference is drawn from the shape of the turning at the bottom of the leg. There is here a bold enlargement to secure strength and room for the slot in which the rocker rests. Early rockers are always secured with wooden pins, never with nails. Several of these chairs have

419. FIVE BACK PENNSYLVANIA CHAIR. 1720–50.

420. Lamp Trammel.　　　　　421. A Six Back. 1720-50.

422–423. PENNSYLVANIA CHAIRS. 1720–50.

424–425. BURL PIECES.

426. ARCHED BACK.

427. DOUBLE JENNY.

428. FIVE BACK.

429. SIX BACK, QUEEN ANNE.

been found, and they are supposed to date from about the end of the seventeenth century, but we fear that the date is at least some forty years later. We have had a report of a chair of this sort made without rockers. What, however, the enlarged bottom of the foot was designed for, other than rockers, we cannot surmise.

No. 397. A lightly turned high desk chair. There are no less than four sets of rungs, including those in the seat, in this chair.

Date: 1710–1740.

No. 398. A turned rush stool. Owner: Mr. Horatio H. Armstrong. Date: 1690–1710. This is an appealing little example, one other being known to the writer. The rungs turned in this decorative form, and well worn, impart a human impression that is very pleasing.

No. 399. The first example of a true joint stool. The word " joint " in this connection is used to distinguish furniture so made from that which was united by bored holes and dowels. The joint means invariably a true mortise and tenon. In other words joined furniture was made by a cabinet maker, whereas turned furniture could be put together by inferior workmen. Joint stools, as found in America, must be closely scanned, as they are likely to be English importations, and of oak. The American examples are seldom if ever of oak. The top is pinned on like a table top, is usually a good deal less than an inch in thickness, and has the thumb nail mold. The overhang at the ends is always considerable. The material of the top may be pine or maple. The hight varies from twenty to twenty-two inches according to the condition of the stile at the foot. There is usually a rake of the legs in one direction.

Date: 1670–1690.

Nos. 400–401. In these chairs we have what is now named the New England slat back. It is a modification of the heavier turned chairs of the earlier period. In that period the number of slats was sometimes two and sometimes three, and the number was not an important matter. In fact the fewer the slats the earlier the piece was supposed to be, other things being equal. When, however, we reach the date here given we must, for good style, never have less than four slats. Five slats are counted much more desirable, because they are more rare and supposedly more attractive. We have known of one or two of these chairs with six slats. In this type there is uniformly a turning between every set of horizontal members, and the posts are all turned throughout rather than having portions left square as in the style last treated.

Owner: Mr. George Dudley Seymour.

Date: 1710–1740. They are from the Captain Charles Churchill

House, Newington, Connecticut, and are now in the Wadsworth Atheneum, Hartford.

No. 402. A fascinating bit of iron for boiling potatoes. It must have been a long tedious task to construct it.

Owner: Mr. H. W. Erving.

No. 403. A heavy cast griddle with short cast handle. These pieces are found in Pennsylvania and are appealing, at least to us. We do not know when they ceased to be made, but it would not surprise us to know that they continued up to the nineteenth century.

No. 404. A five back New England, sausage turned, rolled arm chair. A very good example with a seat of extraordinary width.

No. 405. A New England four back chair with scrolled slats. The date on No. 404 is about 1700–1720 and on No. 405 perhaps ten years later.

No. 406. A slat back chair, curious in respect to the feet, behind, which was apparently designed for rollers or wooden casters. The probable purpose was ease in moving the chair.

Owner: Mr. B. A. Behrend.

No. 407. A turned chair with panel seat and with a cherub carving in the back, above which there is a scroll with turned button decorations. The name is cut on the lower part of the back rail. These chairs are unusual.

Owner: Mr. Edward C. Wheeler, Jr. The date is difficult to fix, but it was probably an eighteenth century piece.

Nos. 408–409. Two very high backed New England chairs in the author's former collection. The left hand example is very perfect in style, the finial being better than that in the right hand example. The latter, however, in the odd spacing of its slats, and in its triple sets of rungs, is a solid and attractive piece. These chairs came in about 1700 and were popular in the higher types, for about twenty years.

Nos. 410–414. On the left is a wrought pot hook with double scrolls. The broiler beside it has an excellently shaped goose neck, and the toaster following it is very prettily scrolled, and has twisted guards for the bread. The next two pieces at the right are fine examples from Mr. L. P. Goulding's Collection. The round one is the largest we have ever seen. The other one is scrolled in both planes on the handle, and has the hollowed bars and trough with spout for collecting the gravy.

Nos. 415–416. Two excellent examples of the serpentine back arm chairs, which were perhaps always rockers. That on the left is in the estate of J. Milton Coburn, M.D. That on the right is owned by Mr. G. Winthrop Brown. A considerable number of these chairs has been

430. ELABORATE FLEMISH SCROLLED CHAIR. 1680–1700.

431. Turned and Tenoned Chair.

432. Four Slat Back.

433. Turned Side Chair

434. Braced Arm Chair.

435. FLEMISH SCROLLED CHAIR. 1680–1700.

436–437.   A Flemish Scroll and a Transition Chair.

438.   Wrought Gift Fork.   18th Century.

found but usually with straight slats. It will be seen that the arm is braced by running to the rung, below the seat rail, and pinning it to the rail. The date may be 1730–1750.

Another characteristic feature of these chairs is that they have short arms not extending to the front posts.

No. 417. A very excellent baby chair in which the free rail usually appearing above the spindle rail is reversed and placed below it, thus making it a Carver variant.

Owner: Mr. B. A. Behrend.

The date is about 1680–1700.

No. 418. A handsomely designed child's wing chair. It belongs to Mr. T. T. Wetmore of Old Saybrook, Connecticut. It is thirty inches high, and has a new seat.

The rake of the sides, the scrolling of the skirt and the piercing of the top in diamonds and hearts are all features which give the chair a great deal of character and attraction. It is almost impossible to date furniture for children. We would only suggest the eighteenth century.

No. 419. A very good example of the Pennsylvania arch slat back chair, to show the characteristic features. The slats are shaped both below and above. The arms are cut away by square incisions and there is left a thin section between the front and the back posts. This is an almost unvarying rule. Also the front spindle is always in decorative turning. Almost always the feet of these chairs have been cut off. The good types should have enlarged balls of a greater diameter than the post above, a kind of reversed mushroom. In the author's former collection.

No. 420. A trammel of wood designed to serve as a hanger for a Betty lamp. We have seen several of these; also we find that they are being largely copied, as they are proving catchy acquisitions. They were hooked from the ceiling, so as to furnish a reading light or a loom light.

No. 421. The rare and much sought six back chair.

Owner: Mr. Francis D. Brinton. The feet have been pieced as in all examples except one which we have seen, and there should be larger balls here. The front stretcher is very fine.

Nos. 422–423. The owner of both pieces is Mr. Francis D. Brinton. The left hand piece is remarkable like No. 428 in having handsomely cusped slats. The right hand piece is a natural complement to No. 421, with its six arched slats.

It will be noted that in No. 422, as in most of the cane chairs, there is an irregularly squared section of wood on the top of the front post which receives the seat rails. We may regard this as a refinement over the plain posts as seen on No. 423.

Nos. 424–425. A bowl of burl and a ladle of the same material. These will be discussed later.

No. 426. A Pennsylvania five back with a somewhat massive effect. The rockers are never original. This piece has very satisfactory lines and massive stretcher. In the author's former collection.

Date: 1700–1730.

No. 427. A double spinning jenny. It is so arranged that two threads could be spun at once. The thread entered in a little hole at the center of the spindle. The distaff could be swung to a convenient distance. It is shown with its flax attached. Found in Connecticut. As to the date of spinning jennies, they were used in the seventeenth and eighteenth centuries.

No. 428. A five back chair, probably one of a set like No. 422, but with arms quite different from the conventional Pennsylvania type.

Owner: Mr. Francis D. Brinton.

Date: 1700–1720.

No. 429. A six back chair with cabriole legs in front. We show this piece with some hesitation as we seek to confine this book to the turned period. Nevertheless, the chair is so rare and good, having its original feet, that we cannot resist it. The ball and ring stretcher and the cabriole leg mark the Queen Anne period. The scrolled board nailed about the rush seat imparts a pleasing finish which indicates a date later than those chairs we have hitherto illustrated.

Origin: A Pennsylvania farmhouse, where it had always been and where it was found by the

Owner: Mr. J. Stodgell Stokes.

No. 430. In this chair we arrive at the fully developed carved scrolled cane chair.

Owner: Mr. H. W. Erving.

When these pieces are good, with the fully developed scroll, that is to say the double Flemish scroll as seen here on the arm and on the leg, they are rich and ornate. A common style mark is the medial stretcher, whence probably the Windsor chair derived its style. On account of the location of this stretcher we find here that the back stretcher is moved to a higher point on the legs behind. It will be observed that in the perfect type, the heavy scrolled front stretcher matches the lighter top rail behind, as here. These scrolls are either single or double and are often worked out like foliage forms. The back rail behind, while in the double scroll here, is simpler, as is the practise, than the other members. In the best types we have the side members forming the back panel, carved as here. The setting of the top rail between the posts is regarded as an older and better design than the setting of it over the tops of the posts. The feet are seen to have protuberances in front in the form of cushions, apparently to take the wear from the scrolled legs.

Owner: Mr. H. W. Erving.

These chairs are a far cry from the simplicity of the turned chair. They were never very common in America. They were nevertheless used to no small extent for the parlors in the finer homes. The caning of these chairs is of the finest character.

Many of the specimens are painted black. The present taste is in favor of natural wood, but we consider that where black seemed so frequent we should not discriminate against it.

No. 431. A very oddly turned chair. The supposition is that it was country made. The rungs are left square at the ends to give a solid shoulder for a mortise. Yet for the main portion of their length they are turned. We have seen one other chair of this kind. The probable object was to secure greater solidity. We do not count it important but rather curious. The date is uncertain, perhaps before 1750.

No. 432. A four back chair with sausage turnings and a neatly turned reinforcing rail below the arm. It has the flat arm, doweled, rather than tenoned.

Date: 1700–1720.

No. 433. A turned slat back of complete and harmonious design. The finials here are better than most of this class, being perfectly satisfactory from the esthetic and historical standpoints.

Date: 1690–1710.

No. 434. This is a good example of the chair with a braced or reinforced arm. In this case the short arm has a support running through the seat rail and doweling into an enlarged section of the top rungs on the sides.

Date: 1710–1730.

No. 435. Owner: Mr. G. Winthrop Brown. The variation between this chair and No. 430 is seen in the leg where there is an extra scroll at about the hight of the stretcher. The arm support is turned however, instead of using the Flemish scroll. The back has only two reversed scrolls. The C in the top and bottom rails is reversed in positions, as compared with No. 430.

The handsome so-called ram's horn arm of these chairs deserves careful attention. It is in a roughly squared section which is turned diamondwise instead of flatwise. The upper edge of this square is softened. The scrolls sweep both outward and downward over the post with a curl quite like a close set ram's horn.

Nos. 436–437.   These chairs are owned by Mr. Edward C. Wheeler, Jr. It will be seen that the front stretcher and the top rail are very closely alike. This chair should be compared with No. 441. While the backs are similar, rosettes appear dividing the scrolls in this chair. Here the feet curve outward and in No. 442 the curve is inward. This scroll is usually called Flemish, whereas the foot of No. 442 is termed English. The distinction is perhaps rather arbitrary.

These chairs are of fruit wood.

No. 437 does not carry out the scroll work in the base which we see in the back, but it is kept wholly to the turned motives. It will be seen that the arm here does not sweep outward. Further it is largely covered by fine carved lines.

No. 438.   An example of the wrought gift forks found in Pennsylvania. Here is the usual heart motive, but the ornamentation is unusually elaborate and suggests carving in wood. We might almost call such a piece a votive gift, to the goddess of the maker's affections.

Nos. 439–440.   A pair of handsomely carved chairs of the second period.

Owner: Mr. Edward C. Wheeler, Jr.

The imposing of the top rail on the back posts should be noted as a change from those hitherto considered, in which that rail is mortised between the posts. It is a question of taste which style one prefers. This style affords a little more room for freedom of design. It is, however, more frail. We see also a change here in the style of the caned panel of the back. In the examples shown it has been bordered by straight lines on the inside of the panel. Here we have scrolls at the top and the bottom. This is the natural progression of design from the more simple to the more complex. The carved stretcher and the top rail are seen to agree quite closely. We have here also another modification in the scrolling on one face of the medial stretcher, connecting the side stretchers.

These chairs are painted black and are in fine condition. The edges of the seat rails should be noted as molded, whereas in the simpler examples it is plain.

Nos. 441–442.   Complementary chairs with the " English " scrolled foot.

Owner: Mr. Edward C. Wheeler, Jr. These chairs are in fruit wood. One should note that the arm chair, as often occurs in this style, has a lower seat than the side chair. We like the bold scrolls of these chairs.

444. Flemish Scroll Chair.　　445. Spanish Foot Chair.

446. Twist-turned Arm Chair of Doubtful American Origin.

447–448. An English and a Flemish Scroll. 1680–1700.

449. ENGLISH SCROLL CHAIR. 1680–1700.

No. 443.   A heart fork formerly owned by Mr. Ralph Burnham of Ipswich.   This is the simplest form of Pennsylvania gift hardware.

No. 444.   A carved Flemish side chair with oval ended panel.

It will be seen that while the chairs hitherto treated had stretchers which did not distinctly arch, this example has a true arch below.   It was doubtless carried out to repeat the oval above.   However, the top rail is pierced and does not attempt to copy precisely the design of the lower rail.   Owner: Mr. Edward C. Wheeler, Jr.

No. 445.   A carved chair with Spanish foot.   The Spanish foot when it is correctly wrought is one of the greatest beauties of early furniture. The proportions require to be very carefully followed, and some examples are extremely clumsy.   Particularly restorations of such feet are often a bad joke.   They need not all follow the same lines, but they must all sweep in graceful curves like the unfolding of the fronds of a fern, reversed.   When these feet were new they showed a fully curved element sweeping about the base.   As that has worn off some chairs show merely a lip on the inside.   The left hand foot here exhibits the lines as they should be.   The very graceful stretcher in the scrolled arch form corresponding to the top of the panel above is good.   This panel suggests a mirror frame of the period.

Owner: not known.

No. 446.   A chair with twisted posts and stretchers.

Owner: Mr. Stanley A. Sweet of New York.

This chair has a strong English feeling.   The band of diamond scratches on the face of the front rail, the carving of the arm, and especially the twisting of the post suggest an English chair.   The question here arises whether any American chair possesses this twist.   The writer owned such a chair in maple but he never felt certain of its origin.   Certainly the motive is very handsome and we can hardly account for its rarity, or perhaps its total absence, in America.   The shell carving on the top rail is very unusual.   We see thoroughly established in this chair the acorn shape of the finial.   Some times this appears in urn form as in No. 448, and sometimes more in the turban form as No. 447.   It is, however, quite distinctively different from the seventeenth century form of the heavy turned chairs.

No. 447.   A side chair with the " English " scroll foot, and a back panel with reeded and carved banisters.   This is a variation on chairs hitherto shown.   The wood is hard, possibly beech.

Owner: Mr. Edward C. Wheeler, Jr.

No. 448.   A chair in the former collection of the author in which the lines of the back panel are obscured by an attached upholstered panel, which is here out of place. The lines of this panel, alike at both ends, are attractively shaped as is also the arched and pierced stretcher.

As to the dates of these chairs, we have seen them dated to the very end of the seventeenth century. We mean that the date was cut in the carving. It may be that there are American chairs of this type as early as 1660, but we very much doubt whether any of them reach back beyond 1680 or 1685.

No. 449. A carved and scrolled chair which, while thoroughly good, does not merit attention as much as some that have preceded it, shown on a smaller scale. One sees here a bottom rail in the back, that is perfectly plain, and also plain reeded banisters forming the sides of the back panel. The seat of this chair, which is rush, was no doubt caned like the back, though it is possible transition chairs existed with a rush seat and cane back.

No. 450. A carved Flemish arm chair. The feature of this chair which emphasizes itself is its extreme hight, between fifty-seven and fifty-eight inches. It is very similar in design to Mr. Wheeler's side chairs already shown. There is much pleasure in following the ramifications of furniture through all its changes. At this period it would seem that there was an effort to carry the chairs up so as to supply a wall decoration. Nobody could possibly require this hight even for a head-rest. We may remember that highboys of the period were also lofty. Looking-glasses, also, tended to slender vertical outlines with highly decorated tops. It was the age when high ceilings were affected, so that long vertical lines in the furniture were almost compulsory.

It is unnecessary to enter into the details of these chairs, sufficiently indicated elsewhere.

No. 450A. and 452. These pieces of decorative iron as used in Pennsylvania are covered with small stamped designs repeated in the form of a border.

No. 451. A handsome Flemish chair. It is reported to have been the property of William Penn. The reader should be warned that in all reproductions of this sort the front of the chair always appears too large in proportion to the back, owing to the foreshortening which is exaggerated by photography. In this example we have the fully developed knob or shoe on the foot, for the scroll to rest upon. We have not observed this knob on the " English " foot. In some of these chairs the connection between the stretcher and the front leg has been unsatisfactory. In this example, however, ample space has been provided so that nothing looks pinched or lacking in completeness of design.

Owner: Mr. Edward C. Wheeler, Jr.

Nos. 453-454. A pair of handsomely scrolled Flemish chairs. Of course the panels of the backs were originally the same, and the seats of both were like that on the left.

Owner: Mr. Francis Hill Bigelow of Cambridge.

The carving is delicate, and that of the scrolled stretcher is more carefully copied from the top rail than that of any other example that we have seen. We have here a molded edge on the lower rail behind. The carving is massed on the top rail, and the reeded panel is left plain at the sides.

Nos. 455-456. A pair of panel back chairs.

Owner: Mr. Edward C. Wheeler, Jr.

In these examples the plain turning and the molded and reeded rails of the back are relieved only by the carving of the top rail in an unusual and striking pattern. The scroll under the seat has been quite generally lacking from the chairs hitherto shown but a somewhat similar scroll appears in No. 458.

The painting of these chairs was decorated with bands of gold. They were found at Salem, and are said to have belonged to Nathaniel Hawthorne, from whose former residence they came. The reader will have noticed the transition from the turned back posts and the handsomely molded post, which appears in these chairs for the first time. In previous examples as in No. 445 we have had a similar molding surrounding the panel itself. Here the molding is on the posts whereas the panel frame is done in a modified reed.

No. 457. A turned corner chair, of unusually heavy character.

Owner: Mr. Mark M. Henderson of Norwalk, Connecticut.

The turnings here are, strangely, not symmetrical. We do not now remember another instance of this kind. We look to see the bottom stretcher correspond with that above it. Corner chairs possess many merits, and we are always surprised at their comparative rarity. In a massive form like this they are extremely rare.

Of course, the imposed and shaped secondary piece at the center of the back is attached to strengthen the chair, where the two sectional pieces of the curved back rail come together in a mortise, on the back post. This is also a method followed on Windsor chairs.

In a later period chairs of this sort would be made with splats instead of slats. The splat is a broad, and usually shaped, thin piece at the back, running from the rail to the seat rather than from side to side in which later case we use the word slat.

The shaping of the slat by steam or hot water or by placing it in a form when green was universal. Hickory was an admirable material for this purpose. Ash, oak and maple and doubtless various other woods were also used. When they were green there was no difficulty in giving them a slight curvature, about the same as that of a barrel stave. In fact, the staves of kegs were often of about the same length and contour as the chair slats, and it is entirely possible that the first slat back chair was an accommodation or adaptation adopted as a makeshift by the cabinet maker. If he found a short keg stave convenient to his hand the inspiration may have seized him to use it in chair backs. Certainly the device was an immense success. Carried too far, however, as is often the case, by a too ambitious scrolling of the slat, splitting off was common.

No. 458.   A scrolled side chair with twin vertical panels.   This beautiful chair, as full of curves as the Meander river, carries to the extreme various characteristic elements.

The top rail rolls over in a graceful spiral. The posts are elaborately molded. The legs in front are a modified Spanish foot.

One observes at the top of the scroll of the leg a turning such as in the chair No. 451, markedly setting off the scroll from the remainder of the leg, which is ribbed on the corner and at the sides.

The side and the medial stretchers are also boldly scrolled, and the back feet have an extreme rake. Of course this conformation gives stability to a chair with a high back, which would otherwise be very easily overset, as we often learn to our sorrow.

The caning in the back of this chair is the finest and daintiest that we have ever seen. The seat rail is done in gilded foliage, which we suppose was original. The chair is painted black.

No. 459.   An unusual pair of small tongs, doubtless intended as pipe tongs. Modern examples of this sort, though lacking some of these elements, are common. Several pairs of tongs with twisted legs have recently been found in the same section of Massachusetts.

No. 460.   A carved chair with Spanish feet and ram's horn arms.

Owner: Mr. Stanley A. Sweet.

This chair is peculiar in that the post, supporting the arm, does not continue in a line with the front leg, but is set back on the seat rail. The center of the spiral on the arm is clearly shown, standing out like a spike, in the best ram's horn design. The turning of the legs and the arm supports is very bold.

No. 461.   Owner: Mr. Stanley A. Sweet.

This very elaborate chair shows every feature of the Flemish style. The scrolled elements of the leg are much more richly carved than is common; the section at the hight of the stretcher being done with imbri-

450. Very High Flemish Chair. 1680–1700.

450a.   451. Flemish Scroll Chair.   1680–1700.   452.

453–454. Pair Flemish Scroll Side Chairs. 1680–1700.

455–456. PAIR CARVED AND TURNED CHAIRS. 1680–1700.

cations. The back is rather intricately carved each side of the panel in a design somewhat different from any we have hitherto shown.

No. 462. Owner: Mr. Edward C. Wheeler, Jr.

A handsome side chair with Flemish scroll, very closely like, but slightly differing from, other chairs in this work.

Date: 1680–1700.

Nos. 463–464. A pair of interesting chairs with Spanish feet.

Owner: Mr. Francis Hill Bigelow.

The feet are in good style. The roll of the top of the rail suggests comparison with No. 458. A touch of carving runs about the molded back in a grooved line, and in a series of four pointed leaf-like forms.

No. 465. It belongs to the style immediately following the Flemish and far more generally seen in Amercia. The banister back chairs are comfortable and have been very popular. In this instance the bottom rail is scrolled with an ogee molding, and all the stretchers are pleasingly turned. We have here an instance of the rolled arm, but in the square section. The chair contains a single element of carving in the back rail.

Date: 1700–1710.

Ownership, now, or formerly: Mr. Brooks Reed.

No. 466. A five banister back turned chair. Here is again an imposed and scrolled but simple back rail.

Owner: Mr. B. A. Behrend.

The dates of the New England slat back and the banister back chairs of this type were coincident. The slat backs, however, began sooner and lasted longer. Perhaps they were somewhat more comfortable. The banisters were elastic enough to give comfort, but if the sitter's back came against the bottom rail, as, in a lounging position, it would do, discomfort would ensue.

The method of turning banisters, especially those of delicate contour, was as follows: two pieces of wood were glued together with a paper between them. They were then turned as a unit, the division being at the center. The insertion of the point of a knife, and a deft twist of the arm, would then separate the pieces, and leave a smooth surface without loss of shape, such as would ensue if the banister were sawed and then planed, both difficult operations.

Nos. 467–469. Three small pieces for children. The little wing chair with ends shaped like a settle; a child's chair, larger than a baby's chair, and a stool with molded side skirts and ogee legs.

No. 470. A well carved Flemish side chair in which the small secondary scroll on the front seems distinctly designed to receive the arched stretcher. The panel of the back here is strikingly narrow, and while arched at the top is straight at the bottom.

No. 471. A very attractively turned high chair with a beautifully worn rung. It was in the author's former collection. The turnings follow the design of the New England chairs for grown-ups of the period of 1700.

No. 472. A cane chair with ram's horn arms, and very wide cane panel. Both the back legs and the panel frame are strongly molded. The stretcher, instead of following the scrolled outline of the back rail, is turned. We see a somewhat restive and shifting variety of mixed designs about this period, which was the beginning of the departure to the eighteenth century styles in walnut, with cabriole legs.

No. 473. A Spanish foot, banister back chair.

Owner: Mr. B. A. Behrend.

This chair is one of a pair. It differs from chairs recently treated in that it has a back with four banisters, and the carving is confined to the top rail and the feet. The Spanish feet were sometimes carved from the solid. In a great many instances, however, blocks were glued on the outside, to be carved as toes. Often these glued pieces, so liable to knocks, have broken off and been lost. It required a much larger post to carve the feet from the solid wood. In the effort to make chairs attractive, old examples with plain turned feet in bad condition have been seen carved into the alleged semblance of a Spanish foot. This trick may sometimes be detected by the failure of the toe to project beyond the vertical line of the leg. A commoner device is to saw off the old foot and attach an entire new one. This also is easily detected. In some instances this addition is legitimate, there having been a Spanish foot in place originally.

Date: About 1700.

No. 474. A Flemish chair owned by Mrs. John Marshall Holcombe of Hartford. It is similar to, though slightly different from, No. 462.

No. 475. A very elaborately turned chair, in which the workman seems to have tried to show us what he could do. The contour of the slats, like the meeting of salamander heads, is in a bold design and very unusual. The lightness and the style of the finial belong to the period.

By such exuberance of turning the worker made a flourish to show that neither he nor nature had exhausted themselves. To secure his effects, however, it is a question whether he did not make the necking of the members of the turnings somewhat too small and so imperil the strength of the chair. However, it has stood the test.

Owner: Mark M. Henderson.

Nos. 476–477. Complementary banister backs. We have here the cresting of the back rail, carved in the earlier manner. Below that point, however, the chairs assume a somewhat later form, although they have

457. HEAVY TURNED CORNER CHAIR. 1700–1720.

458. Spanish Foot Chair. 1690–1710.

459. Wrought, Twisted Pipe Tongs. 18th Century.

Spanish feet. While we have called the chairs complementary, it is a question whether their turnings, which vary slightly, indicate that they were made to go together. One should observe that the huge stretcher of the arm chair often appeared thus, much larger than in the side chair. Indeed, in the arm chair the turner sometimes seems to attempt to show us what he can do. He had a chip on his shoulder. He bubbled over with the love of design.

Nos. 478–483. Six old forms of blind fasteners found in New England. The somewhat flattened S shaped forms are the oldest. The two at the left, attached with plates, indicate a second period. That at the right, used with a spring, is probably as late as 1800. Properly the earlier type was not found in use for blinds, that is lattice work, but rather for the solid earlier shutter, of the seventeenth and eighteenth centuries. The earliest use in New England for the lattice blind is the latter half of the eighteenth century.

No. 484. A turned chair with heart and crown back.

Owner: Mr. George Dudley Seymour.

It has the good feature of the intermediate arm stretcher. We have never seen the back stretcher in an ornamental form in chairs of this type. Even as we write, we find the only exception which is in our possession is a hoax, the ornamental back stretcher being new. The front of this chair is somewhat foreshortened. One should notice the molded arm. We wonder whether an applied scroll on the under side of the arm end may not be lacking. We have, however, seen forms like the one here shown. This chair was found in Milford, Connecticut, and is in the Wadsworth Atheneum, Hartford.

No. 485. This chair is the most perfect of its kind that has come to our attention. The middle bracing stretcher under the arm is turned in the most delicate fashion possible. The turnings between the slats and rungs are cunningly spaced. The ball turning of the front stretchers and the sausage turning of the side stretchers are all characteristic and good. The finial is the best of this period. If we could ask any improvement at all it would be in a slightly better contour of the roll of the arm in front. This beautiful chair is the property of Mr. George Dudley Seymour. At the Wadsworth Atheneum.

The chair was found in the Captain Charles Churchill House, Newington, Connecticut.

No. 486. A chair with five reeded banisters and a crested back rail with three hearts and a crown.

Owner: Mr. James Davidson.

The peculiar bracing stretchers just below the arms have been challenged as being too close to the arms. It is impossible to verify the matter without taking the chair to pieces, but we believe it is all original.

Nos. 487–491. The finest example we have so far seen of the ceremonial gift fork is that showing the fine heart and curl at the top and the elaborate decoration here. This iron is most interesting from the fact that it is drawn out in appearance with a grain like molasses candy. One can see every strand almost as clearly as if it were a skein of thread. The minute copper bowled spoon is small enough for a mustard spoon. We do not know its use. The shovel with the heart opening was undoubtedly to turn the pancakes.

No. 492. A banister back Spanish foot side chair. It was in the Webb House, Wethersfield, in the former collection of the author. The mellow effect of the foot, blending with the leg, and the very handsome and unusual three leaved figure at the center of the stretcher, with the rayed effect in the crest of the upper stretcher are all interesting features.

No. 493. A reversed banister back chair. The intermediate stretcher under the arm, unusual in this type, adds to the interest. A peculiarity is the turning of the banisters so that the flat is at the back, and their advantage is wholly lost. We have seen this in several other examples and regard it rather as a mark of oddity than of merit.

Owner: Mrs. John Marshall Holcombe of Hartford.

No. 494. This shows the first of our chairs with a series of semi-circles in the arched top, formed by well cut molds. The effect is good. It is also seen on the backs of some day beds.

Owner: Mr. Arthur W. Wellington.

Date: About 1700.

No. 495. A chair owned by Mr. G. Winthrop Brown. The long strong bevel of the upper and lower rails is an effective feature, and we wonder that it was not oftener adopted, as it certainly imparts a feeling of style to the chair. The same is true of the great rung, the individuality of which is most striking.

This chair is a good example, which should be carefully noted by the student, of the fact that when the spindles are properly turned they are precisely like the side posts. Thus a line drawn across at any point shows the element of the turnings of every one to be in line with the chair post. Some makers neglected this obvious point of merit. When we have five banisters, the effect is much more marked, and we are of opinion that such a chair is very good in taste and in effect.

Date: About 1700.

No. 496. A candle chair of the New England type of turning. The candle sticks were made open at the bottom with sockets to fit over the

460.   FLEMISH FOOT SCROLL CARVED CHAIR.   1710–20.

461–462. FLEMISH SCROLL SIDE CHAIRS. 1680–1700.

463–464. PAIR SPANISH FOOT CHAIRS. 1700–1720.

465–466. Turned Banister Back. 1690–1710.

467–469. Child's Chairs and a Stool.

tops of the posts, which on these chairs projected somewhat more than usual on that account. The candle sticks were lost from this piece and have been renewed. We have seen such old candle sticks in the market.

Date: About 1700.

No. 497. We have shown this fully scrolled Flemish chair in profile in order to give the effect of the legs. This example is conventional in all respects, and in excellent condition. It is painted black.

Date: About 1690–1700.

Nos. 498–502. These curious little articles are scarcely known out of Pennsylvania, aside from the pipe tongs. The little piece looking like a hammer and a hatchet are a set of utensils probably made as a gift. The knife edge, which was very sharp, is a buttonhole cutter. It was held on the cloth and tapped by the hammer. On the other end of both pieces there is a taper coming to a point, which is used to make holes for embroidery, the size of which was gauged by placing one of these pieces through the other, or by holding the hand at the depth required. The single ornamental cutter is for the same purpose, except that it is more elaborate. We have seen even finer examples. The length of these handles is about three to three and a half inches. The best cutter and the tongs belong to Mrs. M. B. Cookerow of Pottstown, Pennsylvania.

No. 503. This interesting chair is unusual in the excellent shaping of its mushrooms and in the turning below them.

Owner: Mr. J. H. Stiles, York, Pennsylvania.

Date: About 1700.

No. 504. A reversed banister back side chair in which the turnings are rather bold, and the crest of the top rail is done in moon shaped openings.

Date: About 1700–1720.

Owner: Mr. George S. McKearin, Hoosick Falls, New York.

Nos. 505–506. Two little bird trammels. That with four prongs belongs to Mr. Dwight Blaney, and that with three prongs to Mrs. DeWitt Howe of Manchester, New Hampshire. Such small trammels are rare and desirable. They were used in cooking squab or other small birds, as game birds. Yet they are true trammels, to be attached to the crane and adjusted as desired. Eighteenth Century.

No. 507. An excellent pattern of a baby high chair in the New England type. This is the only chair we have seen in which the foot rest was turned, and the short button like attachments reaching from the foot rest to the posts also turned. There is an agreeable effect of wear, and the sausage stretchers add to the interest.

Date: About 1700.

Nos. 508–513. A series of six lanterns. The second is the sort used in the nineteenth century. The fourth is of wood. It could be hung or carried as a sconce. The fifth is a ship lantern designed for a corner. The other specimens are as late as the nineteenth century.

No. 514. A very good specimen of a New England five back arm chair. The effect of uniformity in the back slats is very marked. The failure to turn the front posts below the seat probably marks a date about 1690.

Owner: Mr. Arthur W. Wellington.

No. 515. An unusual banister back, with an interesting crest on the back rail, one or two other examples of which we have seen. Usually, however, the rail is carved as a sunburst reaching up to the scallops. This chair is odd in respect to the slant of its scrolled arms. Other slant arms which we have seen were turned.

Owner: Mr. George S. McKearin.

Nos. 515–527. A series of fireplace and other utensils. No. 516 and No. 523 show good forms of skimmer handles. No. 517 is a good design for the top of a shovel. No. 518 is a small and late pair of pipe tongs. No. 519 is a large pair of kettle tongs, probably. No. 520 shows an unusual trivet designed for use with a round based pot. No. 521 is a pot lifter. No. 522 is a pair of tongs with an ornamental handle, cut in interesting geometrical designs. No. 524 is designed to be used to handle pies in a deep oven. No. 525 we would be glad to learn the use of. No. 526 is a quaint spoon and No. 527 is a very odd design of pipe tongs, the wing at one side being for pressing down the tobacco in the bowl.

No. 528. A fine five back chair. It is very high.

Owner: The estate of J. Milton Cobourn, M.D.

Date: 1700–1720.

No. 529. A well turned and double armed five back chair.

Owner: Mr. Henry S. Stearns.

No. 530. A spinning chair. The seat is very high, and the back is very low to permit the drawing back of the arm, and the sway of the body. It was a wearying task to stand at the wheel all day long and at times the spinner could half sit, using this chair somewhat as a monk's stool was used.

Date: Eighteenth century.

No. 531. A five banister back. The reversed curve of the back rail, and the huge stretcher give the chair sufficient interest to induce us to show it. This and the previous number were in the author's former collection.

Date: 1700–1720.

No. 532. In this chair we have the last example of the transition

470. FLEMISH SCROLL CHAIR. 1680–1700.

471. HIGH CHAIR.   472. SPANISH FOOT ARM. 1700–20.

473. Spanish Foot Banister.   474. Flemish Chair.

475. Salamander Back Turned Chair. 1700–1730.

period between the seventeenth and the eighteenth centuries; for there were Spanish feet, though these are now pretty well worn down. The back, however, follows the lines of the Queen Anne type, having the fiddle shaped splat. With this chair and No. 545 we shall limit the illustration of the period.

Owner: Mr. Edward C. Wheeler, Jr.

Date: About 1720.

It is well decorated in black paint with gold lines constituting an intricate scroll. It has a suggestion of the lacquered furniture of about this date, and probably was painted to approach that style.

No. 533. A handsomely scrolled and decorated door hasp from Pennsylvania. It is 16 inches long. The Pennsylvanians made so much of their barns, and hasps were so unusual on dwelling house doors, that we are not certain to which this piece was applied.

Date: Eighteenth century.

Nos. 534–535. Examples of chairs in the collection of Mr. George F. Ives. The second one is unusual in its ox bow or reversed serpentine back. We feel disposed to bring the dates of these chairs forward from twenty to sixty years in some cases, as we find that chairs for children seem to hold the old design longer, and we have found similar chairs of known date.

Nos. 536–537. Pleasing types of baby chairs holding to the fashions of the larger examples.

No. 538. A banister back chair with scrolled arms which are pierced through at the circle of the roll over. The holes are made on a taper in the form of a countersink so as not to weaken the arm too much. The back is of an odd shape to add some dignity to the plain form.

Owner: Mr. James N. H. Campbell.

Date: 1710–1730.

No. 539. A round about chair. These types are more frequently seen in England. The secondary imposed back or comb turns the piece into what is often called abroad a barber's chair. A chair like this was the true precursor of the Windsor chair in respect to the spindles of the back and the comb. The back is sometimes called a sack back, the thought being that it was to receive a sack or a garment so as to hold it about the figure for warmth, — a kind of temporary upholstery, as a shawl.

Owner: Mr. G. Winthrop Brown.

Date: 1700–1720.

No. 540. A child's wing chair, slanted at the back to render it more stable. The arms were cut for a bar to keep the child safely. There is a good hand hold behind.

No. 541. A joint stool only fourteen inches high. The turnings of this stool are like those on the Thomas Robinson chair, also the bead at the bottom of the rail. The stool probably stood about an inch higher. It is of oak, like the chair, and the legs are vertical. It was found in the same part of Connecticut as the chair and was probably made with others like it at the same time as the chair. It is a very quaint example.

No. 542. A child's chair shown in larger scale than the chair to the right. It is the property of Mr. Chauncey C. Nash.

Date: 1700–1750.

No. 543. The roll over of the arms of this banister back chair is interesting since they are done with a touch of carving in the star pattern.

Owner: Mrs. Niles Lewis Peck of Bristol, Connecticut.

The rockers are, of course, out of place. The posts are maple and the rungs look like oak or ash. The hight is $45\frac{1}{2}$ inches.

Date: 1700–1730.

This chair belonged to the Rev. Samuel Newell of Yale, 1739; first minister of the First Church, Bristol.

No. 544. An arm chair in the Transition Dutch model, which instead of a splat had reeded banisters. The Spanish feet indicate that it fairly belongs within our period.

It was in the possession of Mr. Henry V. Weil.

Date: 1700–1720.

No. 545. A leather back chair owned by Mr. George Dudley Seymour. It is in maple with stretchers of beech. It was bought in Hartford, and belongs to the Transition period, inasmuch as it has a panel with leather rather than a splat.

Date: 1710–1720.

Nos. 546–547. Two Pennsylvanian fat lamps. Various sorts of fat or oil were used in these lamps. When it became hot there was a tendency to spill the liquid, when the lamp was moved about. Such lamps, therefore, are always made on a swivel. They are not, however, gimbal lamps, since there is only one plane in which they swing. These little lamps, seven to eight inches high, with bases from four to six inches broad, are found in an immense variety of styles in eastern Pennsylvania and western New Jersey. Each lamp bears some mark of individuality, and there are large collections of this type. Sometimes the base is a saucer shape, but more often it is a tripod.

There is always some touch of ornament, and the work is always wrought. As to dates we find that Connecticut, called the land of steady habits, must withdraw into the shade in comparison with Pennsylvania, where in rural counties they do things very much as they always did. We

476–477. Spanish Foot Banister Backs. 1700–1710.

478–483. Shutter Fasteners. 18th Century.

484. HEART AND CROWN REEDED BANISTER. 1700-1730

485. NEW ENGLAND FIVE BACK. 1710–30.

486. HEART AND CROWN CHAIR. 1710–30.

487–491. GIFT FORK AND OTHER UTENSILS. 18th CENTURY.

find these lamps in the seventeenth century, perhaps; in the eighteenth century, largely; and probably, also, well into the nineteenth century.

No. 548.   We close our treatment of chairs with this quaint specimen. It has on one post a box built of wood like a sectional bearing, to swing about the post, and to carry a small writing table or drinking table, how do we know which?   It is now appropriately tipped up so that it can hold nothing dangerous.   It is a forecast of the writing arm Windsor, and does not antedate it more than twenty years, probably.

STOOLS

W E HAVE already expatiated somewhat on the use of stools, as preceding that of chairs for people in ordinary circumstances. We do not have in America the long form except as it appears in the pine seats of old church galleries, and in the stick leg puncheon-like benches, found in the Appalachians. In England the long form ran down the back of the trestle board table, and the short form was placed at the ends for one, or at most two diners. We find here only the short form which we otherwise name a joint stool, which distinguishes it from stick-leg or Windsor type turned stools which were so common. The English short forms are common enough, especially in their spurious imitations which flood the country. The top may be of leather or plain wood which latter is attached like a table top. Indeed, it is not always possible to know whether a joint stool is intended to sit on or to use as a table. A wise conclusion would be that such pieces were often used for both purposes.

These stools were twenty-one or twenty-two inches in hight ordinarily.

No. 549. A joint stool with vertical legs and a medial stretcher. It has been presumed that this example is American, but we were not on earth when it was made.

Nos. 550–551. A pair of remarkable stools found at Newburyport. Their turning resembles that of the six legged highboy. We have never heard of or seen any other examples in America. The very fine covers were made by a person now or recently living. The stools, however, with their remarkable cross stretchers which resemble the swastika design, are dainty and add the last touch of charm. The feet vary amusingly as does the whole turning of the post in size, — a common enough occurrence. The stools are the hight of an ordinary chair, and their tops are formed of a circular section, hollow in the center so as to take the upholstery and to receive the dowels of the posts. The wood of these stools is very light, probably bass. The style is scarcely adapted for strength, and if more of them existed one can easily imagine that they would have gone to pieces long before this date.

No. 552. A joint stool of about double, or at least more than half exceeding, the usual length. It has an English feeling and we are not certain of its origin.

If stools are in walnut or oak we think them more likely to be English. If they are of maple we suppose them more likely to be American.

492. SPANISH FOOT CHAIR. 1700–20.

493. SPANISH FOOT REVERSE BANISTER. 1700–20.

494. Arch Rail Banister Back.　　　495. Banister Back. 1700–10.

496. Candle Post Chair. 1700–10.　　　　497. Flemish Chair.

498–502. Decorative Utensils.

Owner: Mr. Chauncey C. Nash.

No. 553. A joint stool owned by Miss C. M. Traver of New York. It shows the usual style of these stools. They spread one way. That is to say their legs rake in one direction but are in a vertical plane the other way. This stool shows clearly the nature of a proper board top, with the thumb nail molding, which is conventional for the joint stool.

No. 554. A joint stool the top of which is not original. We presume the stool to be American. The average length of these stools may be placed at twenty inches. The earliest gate leg tables have been found with turnings like this example. We think that all true joint stools date in the seventeenth century, or if not so they are scarcely over the line into the eighteenth.

No. 555. A joint stool which has lost the turnings of its feet, but which has the original pinned top with the thumb nail mold. In the time when chairs were very heavy, joint stools were more convenient to move about, and sometimes, as we remember, to throw at the heads of bishops!

The wood of this specimen is maple.

No. 556. A joint stool with a drawer. It has lost the turnings of its feet. The present hight is 16¼ inches to which two inches are now added. A piece as low as this could not have been a table. It is even low for a joint stool. The wood is maple. We know no other stool with a drawer.

Nos. 557–566. A series of lighting fixtures. The first is a little copper lamp, the shape of another like it on the wooden stand, the third to the right from it. It was convenient to carry these light whale oil lamps about, and place them on the neatly turned stands when one desired to read.

The second piece in line is sometimes called a hog scraper candle stick, because the hollow disc base was found to be admirable for cleaning bristles, the standard making a good handle. When these candle sticks, as here, have a brass or copper ornamental ring they are counted better. The third piece with the hook could be caught over the side of a barrel by a cooper and one or more candles could be inserted in the scrolled base. Thus he could see whether light showed through between the staves.

The lamp at the right of the standard is so small as to be almost unnoticed but it has a snout and looks like a miniature tea kettle an inch or two high. Doubtless it was a maid's lamp for lighting her weary feet to bed. The next piece with the funnel shaped base and scolloped catch basin, handle and wick snout, is a quaint tin lamp. The saucer candle stick is well known. It appears here in a very broad deep base. The next piece, quite minute, has two sockets, one probably being for tapers and the other for candles, but since we have never used it we are uncertain. The last in line is for a flat wick, probably to burn fluid. In date these fixtures range all the way through the eighteenth and into the nineteenth centuries.

No. 567. We cannot resist bringing in, as a kind of titman at the end, this spider-like very early Pennsylvania Windsor high chair. We have seen one or two other examples quite like it. The medial stretcher turned in the Queen Anne style indicates a date, probably, not later than about 1720. We leave the consideration of the fascinating subject of the Windsor chair to the author's little book on *American Windsors*.

Owner: Mr. Chauncey C. Nash.

No. 568. These pipe tongs are of most unusual construction and are opened by compression. This is a little confusing, but no doubt their owner could have shown us their apt manipulation. The specimen is very rare, and we are not certain of the ultimate origin, but they were bought near Manchester, New Hampshire.

Owner: Mrs. De Witt Howe, Manchester, N. H.

No. 569. A squab stool. The name is derived from the hollowed surface formed by raising the frame around the seat so as to receive a cushion. The piece is remarkable in its single high stretcher. It is inserted here to give strength but omitted from the other side as deemed unnecessary. Thus the whole piece was left so as to permit of drawing the feet under one.

The photograph was made when the piece was in the possession of Mr. Brooks Reed. Its size is not unusual, but it is featured here for its rarity. It is about the hight of a chair.

No. 570. A joint stool belonging to Mr. Dwight Blaney. It is of the good conventional type with the legs raking one way.

No. 571. Another stool of a heavier type and with slight carving under the frame, and at the base of the stretchers. This ornamented frame assimilates this piece to the English style. The date of the left hand piece may be 1670–1690; that of the right hand piece is perhaps 1650–1670. It also is owned by Mr. Blaney.

503. Mushroom Chair. 1700–20.

504. Reversed Banister. 1710–30.

505–506. Trammel Spits.

507. Turned High Chair. 1700–1710.

508–513. Series of Lanterns. 18th and 19th Centuries.

514. Five Back Chair.   515. Rolled Arm Chair.

516–527. Fireplace Utensils.

528–529. ROLLED ARM SLAT BACKS. 1700–1720.

530. SPINNING CHAIR.

531. HOLLOW BACK BANISTER.

DAY BEDS, SETTEES AND SETTLES

THE day bed, which is commonly called a couch in England, and a chaise longue in France, is most aptly described by the last name since it is really a chair with a seat drawn out to the length of a bed. The back is precisely like that of a chair in most instances. The first set of feet under the back are often in a square section like that of a chair back of the period. Thus the true day bed never has its ends alike. A loose commercial term for a single bed with a head and foot is day bed. Doubtless it came in through a desire to render such single beds popular, or perhaps through ignorance. Ancient day beds with two ends were non-existent so far as we know. In England there was a sofa or upholstered settee, as we may name it, in the seventeenth century but it was extremely rare. The only example we have seen in this country is in the Essex Institute, and we do not know that an American origin is claimed for it. We have seen a double ended settee of the Sheraton period. We confine ourselves here, therefore, to the day bed, as it is the only type known in America during its period.

The genesis of the day bed is unknown, like the beginnings of most other things in this world. We have sometimes found a duchesse of a later period, which is built like a short day bed, with a stool which can be moved up at the foot, and built to match it, so as to secure the length of a couch. The charm of a day bed consists in its lines, as they relate themselves to chairs of the period. Such interest has been excited in late years that these articles are practically all gathered in by collectors as rapidly as they are found. Perhaps a score or two are known in addition to the Pennsylvania day bed of which there may be as many more.

It will be observed that they never have a back. The head is the back.

No. 572. A day bed belonging to the Metropolitan Museum. The stretchers are carved and pierced and arched in a manner practically the same as that of chairs in the Flemish style, dating from 1680 to 1700.

A feature of the construction is that we do not find a scrolled stretcher at the foot. The piece was intended, of course, to be placed at the side of a room. The foot stretcher is set low to correspond with the cross stretchers, between the others pairs of legs. As a rule these pieces are made on both sides alike. That is, they had no backs except the head, and were symmetrical and appropriate wherever placed. In the more elegant pieces as here the back and the seat are caned. In this example the legs are turned, though the principal stretchers and the back or head are carved.

Another feature of these day beds is that the head is usually hinged, swinging down at the top on dowel pins which run from the frame of the head into the posts near the main frame of the day bed. These features are occasionally absent, and where they were originally present we sometimes find that the swinging head has been fastened in an immovable position like a chair back. The swing of the head was regulated by a chain which passed through the posts or was attached to them so that the head might be thrown down into a horizontal position or given any angle for comfort. Possibly this arrangement was made in deference to the occasional use of the day bed as a bed. The frame is usually a little short for a bed, and the letting down of the head serves to lengthen the frame. The specimen before us belongs to the walnut period.

No. 573. This simple day bed shows the method of lacing or trussing the canvas where such a basis was used for a cushion. We may presume that the cane seats were often provided with cushions. At least they would otherwise have gone to pieces quickly. The arrangement to receive the cushion here is similar to that in many old fashioned beds, using a canvas instead of a rope support.

Owner: The Metropolitan Museum.

Nos. 574–576. A room in the Captain Brown House, the house of the Antiquarian Society in Concord. The remarkably handsome day bed shown in the corner of this room belonged to the Rev. Peter Bulkeley, the first minister of Concord, and the chair which is seen to match it was his chair of dignity, appertaining to his office. These pieces, having been designed to go together, are among our richest treasures of that period. In fact, the collection of this society, though smaller than the collections of the great cities, consists of a good number of very choice specimens, so much so that it is perhaps not rivaled in New England by any other public collection.

No. 577. A simpler day bed belonging to the George F. Ives Collection. It will be noted that this is all turned and that even the post at the back is as near like the other posts as it may be and still afford a space for the mortise of the main rail. Upholstery on these day beds is very rare and probably always out of place. We do not believe that in this case the upholstery should be attached. It will be noted here that the head is rather plain and composed of three splats, if we may use that term of wide banisters.

Specimens like this or indeed any of the day beds are very light and easily movable, by which we infer that it was the intention to place them temporarily where they were most convenient.

No. 578. A turned day bed, the property of Mr. Edward C. Wheeler, Jr. This bed shows a proper cushion added to a foundation such as that of No. 573. The true stretchers at the head are a very unusual feature. One also sees here that the rails are mortised into the post at the foot, and do not run over the foot posts as in the other examples so far shown. This assimilates the day bed more closely to the chair. The bulb and ring turning is the usual style of the end of the seventeenth and the beginning of the eighteenth century, unless we have carving.

No. 579. This day bed gives a good example of the development from a chair. Thus it will be seen that the back or head has legs precisely like a chair of the period, and that the front end or foot has Spanish feet, like the front legs of a chair. The intermediate sets of legs are plainly turned. The head in this case is the true Dutch fiddle back, Dutch in this connection referring to the types brought in under William and Mary and Queen Anne.

The upholstery here has now been removed and a leather cushion put in its place. The canvas bottom is found. The day bed is of walnut. There was an inscription attached to the underside stating that the piece belonged to Clarissa Griswold of Killingworth, Connecticut, from which state the piece came. This piece is longer than usual, being 74 inches over all. The width is $21\frac{3}{4}$ inches. The hight of the head is $37\frac{1}{4}$ inches. The frame is 14 inches high.

No. 580. A prettily turned day bed with a paneled head. This panel being solid differentiates it from other examples. Here also is first seen plainly the arrangement for swinging the head.

All the specimens we have so far shown have eight legs, a style more sought for and regarded better than the six legged type.

Owner: Mr. L. G. Myers.

No. 581. A heavily turned day bed. We have here the Dutch splat in the back, which in this case seems designed originally to be fixed.

It will be seen that in the framing of a piece like this it is important that the cross members should enter the posts at a different level from the lengthwise stretchers. Thus there is ample room for mortises without weakening the legs. As an example of turning, this is an attractive day bed. The maker was called upon, owing to his chosen method of construction, to devise a very long turning for the side stretchers, which he has successfully accomplished.

Size: 72 inches long, $26\frac{3}{4}$ inches wide, $16\frac{3}{4}$ inches high on the frame. The head is $36\frac{3}{4}$ inches high.

Owner: The estate of William G. Erving, M.D., of Washington.

No. 582. A Spanish foot day bed with an extraordinary number of stretchers. We have never elsewhere seen anything like the two additional longitudinal sets which are mortised into the cross members below. The effect is not unpleasing. A much greater degree of strength was secured. In this specimen we have for the first time all of the feet carved in the Spanish fashion, and very well done. Of course, the original thought of the chaise longue was departed from in carving the feet at the back or head.

The head here is elaborate and handsome. The wood is walnut, as in most cases of elegant construction. We are more apt to find maple in the simpler specimens.

Owner: Mr. Martin Gay of Hingham.

No. 583. A Pennsylvania day bed. These specimens are interesting for themselves and also because they undoubtedly foreshadow, and at no distant period, the beginning of Windsor construction. In fact, the "blunt arrow" type of construction found on the feet, and the general turning of the leg, is precisely like that found in the earliest specimens of Windsor arm chairs, though of course the posts here are larger. There is the curious effect in this specimen of slanted back posts, which omit the usual angle at the frame. That angle required a rather special adeptness with a lathe.

The head is of reeded banisters running above into an arched and molded rail. The average size of the turning of the legs in Pennsylvania beds is about two and a half inches. The same heavy bulb and ring stretcher is used as appears in the Queen Anne furniture. The top rail of the back was made long enough to strike against the posts when the head was drawn up, and thus to prevent the head falling forward on the seat.

In some specimens the central pair of side stretchers on the Pennsylvania beds is set at a different hight from the side pairs, in order not to weaken the wood. From a structural standpoint this scheme is good, but to borrow an expression from automobiles, it loses the stream line effect.

In all the examples we have seen of the Pennsylvania day bed the seats were covered with rush. The pieces are very comfortable, substantial and quaint articles of furniture.

Owner: Mr. Hollis French.

No. 584. A specimen of the Pennsylvania day bed, in which the reeded banisters of the back enter a semi-circular crested top rail, which is heavily molded to correspond with the outline of the arch.

532. TURNED DUTCH CHAIR. 1720–30.

533. A PENNSYLVANIA ETCHED HASP. LATE 18th CENTURY.

534–535. A Dutch and a Serpentine Child's Chair. 1710–20.

536–537. New England and Pennsylvania Child's Chairs.

538. ARCHED BANISTER BACK.

539. COMB CORNER CHAIR.

540. CHILD'S WING CHAIR.

541. Very Early Joint Stool. 1640–60.

542. Child's Chair.

543. Banister Back.

In neither of these Pennsylvania day beds that we show does the ball at the foot of the post exhibit the best characteristic mark. In a specimen of the author's collection which is not shown, this ball is very markedly larger in diameter than any other part of the post, and the appearance is distinctive.

We see here that the back posts, while turned above, are of a square section below, after the analogy of the chair. As a kind of concession, however, to the rest of the construction the square legs are roughly notched near the bottom.

This piece was in the former collection of the author.

The owner is not known to the author.

No. 585. A day bed in the estate of J. Milton Cobourn, M.D. This singular and interesting piece is evidently a country made specimen. The stretchers instead of being turned or carved are cut like the skirt of a table, and are run around the entire frame at the same level. The head also is not made to swing but the top rail is imposed upon the posts, and a large number of banisters or spindles are inserted. Nevertheless, the legs have turned sections, as well as the upper parts of the head. We may presume that the maker was removed from the direct influence of an established style, and therefore worked from memory or from his own ideas.

We may remark as we close the subject of day beds that their existence indicates that our ancestors had not the iron constitutions with which they have been credited. The day bed indicates that they sometimes found it agreeable, and did not consider it immoral, to enjoy a siesta. We might, it is true, point out that the shortness of the couch portion may indicate that these pieces were used for resting in the bed chambers, and by the ladies only. We do not know that there is any ancient evidence as to the rooms in which these pieces were usually placed.

No. 586. A day bed in the full Flemish design. This beautiful piece in walnut carries out completely the Flemish scroll in the design of the leg, and the stretchers It will be noticed that the arch of the carved stretcher in this case is filled with a pair of scrolls and is pierced. Undoubtedly this method of construction was in the interest of strength and we believe it is sometimes found in chairs. This elegant piece has often been seen at the annual exhibit of the Arts and Crafts Society at Hingham. It is in good condition, and the existence of the balls or shoes on the feet indicate that it has always had good care. The head of this piece does not show very well but it is excellently carved.

Owner: Mrs. Rogers of Hingham.

No. 587–588. No. 587 is a child's settle. We see here the analogy of the pine chest, in that the settle has no frame, but that the front board is nailed directly to the scrolled end.

The finger holes at the back corresponding with that of the wing chair on the right are interesting. Although these pieces are now found together we cannot suppose that they were made to go together, otherwise the scroll of the wing would match in both specimens. The boring of the holes rather than cutting out a larger piece is in the interest of retaining the strength of the wood, for the material here is pine.

Although we have called the larger piece a child's settle it is entirely possible from its size that it was a pung seat. Indeed the author owned such a seat in precisely the same construction, which showed on the outside of the ends the wearing away of the red paint where the end had come in contact with the side board of the pung.

The settle in its pine board form was the furniture of persons in moderate circumstances or, since it was placed as a rule in the kitchen, it was made thus simple for every day use.

We have not seen an American carved settee or settle, though we have seen such a settee on which new carving had been done to pass it off as an unique American piece.

No. 589. A small scrolled settle. The shape of the scrolls on the end boards of this settle suggest somewhat the crude carving in imitation of the limbs of an evergreen. The shortness of the piece adds to its interest.

Owner: Mrs. De Witt Howe of Manchester, New Hampshire.

The material is pine.

No. 590. A miner's candle stick. The flat scroll which receives the candle is made as a spring to grasp closely. The candle stick could either be thrust into the wall of the mine or hung up. Very elaborate specimens of these miner's candles are known in Pennsylvania, one of them being a work of art.

No. 591–592. A settle bed. At this writing this piece is the only one known of its kind in America. The author owned this for some time before he knew what it was. Below in No. 593 it is shown as used in the day time. An Irishman who happened one day to see it exclaimed, " Well, if there ain't a settle bed! I was raised in one of them things." It is said that they are found in Ireland in oak, and there is a report that they are known in Poland.

This piece is in hard and soft pine. The eleven deep panels of the back are framed and pinned so far as their rails and stiles are concerned. One board, however, covers the length of all and is of course not a true

544. Spanish-Dutch Chair.　　　545. Early Dutch Chair.

546–547. Pennsylvania Lamps.

548. Slat Back with Writing Arm. 1720-30.

549. Turned Joint Stool.

550–551. Pair of Unique Chair Stools 1690–1710.

552. A Long Turned Joint Stool. 1680–1700.

553. SPLAYED JOINT STOOL.

554. HEAVY JOINT STOOL.

555. LIGHT JOINT STOOL.

panel. The panels in front are true. The seat swings out and down and is boxed at the ends, and was never built into the frame of the settle. It was attached by hooks and staples, a portion of which still remain in place. A feather bed was used, so that the bed and the covering would easily shut up into the confined space. The ends have panels like those on the front. The arms are of the wainscot chair type but are of pine. The front edges of the frame at the ends under the arms are very strongly molded.

Size: Length outside 74 inches. The back is 36¾ inches high. The seat is 14 inches wide and 17¾ inches high. The frame at the ends and the arms are 1⅝ inches thick.

Origin: Found on the North Shore of Massachusetts in 1922.

We have here, therefore, a framed settle or more properly settee, a term which is restricted to framed seats.

The quilt is of a quaint pattern.

No. 594. A framed settee. The wood is maple, as to the turned parts. The seat and panels and frame in the back are of yellow pine. The back sill is of oak. This piece was found in Connecticut in 1922. So far as it has come to our observation it is the only framed settee analogous to the English type. It supplies the long desired missing link, to go with our rare American wainscot chairs with the scrolled arm.

Size: Length over all, 75 inches; width over all 27 inches, which includes the rolled end of the arms. Hight over all including extension of back posts, 50½ inches. Width of seat 20½ inches; hight of seat, 18¼ inches. The square of the turned posts is 2¼ inches. The back posts are 1¼ inches by 2½ inches. The arms are 1½ inches thick.

No. 595. A New York wagon seat. We give these seats the name because most of them seem to be derived from New York state, though they have been found in western Connecticut and Massachusetts and probably in northern Pennsylvania and New Jersey. They were used alternately as seats in market wagons, held in place by the side boards, and as small love seats in the dwellings. A characteristic is the middle post, which is made larger than the end posts.

This specimen is from the collection of Mr. Chauncey C. Nash.

Size: 29 inches high. The seat is 13 inches high, wagon seats always being lower than chair seats. The surface of the seat is 14 by 33½ inches. A great many of these specimens have been brought into the market within recent years. The seats are mostly in rush, but we find an occasional one in splint.

No. 596. An amusing spring wagon seat.

Owner: Collection of George F. Ives.

The construction is sufficiently obvious to need no explanation, but we may say that ordinary wagon seats were often built with the same spring construction. The turnings here are very much better than we ordinarily see.

No. 597. A quaint small rocker settle. The foot rest is concaved. Doubtless the intention was to raise the feet from the floor for the sake of warmth. The settle seems to have been " built for two." The immediate derivation is from New York, but we presume it is a Jersey or Pennsylvania piece.

Relating to the date it might be, judging from the habits of the people of the region, any time in the eighteenth century.

No. 598. New York wagon seat with spindles. In this specimen some effort has been made at ornamentation by setting a portion of the spindles on a diagonal. It will be noted that we have here an arm which runs over the top of the post and is connected with it by a dowel. On the other hand in No. 596 we have the earlier method of construction by which the dowel runs into the side of the post.

Owner: Mr. Rudolph P. Pauly.

No. 599. A cradle in oak, perhaps English. We show it here in order to give a progressive demonstration of the development of the cradle as it was found in America.

No. 600. A pine board settle with panels. A piece of this sort made with two rows of panels is now considerably sought for.

Owner: The Collection of George F. Ives.

One notices the method of setting the little candle sconce in the center. The settle ends here are very high.

Size: 64 inches long, the back is 52 inches high. The seat is 16 inches deep and the hight is the same. The arms are 35 inches high.

The advantage of paneling the backs of settles was slight, so far as use was concerned. Paneling was somewhat more finished but entirely unnecessary. Of course, when found paneled, as here, they are successors of the English tradition of oak paneling.

We do not seem to find cushions for settles, but no doubt they were sometimes used. The seats are never shaped, and therefore are rather uncomfortable. Usually the seat was hinged when the settle was boxed in below. In this case the base was used, sometimes for a wood box, as the piece was kept near the fire, or sometimes for a grain chest. Indeed, the development of the settle from the chest is obvious.

No. 601–602. This is the only example that we happen to have seen of a built in settle. It is in a seventeenth century house in Wrentham, and has a single end only. It is set back over the sill of the house and

556. Joint Stool with Drawer. 1680–1700.

557–566. Candles and Lamps.

567. WINDSOR HIGH CHAIR. 1720.

568. UNUSUAL PIPE TONGS. 18th CENTURY.

569. HIGH STRETCHER SQUAB. 1680–1700.

570–571. JOINT STOOLS. 1660–1700.

572. SCROLL STRETCHER DAY BED. 1680–1700.

573. ALL TURNED DAY BED. 1690–1700.

the sheathed paneling of the outside wall forms the back.   It is quaint and small and most interesting.   The door handles and latches here shown are original on the house and are of wood.   We know no reason why we may not consider the settle as contemporaneous with the house.

No. 603.   A large pine paneled settle, the property of the Rhode Island School of Design.   The knob-like terminals of the scrolled end boards are interesting.   Also one should notice that there is a board laid over the back at the top in the form of a hood.   Of course the object was to keep off the wind, as these pieces were drawn up before the great fireplaces.   There was a frost line on the floor in bitter weather, as referred to in Whittier's " Snowbound."   In these settles the back board behind the seat usually ran to the floor to stop the movement of cold air.   In many cases the end board was not scrolled as here but was made solid for purposes of protection against cold.

If we consider the settle in its modern use we feel that it interferes with the unity of the house, as it cuts off the view of the fireplace.   It shuts the fireplace away from the rest of the room.   Therefore, in the arrangement of a settle in an old house it is better to place it on the side wall at right angles with the fireplace.

The Rhode Island School of Design possesses a second settle very similar to this.

Size: 74 inches long, $53\frac{1}{2}$ inches high, and 20 inches deep.

CRADLES

W E DO not know when or where the cradle originated. We regret its discontinuance as an article of household furniture, because about it is enshrined so much of sentiment. After all is said and done, the sentiment in relation to antique furniture is, to us, at least, a great part of its charm. It is said that cradles are not good for the health of a child. Happily, we do not have to pass on that subject. The hand that rocked the cradle now places the child in a bed or crib, theoretically; but practically, most mothers put their children in baby carriages, to do duty instead of cradles.

There is an interesting question as to the origin of the rocking chair. An Englishman told the author that his mother had bounced back and forth with him in her arms, on a flat-bottomed chair, until she had worn the base into a roughly rounded form. This is a very amusing sidelight upon the lack of rockers in England. It raises the question whether or not rockers in this country may not have come in about the time that cradles began to go out. It may be that their original use was to carry out the idea that the English mother was working out so blindly. At any rate, the cradle was not rocked with the hand, as the politicians would tell us, but by the foot, so that the hands might be available for knitting or mending. In practice, of course, the cradle would be for the most part rocked by an older child.

We do not often find cribs in the earliest American period. In fact, no such article has come to our attention. We may safely assume that the cradle or the trundle bed served instead of cribs. The cradle was a necessity in the home room, or the fire room, because there was not room in it for a bed, and there was no heat in the bedroom. The child must be under the mother's eye and in a comfortable place. We have seen cradles which bore at the foot the mark of heat blisters from the effect of the fire.

The hearth really became the sacred spot in our ancestral history. The baby was born by the hearth, was rocked there, and later crept about it, and got his first lessons in chemistry and poetry by watching the blaze. At a later period, it was at the hearth that his education began, as he stood between, or sat upon, his grandfather's knees, and heard the tales of long ago. There, also, he conned his horn book, or read of Bunyan's Pilgrim, by the light of pine knots. At the hearth, as a youth,

574–576. Day Bed and Corresponding Chairs. 1680–1700.

577. Day Bed, Banister Head. 1690–1710.

578. Turned Day Bed. 1690–1710.

579. Turned and Spanish Foot Day Bed. 1690–1710.

580. Unusually Turned Day Bed. 1690–1710.

581. A Six Legged Dutch Day Bed. 1700–1710.

582. Double Stretcher Day Bed. 1690–1710.

583. Pennsylvania Day Bed. 1710–30.

he held his sweetheart's hand. Here he was married. Here, surrounded by his children, he passed the evenings of his middle age. Here, as an ancient, he sat in the chimney corner, in the cool days of the early fall and late spring, and warmed his hands at the small fire kept up for his comfort; and here he passed on to his fathers.

The cradle, the beginning of the seven ages of man, is, therefore, for us Americans, an object of no little interest. Nevertheless, the mahogany or light maple cradle, which is found in almost every attic, is scorned by the collector, because it is not ancient nor rare enough to attract us, nor is it wanted about under foot. A use, indeed, has been found for it of late. We notice in a great many households where antique furniture is used, that the cradle has become the woodbox for the fireplace.

Of course, in this volume, we confine ourselves to the very early examples which are either so ancient or so good in themselves as to be highly regarded.

No. 604. A walnut cradle, originating in Pennsylvania. It has a scrolled head and foot board, with a heart-shaped hand hold for lifting about. There is also a scrolled bracket at the head board. The piece is framed, having large corner posts ending in rude balls. One notices the knobs at the side, which were used to button down the coverlet. In Pennsylvania, cradles were used to a date later, probably, than in New England. We do not know, when we reach Pennsylvania, that someone may not be making furniture as his first great-grandsire did at the time of the settlement. They love the old ways even more than the people of Connecticut. It is safe, however, to place a cradle of this sort in the eighteenth century, with the caution that similar cradles may have been made much later.

It is apparent that the sides of this cradle are raked, that is, splayed. We shall see later that the very earliest cradles had vertical sides.

No. 605. A cradle with a gallery and with spindles at the sides of the hood.

Owner: The Rhode Island School of Design.

This cradle is remarkable in having a fascinating low gallery around the sides and the foot. It terminates near the hood against brackets. The balls of this cradle are in excellent condition. It requires slight attention to see that cradles of this sort were made after the analogy of the chest. It has its panels, its corner posts, and its channel molds on the rails and stiles. This cradle probably had some sort of a cap to its hood. In the uncertainty as to its precise form, however, it is better to leave it as it is. It is said to have been found near Abington, Massachusetts, about 1920. Its sides are vertical.

No. 606. A flax breaker, such as was used in the seventeenth, eighteenth, and probably the beginning of the nineteenth century. The flax was placed in the form in which it came from the field, under the huge wooden maul, which by repeated blows disintegrated the stem into fibres, until, through the use of the hatchel, it was at last reduced to a sufficiently fine condition to be spun.

No. 607. The Dr. Samuel Fuller cradle. Although no lives have yet been lost in battles around this cradle, it has excited so much interest and controversy as to be a kind of monument among antiques. It was through one of the Alden family that the author was referred to the Cushman family, related to the Aldens, as the owners of this cradle. The Cushmans inherited it through intermarriage with the Fullers. There is an unbroken tradition that it came from Dr. Samuel Fuller of the Mayflower. So far, the tradition seems thoroughly credible, because the manifest age of the piece should take it back to 1650 at least.

The tradition then goes on to say that Peregrine White was rocked in this cradle on the Mayflower. As Peregrine is also said to have been rocked in a wicker cradle now in Pilgrim Hall, Plymouth, and even is, by some, said to have been rocked in the cradle in a glass case in that hall, we must conclude, if any of these tales are true, that Peregrine was, to use a Southern phrase, the rockingest child, as well as the first white child born in New England. First he was rocked in the cradle of the deep, and being born in Provincetown Harbor, was supposed to have been rocked in the cradle here shown, since it was handily available in the lading of the Mayflower, whereas the wicker cradle was hard to get at. It was, of course, presumed that the arrival in America would long precede the birth of the child.

An artist who has painted one of the large Pilgrim pictures at the Hall has shown one of the Pilgrim fathers wrestling with a cradle as he gets it aboard the Mayflower. We use the word "wrestle" advisedly, because, as a friend of ours said, with a sardonic grin, the cradle is large enough to rock a bull calf in. However that may be, the cradle is purely American. Its side panels are all pine, though its end panels are all American oak, and of course, also, the frame. The hood, however, is of pine. It is notch carved on the ends, and molded on the front and back, and a border is scratch carved in a diamond pattern. This is one of the important features of the cradle, since so many ancient examples have lost the cap board of the hood.

A second feature of great importance, and possibly marking uniqueness in American cradles, is the carrying of the gallery around three sides of the hood. The gallery at the back is composed of short spindles. The

584. PENNSYLVANIA DAY BED. 1710–30.

585. COUNTRY MADE DAY BED. 1710–40.

586. Flemish Couch. 1680–1700.

587–588. Child's Settle and Wing Chair. 1730–80.

589. SMALL PINE SETTLE, SCROLLED END. 1730–80.

590. MINER'S LIGHT.

591–592. SETTLE BED MADE UP. 1710–40.

593. SETTLE BED CLOSED. 1710–40.

supposed purpose of the gallery was to allow the mother a peep at the child from whatever angle she viewed the cradle. The turnings of the spindles are practically identical with those found on the earlier Carver chairs.

A third item of great interest is the split spindle, not so rare on the inside of the gallery opening, attached to the frame; but unique, up to the time of the present writing, as attached in the form of a long, specially turned drop or split spindle on the front of the hood. The sides of the cradle are vertical, and it is very deep. The stiles and the rails are strongly cut in channel molds and double pinned. There is a chamfer around the panels. In fact, what we have here is really a chest in which a hood is substituted for a lid; that is to say, the chest construction is modified sufficiently to form a cradle. The projecting foot-posts are in the earliest form of turning. The cradle has never been painted. An interesting feature is observed here in relation to the quartering of the oak of the frame. Those portions which are featured show dark. In a piece that is finished by shellac or varnish, they show light, as compared with the rest of the wood.

Of course the cradle was made in America, and in Plymouth, but whether by John Alden or Kenelm Winslow, we, of course, do not know. An amusing fact in relation to this cradle is that there is now being sold in Plymouth, as has been the case for many years, a picture of the cradle as being the one now in Pilgrim Hall under the glass case. We are assured by a lady who was rocked in this cradle as an infant, as have been every one of her American ancestors, that she knows absolutely the whereabouts of the cradle during her life, and that it has never been in Pilgrim Hall. Certainly it is quite unlike the example now there, which is not a paneled cradle. On it thin strips of maple or beech are applied and nailed to form false panels on the pine boards beneath. One of these strips at the foot has become detached, and the observer can plainly see the discoloration of the wood where it once was. The old stories indicate how cursory and uncritical, and in many cases, really untruthful, matters connected with antique furniture can be.

The cradle in Pilgrim Hall has very pretty spindle work over the head, instead of a cap for the hood. In that particular it is important. It is also, doubtless, important for a historical reason in connection with another branch of the Fuller family.

Our Samuel Fuller cradle is a most satisfactory specimen, from the mellow and worn condition of the wood, and from its Pilgrim origin, and especially from its intrinsic merit.

A number of years since, the author replaced the missing rockers with oak cut from the face of an exposed beam in the Marsh House, Wethersfield, the oldest house in town. This oak is of precisely the same color and consistency as the rest of the cradle, so that, unless one points out the inner surfaces of these rockers, it is hard to persuade even a critic that they are not original.

Size: The square of the posts is $2\frac{1}{2}$ inches. The cradle is $34\frac{1}{2}$ inches long, 33 inches high, and $19\frac{1}{2}$ inches wide. These dimensions do not include the side extensions of the rockers.

Nos. 608–611. A picture showing an early eighteenth century room. The bed is of the second period, when the hangings were still retained at the head, but were reduced at the sides and the foot merely to an upper and a lower valance.

The quaint little child's chair before the fireplace is worthy of attention. The chair nearest the bed has its back posts running up above the main frame of the back section, as is the fashion in Spanish chairs. Hence this chair is not otherwise shown. A quaint little looking glass on the wall has a leather frame.

No. 612. A cradle in maple, swinging on posts. This quaint and odd device is sometimes seen on later mahogany cradles, as in one beautiful specimen at the Essex Institute, Salem. In the cruder form here exhibited we have the shoe, or base, run crosswise at the ends below the posts, and a longitudinal stretcher on the floor. The cradle swings on heavy wooden pins. We are at a loss here, as usual, about dates, and even more than usual. The piece is absolutely in the rough.

No. 613. A cradle of Pennsylvania origin, with stenciled discs and other decorations. One quaint feature here is also the roping of the bottom. We have seen a chair similarly roped. The method is precisely like that used in beds. The stenciling is similar in design to that found on a few small boxes of pine, on one or two "Bible" boxes, and, on a larger scale, on the barn decorations of eastern Pennsylvania, which are to be considerably elaborated in the author's "Pennsylvania Beautiful."

No. 614. An oak cradle with raised panels. The ends of the raised portions of the panels are gouge carved, whereas their sides are handsomely molded. This is a detail we have not previously noted in antique furniture, and we have not yet been able to learn whether similar examples are found abroad. The heavy channel molds or beads on this piece, and the general system of construction, together with the tall foot posts, as purely Gothic as if they were made in the thirteenth century, are features of much interest. These foot posts are in what is called the square turning; that is, the maker did not have a lathe, and he contoured the sides of the square of the post so that it should agree with the outline of a

594. FRAMED MAPLE AND PINE SETTEE. 1720–30.

595. NEW YORK WAGON SEAT. 18th AND 19th CENTURIES.

596. SPRING WAGON SEAT. 18th AND 19th CENTURIES.

597. ORIGINAL ROCKER SETTLE.

turning. The hood of this cradle is somewhat of a puzzle, as we presume it once had a cap, it being cut on the paneled end in the form of a gable. There are a few tacks in the edge of this gable, but no other marks to hint at any attachment of wood. The rockers are neither original, nor are they placed in the proper position. Undoubtedly the posts were extended in the form of legs, and were then bifurcated to receive rockers. We speak thus positively in spite of the appearance of the example to follow.

The cradle is said to have come from Wethersfield, Connecticut, and to date from the time of its settlement, but we have no reliable data. It was bought in Worcester, in 1923.

Size: The posts are $2\frac{3}{8}$ inches by $1\frac{7}{8}$ inches. It is $38\frac{1}{2}$ inches long, 30 inches high, and $16\frac{1}{4}$ inches wide.

No. 615. A cradle, presumably in beech. It is composed of true panels, which are interesting in the construction about the head, formed like five sides of an octagon. The cradle belongs to the Plant family, from the Mill Plain district of the town of Branford, Connecticut, where it is on exhibition in the public library. It has been traced to Jonathan Barker, born 1705. The sides are not quite vertical. The condition is somewhat dilapidated. The rockers seem not to be original. It will be seen, however, that the head and foot posts are turned in the same pattern, and that the head posts, unlike previous examples we have shown, extend above the frame. Of course, this is owing to the manner in which the cap of the hood is attached. The extended and turned posts at the head, however, are a feature of still earlier English cradles.

BEDS

W E HAVE in America no great elaborately turned high posters, such as were found in England at the time of the American settlement. We have records of such beds being ordered from England. Such importations of an ancient period have disappeared. Of course they lack wholly the American feeling, and as we can see such beds in England, the loss is not as great as it might seem at first.

The earliest beds known in America are simple as regards their posts. They are always square in the earliest examples, below the bed rail. Above that rail they may be either square, octagonal or turned, but the turned specimens may be later than the other forms. In every instance the posts taper, and are small. In the square at the frame, the most usual dimension is $2\frac{1}{2}$ inches. We have never seen it exceed $2\frac{3}{4}$ inches on very ancient beds. This dimension continues to the floor without change. Beds turned below the frame are more likely to be of the nineteenth century, especially if the posts are heavy. The Sheraton type, indeed, and sometimes the Hepplewhite, have turned legs. In our period, however, we have not noted an exception to the general rules above. Any delicacy of turning, or any urn turning, means an approach to the end of the eighteenth century. The continuation of a large post to a point near the top is always late and poor, whether it be carved or not.

At the same time it is wholly impossible to assign the plain bed to a date anywhere nearly exact. This arises from the fact that it was in a manner styleless and continued, probably, from 1670 even through the eighteenth century, with practically no change except some slight marks such as we have already mentioned, regarding bolts, etc.

Of course the purpose of the tester and curtains was a double one — to secure privacy, and to shut out drafts. Some of the ancient houses, being the homes of large families, required more than one bed in a room. Indeed, attics, to which the children or the hired men were often consigned, were known not infrequently to have four, and sometimes six beds. It was regarded as effeminate to heat a bedroom for people in health, though for guests or elderly persons the fireplace, almost invariably found small in bedrooms, might be used. It scarcely raised the temperature above freezing. As fashions changed, first the side and foot curtains, and finally the whole top, were dispensed with. In the effort to

598. New York Seat with Spindles.

599. Oak Cradle.

600. Ten Panel Pine Settle. 1710–50.

601–602. Built-in Settle.

603. TEN PANEL SETTLE. 1730–80.

604. WALNUT PENNSYLVANIA SCROLLED CRADLE. 18th CENTURY.

605. CRADLE WITH GALLERY. 1680–1700.

606. FLAX BREAKER. 18th AND 19th CENTURIES.

ape, rather than to imitate, the ancient fashions, modern beds are put on the market with high posts, but without canopies. This is a makeshift which can scarcely be justified either in logic or taste. If persons desire to have the really ancient beds with canopies, they may omit the lining below the fish-net stitch, and secure a circulation of the air, so that they may still have the old fashion without transgressing sanitary demands.

Some of the old canopies were composed of very rich work, so that the inheritance of a bed, by a special clause in a will, was counted an honor. The bed, with its furniture, a phrase which included everything aside from the woodwork, was the most considerable object of value in the home, even exceeding that of a cupboard.

Nos. 616–618. A four-poster bed formerly in the Hazen house, Haverhill. All the parts of these hangings and the canopy were beautifully laundered and laid away in a box when the bed was purchased. The tester proper was attached on its four sides by laths like old curtain sticks pushed through the open-ended wide hem, and then tautened by straining them over the iron pegs of the tops of the posts.

One sees the trundle-bed head at the foot of the large bed. On the right, in the rear, is a quaint early high chair, and on the left a good New England slat-back.

Why beds are called four-posters is one of the unsolved mysteries, since we can scarcely conceive of beds being constructed without four posts. Perhaps those who gave the name thought of a post only as a high post, and if it was short, called it merely a leg. It is necessary, however, to run one's forehead against one of these posts in the night, fully to appreciate the name.

Of course the only object of the high post was to attach thereto the curtains. In the case of the bed before us, these curtains were held up by strings running from the posts and caught at the centre of the tester in rings. The ordinary method was to tack the curtain to the side lath.

No. 619. A jointed bed, otherwise called a press bed or a slaw bed. These beds were intended to have their heads set in a shallow closet, with two large doors. The bed in the day time was thrown up on the joints of the secondary set of legs, and the doors were closed. The bed is shown without furniture, in order to give an idea of this method of use.

There is an amusing sameness between the needs of the present generation and those of the first generation, in respect to scanty house room. Our remote ancestors, as the family grew large, were hard put to it to provide room for all. Hence we have the scheme of the trundle bed, the settle bed, the press bed, the trestle board, the trammel lamp, the chair table, and various other devices to accommodate many people in a small space.

In fixing the dates of beds it will be observed that in the earlier styles there were no bolts used at the corners, but that the frame was held together merely by the tension of the bed cord. There are two tools, a straining wrench and a special wedge, together, of course, with a mallet, that are used in cording a bed. It is necessary, in case of a new rope especially, to increase the tension of a bed after a few days.

Another detail to be noticed is that the makers sometimes cut a groove into which the rope sank between holes. We are not clear whether this was an improvement or an original plan.

Small beds with low posts got the name " hired men's beds." They were the sort commonly in use for the small chambers.

No. 620–624. A low post bed with a double arch in the headboard, to indicate where grandpa and grandma should sleep. There is also a trundle bed, but without a head. The woven spread shown on the trundle bed seems to have been a great favorite. Multitudes of these spreads still exist, blue being perhaps most preferred.

The bird cage in the remote background is of wicker work, such as was commonly employed in the old days. On the right wall are hanging rope shelves.

No. 625. A trundle bed with a paneled head. Owing to the heavy bar across the head, we consider this an early specimen, but the side bars above the main rails are missing.

No. 626. A bed unique in our experience, sharing in its interest with the settle bed previously shown. Here we have true settle ends, with ogee contours at the feet, but the back of the settle is elongated into high posts. The bed frame hinges on the front of the end boards. When the bed, therefore, is lifted up, as here shown, the counterpane is drawn down over it to cover it. We have purposely exposed the scroll of the settle end to show the arm. The bed is painted blue. It was bought in Worcester in 1923. We know nothing whatever of its age. It is obvious however, from the method of construction, that it was not to be set in a press but to stand free in a room. Of course it could not be used as a settle. At the same time, it is a quaint conceit, and when made up for the night, is of somewhat pleasing outline. At the top there is a shallow frame sustained by a diagonal strut, forming a bracket on each post, over which the coverlet is drawn down.

No. 627. A famous bed, now in the York jail, the Museum in the town of that name in Maine. It is one of the few examples shown in other works. The crewel work and the colors are very rich, especially the greens and reds.   The counterpane and valance are a part of the same work, with uniform colorings, done, of course, on old linen.

A feature giving much flavor to this bed is the use of texts or poems in crewel work, around the upper valance.   The sentiments are such as might appear on samplers.

We are glad to present so clear a picture of this ancient piece, which dates from 1745.   At the jail various details regarding the bed and its donor are preserved.   We are especially glad of the existence of this beautiful example, because it forms a connecting link with the stately beds of the sixteenth century.

Nos. 628–633.   On the left is the only American oak high poster that has come to our attention, or to that of our friends.   It was found in the attic of the Webb House, Wethersfield.   Mr. Welles, who owned the house, when a boy sawed off one of the posts as a ball bat.   Aside from that, the bed is in its original condition, and is an amusing instance of the persistence of the Connecticut taste for oak.   The posts rise in a perfectly plain taper, and the bed is held together by cording only.   When this bed was on the market some years since, the general public entirely overlooked its importance.

In the same picture appears a wing chair made in precisely the same fashion as a settle, except that it has a single seat.   It is of pine, and covered with figured cotton goods.   The chair before the fireplace is of an early turned type.   The chair at the left is of the Dutch turned style, with a kind of stump foot, somewhat later than our period.   Of course the Windsor chair and the stand do not come into our view, but the braided rug and the rag rug go back to a period the beginning of which we are unable to trace.

Nos. 634–636.   Sets of andirons from the George W. Ives Collection.   The Hessian andirons are reversed.   We are informed that if the backs are hollow, the andirons are not very early, and that the original Hessian or other cast type was puddled iron; that is to say, the iron was poured into an open mold and filled in on the back.   The Washington andirons on the other side are of interest.   The middle pair are odd in respect to the so-called square turnings with which the flat members of the posts are tipped.

Nos. 637–639.   A high-post bed in which the posts are made in two sections, the upper part doweling into the lower part, and made detachable.   The upper sections are called poles.   It is possible that the phrase "tent bed," usually describing a round topped bed such as we shall presently show, had some connection with the phrase "bed pole."   It is to be seen here that this bed is turned near the foot.   Its other ornamental details indicate a late date, but the canopy in blue peacocks is very interesting and rather early.

The scrolled-leg chair immediately in front of the lady standing is a good example, as is also the Spanish foot fiddle back chair in the immediate foreground on the right. The ram's horn arms on this chair surpass, in the way of carving, any others we have seen, in respect to the spiraled terminals of the horns.

No. 640–642. A bed with its original canopy of linen. The method of draping the bed, by the use of cords attached to the laths running around the frame, is seen here, also the fashion of attaching the fringe both to the upper valance and to the curtains. The quaint stool at the foot is of the earliest Windsor pattern.

No. 643–645. It would seem that the pudding stick here should be enshrined as a kind of fetish with the Harvard Hasty Pudding Club. The design was worked out in wood probably in imitation of an iron design. The rolling pin in its early form was turned with a knob at one end only. The wooden spoon was common for mixing purposes, as now.

No. 646–649. A folding or jointed six-legged bed, in the George F. Ives Collection. The bracketed head or canopy is quite like that in No. 626. It is designed, as in that case, to hold a screen or coverlet for daytime use, and to be drawn down over the bottom of the bed, whose legs at the foot were jointed if long, or otherwise could shut without folding inside the canopy. A peculiarity of this bed is that there is a jointed frame at the head with a shoe or bottom member connecting the main posts with the secondary set of posts. Further, there was a drawer in this section for bedding. Of course it was available only when the bed was closed, as in the daytime.

We have seen another very handsome bed, something of this sort, in Woodbury, Connecticut. There is also a very pleasing specimen in the rooms of the Dartmouth Historical Society in New Bedford.

The clock at the left is a so called wag-on-the-wall, most of which were imported. It is said that the little chest at the foot of the bed was often used for the extra bedding. The candle stand of wood on straddling legs is a dateless and sometimes styleless article which is nevertheless much sought for.

No. 650–653. A bed in the dwelling in Duxbury, said to have been built by the grandson of John Alden. In this house, though not in this room, but in the bedroom off the kitchen, it is said that John and Priscilla passed the last thirteen years of their life. It is probable that John Alden assisted, by his hand or by his brain, in the framing of this house, supposed to have been built about 1653. Alden was at this time about fifty-three

607. Samuel Fuller Cradle. 1620–50.

608–611. Slender Post Bed. 18th Century.

612. SUSPENDED CRADLE. 18th CENTURY.

613. PENNSYLVANIA DECORATED CRADLE. 18th CENTURY.

614. Oak Cradle, Gouged Carved Panels. 1635–50.

615. Paneled Hood Cradle. 1680–1710.

616–618. Canopied Bed and Trundle Bed. 18th Century.

619. Folding Press Bed. 18th Century.

years of age. The massive character of the framing and the gun-stock post are shown in the corner through the bed. The bed has upon it a counterpane of the drawn-in candle-wick design, all in white and now so rare. The figures here are not as elaborate as are frequently found. The floral pattern is the most highly thought of. A stool of early but uncertain date and a banister back turned chair, hooked rugs and a braided rug form the remainder of the furniture.

This house is being honorably treated by a Mr. Charles Alden, who has a long lease of it. He is attempting to restore it absolutely on the lines of the original design, and deserves much credit for the wholly new plenishing which he is providing from time to time, as he is able to find suitable examples.

No. 654. A high-post bed in which the chamfering of the posts is quite evident.

Owner: The George F. Ives Collection.

The plainness of the posts in ancient beds is justified by the fact that they are shut in by the curtains. As they were not visible, there was no special reason for working the wood into decorative forms.

In this connection an amusing instance is that of a buyer of an old bed, who indignantly returned it to the seller on the ground that the head posts were plain, and that he would not bear having put off on him a spurious article. The bed was all original. The foot posts were turned, as was the custom in the second period, because they were to be visible. The head posts, on the other hand, being draped, were left plainly octagonal. The bed concerning which the buyer complained was far more valuable, because earlier, than it would have been had all the posts been alike.

CHAIR TABLES

THE chair table, sometimes called when the box is too high to sit upon, a hutch table, is in its best forms a very interesting and important article of furniture. It does not, however, in simple designs seem to appeal strongly to American collectors. It is one of the instances in which fashion has played some part. We show several very important examples. These chair tables were quite common on the New England coast. The appeal to our ancestors of economy in space made chair tables popular, as of course the purpose was to place them against the wall when they were not being used as tables. The oldest specimens have oak frames, but for the most part the frames were maple, or the pieces are mere six-board chests on legs, with table tops of maple or pine.

No. 655. An interesting oval top hutch table in the George F. Ives Collection. The meritorious points are the ogee scrolls on both faces of the legs, and the shoe and stretcher on which they rest. It will be observed that the board which forms the side of the hutch is made on the ends in the form of a single large dovetail, and that there is a lid to the hutch. The cleat, otherwise called a batten, which attaches the parts of the top together, is scrolled so that when the table is used as a chair a decorative feature may appear.

The word "hutch" is not precise in its applications, and has a more general use in England than in America. Even a hutch such as is shown here could be used as a seat with the help of a stool.

No. 656. A remarkable chair table said to have been found in New Jersey. It is of oak, and the top, shown in 657, is scrolled or contoured or shaped, phrases loosely used to denote the same thing, and finished with a thumb-nail mold. The turnings resemble those on two examples of stretcher desks which we have shown, and suggest the William and Mary period. The especial object of importance in this piece is the scrolled X stretcher, a feature we have not elsewhere seen in American chair tables. This example was sold to a museum. It is said that when it was uncrated the finial was missing, and that the piece was therefore rejected. It is all original except the finial, which was constructed by the use of the photograph which showed it before the original finial was lost. The drawer closes flush. The seat is molded like the top. The feet are of the heavy ball type as shown later in a court cup-

620–624. Low, Double Arched Head Bed and Trundle Bed.

625. Paneled Head Trundle Bed. 18th Century.

626. SETTLE END FOLDING BED. 18th CENTURY.

board table. It will be noted that the tops of these chair tables are attached with large turned pins, similar to those in the Pennsylvania library tables. The large turnings and the ogee scroll on the skirt or valance provide the finishing touches on a piece of the highest interest. We have not been able to make out the abbreviated legend on the under side of the leaf. Certainly the date is not, as it might appear to be, 1777.

Nos. 658–664. On the left there is a hutch table with a shoe prettily scrolled in the ogee pattern. In the foreground there is a child's wing chair of pine. The back is unusually high and quaint. At the right is a maple chair table with a square oak frame and a drawer, an unusual specimen. In the rear there is a cupboard with a drawer paneled from a solid. In the right foreground is an arch slat back chair of the Pennsylvania type.

This room is one of two which we have seen showing openly the great braces of the frame at the chimney girt. The method of hanging a lantern in the kitchen, as we know was frequently done, is also illustrated.

No. 665. An all pine American Gothic chair table with curved panels in the frame. This piece, which belonged to the author's former collection, he found in the hands of a small dealer in Freeport, Maine. A most astonishing cleat, in the true Gothic pierced form, runs across the top in the dovetailed conventional slot, to prevent warp, and also to avoid the necessity of nailing.

The piece stands upon shoes and the curvature of the panels is obvious. There is a lifting seat. We have never seen another piece of this character, and regard it very highly.

No. 666. A room in the Hazen Garrison house, with many objects appropriate to the date, 1690. A little wing chair, a butterfly table, a straddling high chair, a scrolled pine cradle, a hornbeam barrel, and other features appear.

No. 671. A chair table of the more usual type such as is found in eastern New England. This specimen has gouge carving at the ends of the shoes.

No. 672. A rack formed like a cone. It is designed to hang dipped candles and its construction, it being a homemade affair, is obvious. It is the property of Mrs. De Witt Howe.

TABLES

Persons who have ever camped will have learned the genesis of a table. Some sort of trestle is provided and a board is placed on it. Here, then, is the table as it was used for many ages. In a Greek dwelling of the higher character the table was thus brought to the banqueting apartment and then removed after a meal.

Leonardo Da Vinci's celebrated "Last Supper" shows a board on a trestle of carved shape, but precisely like the ordinary carpenter's horse as to main outlines. The last table known in the Middle Ages was a trestle-board. Early American inventories mention such boards in considerable numbers. They are found in ancient homes in England today. Mr. Bolles found the first one in America at a time when he was probably one of a very small number who would know what it was that he had found. The story of his discovery of it, in an attic where it was necessary to remove some of the structural features to get it out, is one of the epics of collecting.

In the third chapter of *Ivanhoe* one reads how the servants came in and removed the trestle board after a meal. Our ancestors did not feel any special need of fixing the table's top permanently in position, and this is not to be wondered at. With large families it was a convenience to have the long board removed. Of course the trestle-board necessitated a narrow table. The presumption is that the service was from one side, and that the diners did not sit facing one another. The ends of the table were occupied by joint stools, one at each end.

Tables in a fixed form indicate a civilization which has come to a quiet period and believes in stability. A very large table means a great house, with large doors. The first and principal use of tables was for dining. They undoubtedly derive their form from the long tables in the refectories of monasteries. The tables were placed in the parlors as places where conversation was allowed. The long board then adopted in the halls of nobles was required for the great number of retainers. The family of the lord would perhaps have such a table on the dais or raised platform at the end of the hall, at which his family and dependents or guests would sit. His men-at-arms and servants would occupy one or more trestle-boards in the body of the hall. The word "board" is of sufficient explanation of the origin of the table and of our common phrase

627. CANOPIED BED WITH CREWELWORK. 18th CENTURY.

628–633. An Unique American High Poster. 17th or 18th Century.

634–636. Hessian, Square Finial and Washington Andirons.

637-639. CANOPIED BED, SECTIONAL POSTS. 19th CENTURY.

640–642. Canopied Bed with Netting. 18th Century.

643–645. Hasty Pudding Stick, Spoon and Roller. 18th Century.

" board by the day," and analogous terms.   The ancient legal phrase
" bed and board " is also referable to the same origin.

The word " table " is pure Latin in origin, and thus etymology en-
forces the fact of the foreign origin of the table itself.   We often forget
that the majority of people on earth need no tables.   They sit on the
floor.   A table, therefore, is not the earliest article of furniture, and it
naturally comes under the last great division of our book.

The first table designed as a fixture was called a standing table, and
was so described in the old inventories.   With its great bulbous legs,
elaborately turned or carved, it was a ponderous and obvious article in
the homes of the wealthy.

As far as we know, none of the great foreign bulbous tables of ancient
time is found here.   If any such existed in America they have gone the
way of the huge beds.   The larger an object of furniture, the less likely
was it to be imported.   The abundance of woods in America stimulated
American manufacture and gave freedom to American design.   Great tables
were precisely what a new country could not afford to import.

It is a curious mark of growth that the first standing tables that we
know in this country were made with removable tops.   The posts were
prolonged, either wholly or in the form of tenons to engage in mortises
in the top, which could be lifted off.   It was thus convenient to move
a table in two parts from one room to another, as the early doors were
rather narrow and low.

The table affords rather meagre space for carving.   We do not know
of an instance of a table leg carved in America.   A table frame with much
decoration would have interfered with the knees.   The table frame was
further more or less masked by the overhang of the top, so that it was
not a place to encourage carving.

Undoubtedly the introduction of tables with leaves follows naturally
from a desire to secure substantially the same results as by the use of a
trestle-board, but with less trouble.   Thus the gate-legs and the chair
tables came in.

Some of the gate-leg tables are intricate and huge, and found in
England.   The author remembers, when he was a boy, it was the custom
in country houses, everywhere to drop the leaves of the dining table, and
to set it against the wall between meals.   There was no possible reason
for it then more than now.   It was a continuation of an ancient habit,
that is all.   We remember one ancient and huge kitchen where two members of the family were left.   Invariably the dining table was closed and
pushed to the wall after every meal, leaving a great empty space of no
possible benefit.   Our grandmothers would as soon have thought of leav-

ing the dishes unwashed as of leaving the table in the floor. It is one of the most curious instances of the failure of the human mind.

The trestle style of table survived in small gate-legs sometimes, and also in a few tavern tables, but the tops were in all cases attached. Pins of oak were the ordinary method of securing the tops in position. It was not until the Sheraton time or thereabouts that we have table tops secured by screws from beneath. If we find an old table top nailed down, we may be sure that the nails are not original, although they may be old. We do not remember at this moment having seen an American table with an oak top, although many such may have existed and some may remain. Oak was a very poor material for table tops, especially if one desired a single board. It was inordinately heavy and hard to work. We find pine very early in table tops, imposed on maple frames. We also find maple used to a great extent, although not so much probably in the seventeenth as in the eighteenth century. Maple is a very smooth but very warpy material. Many of the ancient maple table tops are curved like a bow, to a really humorous degree. Incidentally it has been learned that there is no material so good in the manufacture of violins as these warped table tops. Their wood and contour and their age all make them ideal for the purpose.

In the walnut period the entire table was constructed of that wood. The finding of a maple or a pine top on a walnut frame is always suspicious, and generally an evidence that the top is not original.

We cannot too emphatically point out the danger of asserting that a table has its original top. There is no possible method of proving such an assertion about any table. If one removes the top and finds that there is but one set of pin holes in the frame, the probability is strong that the top is original, but if an owner is persuaded that his top is original, he will not remove it to prove the fact. Further, it is entirely possible, by inserting pins, and placing a second top over them, to use the same holes. We have known of instances where old, but not original, tops have been been passed off as original by this method. Pine tops were especially liable to disintegration through wear. We can often be morally certain that the top is original, and oftener still, we can state that there is a strong probability of its being original. Ancient table tops, however, are often found and are easily adaptable to ancient table frames, especially in the case of the tavern table with its one piece top.

Nos. 673–674. The author had the good fortune to discover the table here shown. It was the second trestle-board to be found in America; the first, found by Mr. Bolles, being in the Metropolitan Museum. The main features of such tables clearly appear here. The trestle itself is in

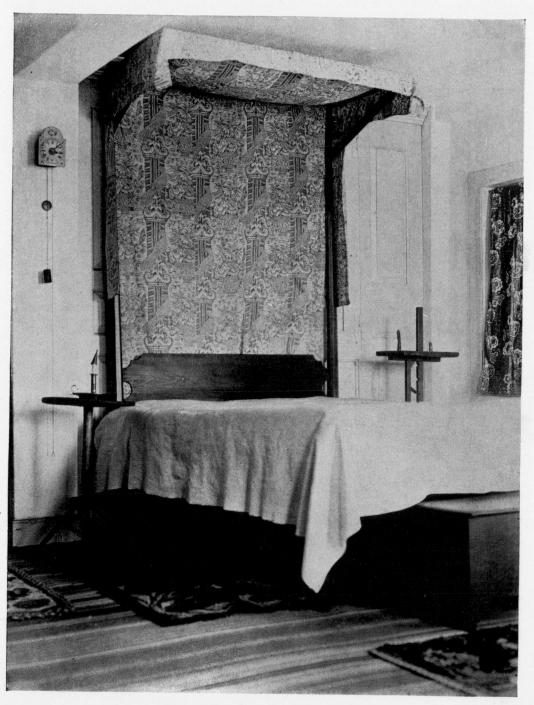

646-649. FOLDING BED WITH SHOE BASE AND CRANE HEAD.

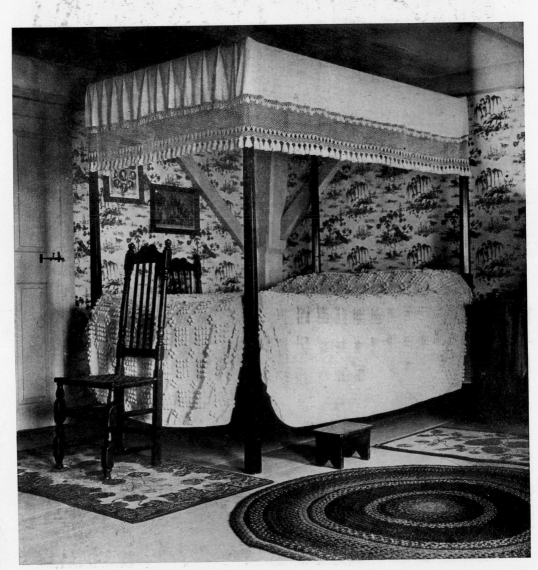

650–653. CANOPIED BED, JOHN ALDEN HOUSE. 18th AND 19th CENTURIES.

654. CANOPIED BED. 18th AND 19th CENTURIES.

655.   SCROLLED HUTCH TABLE, ON SHOES.   18th CENTURY.

the form of a double T. Two or three such pieces were connected by a truss along the centre. In the instance before us, there are two spindles, resembling early turned chair spindles, inserted at intervals on the truss, and running to T heads which are in section like the heads of the main trestle. The board is about 25 inches wide. The tops were ten to twelve feet long. The board here is pine. The frame seems to be of maple. The truss was originally held in place by pins run into the post by hand and temporarily holding the table in place.

Owner: Mr. B. A. Behrend.

The table was preserved at the Richardson Tavern, Medway, because Washington had once eaten from it. It was put in the attic, and on the occasion of an auction early in the twentieth century, it was brought out, photographed and sold. Persons from each part of the ancient town, which had been divided, bid on the table. They ran it up above ten dollars, and, the bidder being judged insane by most persons at the auction, it was knocked down to him. The object of the buyer was merely to preserve a Washington relic. No one present knew of the great importance of the piece. The author saw by accident a photograph of the table, and traced it into the West. After an exciting chase and fevered expectancy it was secured. One end of the board is chamfered, while the other end, perhaps, has been cut off a little. In other respects, it is practically in its original condition. It is possible that the tenon of the truss originally ran through and was pinned on the outside, as on the Bolles example. The pins are at present fixed and cut off, and we never sought to withdraw them.

Upon this table there are placed various trenchers of wood and bowls used for mixing or serving food.

It ought to be pointed out that a considerable number of trestle-board tables has been found within a short time, but for the most part, they have been traced to the Shakers, and date around 1800. They sometimes have turned posts. We hear rumors of one or two ancient examples, but we have never seen them.

Nos. 675–676. These illustrations show, on the right, the earliest, and on the left, the next earliest, methods used in America of attaching the sides of drawers to their fronts, in court cupboards or tables. The oak was gouged out so as to get a better hold for the nail driven into the rabbeted end of the front. It thus appears that in this country, at least, the use of nails in drawer construction was earlier than that of the dovetail. The dovetail on the left, one notices, is single. The groove in the side of the drawer is very clearly shown. It engaged a strip of hardwood attached to the inner frame of the table.

No. 677. This table, the property of Mr. George Dudley Seymour, is at the Wadsworth Atheneum, Hartford, and is the only one that we have noticed in this style. It was no doubt suggested through a memory of the trestle table, because its leaves are on the ends instead of on the sides. When these leaves are extended it has quite the trestle-board appearance. It is, therefore, a connecting link between the draw-table and the gate-leg table. The obvious thing for us would be to place leaves at the side of a table.

There is in the rooms of the Connecticut Historical Society at Hartford a table, very massive, its legs being nearly five inches in diameter, which was built as a draw table; that is to say, leaves were drawn out from each end, sustained on elongated cleats, allowing the central portion to drop to their own level. Such tables are known in England, and have of recent years been imported. Lyon illustrates this Connecticut table, which has lost its leaves.

The specimen before us, however, is a modification of that table and an advance upon it, as the leaf attachment is simpler. Most persons who can remember fifty years know that it was a common thing to extend ordinary tables by the use of such leaves with prolonged cleats or tongues, which were thrust into holes cut for them in the table frame immediately under the top. It was a kind of early accommodation answering the purpose of the extension table of modern times.

No. 678. This form of the trestle table, found in a good number of instances in New Jersey, in which the X or so-called stretcher is slightly scrolled, is a good example of its type. One notices, however, that the date is about one hundred years removed from the trestle-board forms we have previously considered.

Owner: Mr. Willoughby Farr of Edgewater, New Jersey.

Nos. 679–680. A pair of trestles and a board about six feet in length, owned by Mr. Harry Long. The ingenious stiffening brace is located at a point where it is wholly out of the way. It is also very effective. It is let down into a slot in the trestles. The two stools are half-moons in shape. The writer does not know their origin.

No. 681. An oak "court cupboard" table. It is, so far, unique in the annals of American collectors. It is reported to have been found in the attic of an ancient house on the North Shore, within a very recent period. It was somewhat fully described in *Antiques*. The author, however, made the illustration here used, before that publication. We have already referred to this table under court cupboards, to show the similarity of the applied turnings to those on such cupboards. This specimen had a drawer at the center, and appears to have one now but only

656. Oak, Cross Stretcher Chair Table. 1700.

657. CHAIR TABLE WITH TOP DOWN.

658–664. CHAIR TABLES, CHILD'S CHAIRS, ETC.

655. American Gothic Paneled Pine Chair Table. 17th Century.

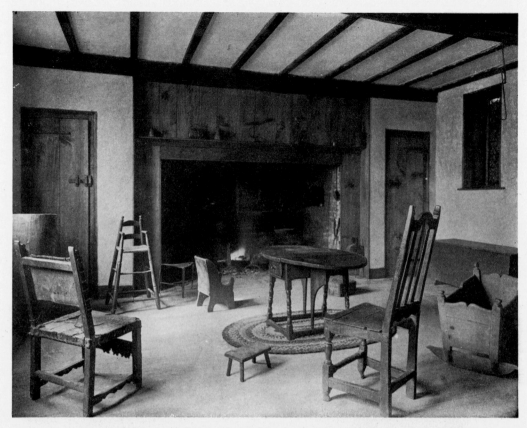

666–670. ROOM OF THE PERIOD OF 1700, HAZEN HOUSE.

671. CHAIR TABLE, 18th CENTURY.

672. CANDLE RACK.

the front is in place. The drop under the frame was convenient, as far as this central drop is concerned, to serve as a drawer pull.

The top of this table is practically circular. At the present time it is painted in imitation of marble, but we assume that it was earlier in its natural state. The balls of the feet are quite like those in the oak chair table recently discussed. In the present instance they appear to have lost about half their thickness. They are cut down to allow the insertion of casters. In this instance they should be restored, as the elevation of the table and the rounding out of the feet would add very much to its dignity. This table has a subordinate and smaller gate-leg in the rear, on which, when the double top is opened, it rests. There can scarcely be a doubt that this table was made for a room containing a court cupboard, its turnings being so nearly similar.

The diameter of the posts, about 3½ inches, is detailed more fully under turnings. The curious hinges we believe to be original.

It is difficult, of course, to trace the origin of a piece so old. It is not impossible that it came from England along with a court cupboard. It certainly, however, has been in America a very long time, and might easily be American so far as its wood is concerned. It is very curious in this connection that Englishmen tell us that the wood of some of our American pieces is English oak, whereas we are able to point out the error. This statement is not made with any sarcastic intent. We mean only this: that the English, unconsciously, perhaps, wish to establish the English origin of an American piece, whereas we are just as unconsciously leaning to the other side. Those people who absolutely know oak would of course contemptuously brush both contenders aside. This sentence is intended to bear a touch of sarcasm.

Owner: Mr. George B. Furness, Douglaston, Long Island.

Size: 27½ inches high; 36 inches diameter of top.

No. 682. A large table of uncertain use. Probably it was for dining purposes.

Owner: The estate of William G. Erving, M. D. Features of especial interest are the unusual size of the brackets, and the central scroll on the frame, the brackets adding to the strength, and brackets and scroll adding to the appearance. One sees here a medial stretcher rather than the outside longitudinal stretchers.

The tops and rails are pine, the stretcher is ash. The top is 32¾ by 64 inches. The frame is 24½ by 54¾ inches. The hight is 27¾ inches.

No. 683. The table previously described and this type are often called refectory tables. There is a confusion in the American mind between the refectory and the communion table. Refectory tables are not known by that name in the old inventories. There they were called "long, standing, jointed." The term refectory refers to the frequent use of such tables in college commons, or the like. It is a somewhat stilted and un-American word. A long table would be a better term. Such tables are very scarce in America, so much so that when we pass from those of the type of No. 682, which might be called a long tavern table, to the communion table, the room between the two for a true refectory is small. The communion tables are all too high to be used for dining tables. We think it is very much better, therefore, to call them frankly communion tables. The table before us was owned by Mr. I. Sack. We believe the posts are maple. The top, as we show it, was of two pine planks. We believe it to be a communion table, for if, as we are told, the fashion in the ancient day was for high tables, why are not the trestles high? This table was even higher than it is now, it having had balls on the feet, which would have given it a hight of about 34 inches.

Nos. 684–686. We here interpose a picture of a room with cross stretcher furniture, the greater part of which has already been described, although the clock on the left, formerly supposed to be of Knickerbocker origin, is now known to be Spanish. The clock seen through the doorway has always been known to be English. We are omitting clocks from this work, for separate treatment.

No. 687. A kitchen table with a leaf at the end.

Owner: Mrs. F. Gordon Patterson of Boston.

The brackets stiffening the frame are a feature of merit. The slide is missing.

No. 688. An American all oak square topped table. It was found at 59 Central Street, Andover, Massachusetts, in the basement of a very ancient house, said to be of the seventeenth century. The table is supposed to have been there for a long time. There is no possible reason for regarding it as a communion table, as its shape would be wholly different from what we have been led to expect.

An outstanding feature of the construction is the large bulb upon the legs. This turning resembles somewhat the turnings of the one or two known cross stretcher desks and the cross stretcher chair table already described. It is a good deal smaller than the bulb of the Virginian court cupboard described. The color and the texture of the oak, the figure of its beautiful quartering, and the location of the table, so long in one place, have induced the belief that the piece is American. This belief is further reënforced by its style, especially its turning.

The top is made to lift off, small mortises engaging a section of the

673–674. Trestle Board Table with Spindles. Early 17th Century.

675–676. 17th Century Drawer Ends.

677.   A Modified American Drawer Table.   1690–1710.

678.   X Trestle Table.   1720–50.

679–680.   Trestle Table and Stools.   18th Century.

681. Unique Table, Court Cupboard Style. 1660–80.

682. Medial Stretcher Table. 1690–1710.

683. Communion Table, Maple or Birch and Pine. 1660–90.

684–686. A Cross Stretcher Room. Period of 1690.

687. Kitchen Table with Slide, Drop End, etc. 18th Century.

legs extended in the form of a tenon. It is thus of the period when the evolution was proceeding from the trestle-board to the standing table. All the boards of the top are apparently from one piece of timber, such is the sameness of the quartering. The method of attaching these boards, seen in No. 689, was through long dowels running from the end cleats into the center of each board. In the passing of time, a shrinkage has made it possible to work these boards much as a swivel blind is worked! The only part of the top that is not original is the wider of the two outside boards. The other restorations are two of the balls of the feet, and two out of twelve of the applied scrolls ornamenting the drops. The brackets are amusingly constructed. On the end next to the post they are thinned into wedge shape, on their backs, so as to be driven into the mortise. The brackets are fastened on the outside and in the usual way, by a nail driven into the frame. The stretchers are molded inside and out.

The interesting method of forming the top, so as to leave no end wood, is obvious. It was of course necessary to nail or pin at the corners of the top. The under side of the top and the inside of the skirt aprons and brackets are hewn and left in the rough. These features of construction belong to the earliest style and throw much light on methods.

Every part of the table is in quartered oak except the legs and the stretchers, and there is a trace of quartering even in them. The fine grain and quiet character of this quartering and its blending from board to board, produces one of the handsomest effects we have ever seen on a piece of ancient furniture.

At this writing we know of no other American table so large and at the same time with as much contrast between the square of the turning, which it will be noted is small, with the large size of the bulb. The hight of this table puts it part way between the ordinary hight and the communion table.

Size: The largest bulb of the leg is $4\frac{1}{8}$ inches in diameter; its square is $2\frac{3}{4}$ inches, scant; its smallest diameter is $1\frac{3}{8}$ inches. The foot is of the same size as the great bulb. The top overhangs about 8 inches, and is $45\frac{1}{2}$ by 46 inches. The hight is $31\frac{1}{2}$.

The authority for the location is Mrs. N. E. Bartlett, whose ancestors have owned the table and from whose house in Andover it came.

No. 690. A long table with brackets and drops.

Owner: Mrs. John Marshall Holcombe. This example was used in the Grant family of East Windsor Hill, Connecticut, as a dining table, before 1700. It was possibly the property of the settler, Matthew

Grant, who was a surveyor, and whose tripod was among the family treasures. The channel mold on the frame is the same as that appearing on American oak chests.

The frame is oak. The style of the turnings is close to the earliest American work.

Size of top: $32\frac{3}{4}$ by 70 inches; frame, 32 by $58\frac{1}{2}$ inches; hight, 31 inches.

Nos. 691–693. A room containing seventeenth century furniture, or early eighteenth century examples, most of the individual pieces of which are described in this volume. The sheathing is of the character common in houses of that period, but the shutters are somewhat later.

No. 694. A communion table used by the church of Sudbury, Massachusetts, and dated from the second edifice, which was completed and in service in 1655. This table was described in the first edition, but some facts were withheld, since the church did not wish to be annoyed with inquiries. By an arrangement for a fund, the interest of which is to be applied in support of the church, the table was passed into the author's hands. It is, perhaps, the oldest table whose ancestry can be quite precisely traced to so early a period in American history. While not as important from the standpoint of style as No. 698, it is more " in the rough," and, to a certain class of collectors, is of greater interest on this account. We confess to belonging in that class. The original church in the town of Sudbury was in what is now Wayland. When the Sudbury Center church was set off as a new parish, a part of its inheritance from the older association was this table. The top is of yellow pine, and was in one piece. It has been split, but in such a way as obviously to indicate that each section belonged to the original part. It is of pine and an inch and a half in thickness.

Its dimensions are 29 by $84\frac{1}{2}$ inches. The hight of the table is $33\frac{1}{4}$ inches, from which probably $\frac{3}{4}$ inch has been lost by attrition and decay. The end overhang is $6\frac{1}{2}$ inches, and the side overhang is $2\frac{3}{4}$ inches on the front and but $\frac{3}{4}$ of an inch behind. This indicates that it was intended to show on the side of the wider overhang only. The posts are $3\frac{1}{2}$ inches square. The stretchers are 2 by $2\frac{3}{4}$ inches. The frame pieces under the top are $3\frac{3}{4}$ by $1\frac{1}{2}$ inches on the sides, whereas the end pieces are 4 inches wide. The posts extend above the frame $\frac{1}{4}$ inch and are let into shallow mortise holes in the top to give rigidity and to prevent a sliding of the top. Every part is original.

No. 695. A kneading-trough table. It is in the Metropolitan Museum. There is a drawer and cross stretchers. The front of the drawer carries quaint carvings. The huge wedges which hold the middle truss

688.   SQUARE OAK PARLOR TABLE.   1670–90.

689.   QUARTERED OAK TOP OF PARLOR TABLE.

690. Refectory Table, with Brackets and Drops. 1650–80.

691–693. Room of the Period about 1700.

694. Communion Table of White Oak and Pine. 1655.

695. Kneading—Trough Table, X Stretcher. 1700–40.

696. PANELED FRAME TABLE. 17th CENTURY.

697. LIGHT REFECTORY TABLE. 1700–30.

in place carry out the sturdy effect of the piece. The cross stretchers are slightly scrolled. So, also, are the straddling legs. The material is pine.

One is naturally prone to the opinion that this piece was a gift constructed by a young husband for his bride. We do not certainly know the origin, but it is probably of Knickerbocker or Jersey derivation.

No. 696. A remarkable table owned by the Metropolitan Museum. It contains a box or hutch below the top, which latter is made to slide, the cleats being dovetailed. The panels are encroached on at the bottom by the base molds of the frame, a thing which we can hardly understand because the table was evidently a thoughtful composition. The turnings are very early and quaint. There is apparently something missing at the bottom, since the flat stretchers were not intended as shoes. Had they been so intended, they would have run under the feet. The top is made with mitered ends to avoid any end wood. It has been thought that the table is American, but we do not feel competent to judge.

It is an odd feature that the only method of gaining access to the hutch is by sliding the top, a thing one would not do with ease, if it were covered with articles.

The top handle of iron is like what we see in English pieces. This table serves to point the statement that early tables were made without leaves. If larger tables were wanted, two or three were put together, and that method continued down through the year 1800. When tables with leaves finally came in, they speedily drove out of use all large tables with one-piece tops. Hence the extreme rarity of such tables.

No. 697. We may name this a light refectory table, as it will do as well as any other term. Still, it is the type of a long tavern table. The objection to using the term tavern table of these large pieces is that they could not, of course, be moved about readily for the use of individuals, a requisite attached to the name and use of the tavern table.

The frame of this table is oak, but the top is pine. There is a good overhang all about, making the table convenient to sit at.

One sees in this table an approach to the gate-leg style of turning. Its plain stretchers, however, hold to the earlier type of the standing table. The plain stretcher was stronger than the turned stretcher, a very important matter if the stretcher was long, as here.

A frame of oak usually points to an earlier date than a maple frame. Still we cannot be too dogmatic on such matters. Old traditions died out slowly in some parts of Connecticut.

Size: The top is $29\frac{1}{2}$ by $67\frac{3}{4}$ inches. The frame is $20\frac{1}{2}$ by 47 inches. It is $25\frac{1}{2}$ inches high, and has, obviously, lost something of its feet, which would be proved also by the fact that it is too low to sit at as a dining table.

No. 698. The Salisbury communion table. This very remarkable table, all in American white oak, with carving on the front of the frame, the author saw brought in by the dealer who discovered it. At that time the top was loose, showing the joints between its boards. On the occasion of its sale, the purchaser desired those boards jointed and cleats applied, which was done. Later, when it was resold, a purchaser threw it back upon the seller, on the ground that the top was not original. The inference was natural enough to one who did not know the circumstances.

The table is unique at the time of this writing, in respect to the fact that it is the only American table found with carving on the frame, which also has its original base, practically at the full hight. The table also solves the question whether or not there were ever American tables whose feet terminated in squares, and were not turned. Tables found with square feet in England, we were accustomed to think, had lost the turned feet in most cases. We believe that in some instances the feet were originally square. We did not feel certain that any table of the type existed in America.

The carving consists of interlaced straps, within which are rosettes, technically called a guilloche design. The design is said to be a symbol of eternity. The spandrels are also stippled. As this table stood in front of the pulpit and probably on a dais, elevated at least one step above the hight of the pews, and as the table itself was about five inches higher than a dining table, the carved member was impressively exhibited to the congregation, as they sat. It is for this reason that carving on a communion table was particularly appropriate. The style of the turnings is the earliest American. The only restorations on this table, aside from jointing the top as above mentioned, are the two brackets at the junction of the frame and the posts on the front. Mortised slits in the posts were found, giving the precise width of the original brackets. Broken off nails were found on the frame, showing where the bracket had been nailed in the conventional manner at its inner end against the frame. We were able, therefore, to make a very exact restoration, which greatly increases the beauty and sense of completeness of the table. The construction of the frame is heavily mortised and pinned, there being two pins at every joint on the upper part of the frame. There is a $\frac{3}{4}$ inch mold all around the edges of all the members of the frame, top and bottom. This molding is worked on as in the case of chests, a part of it being done after the frame was assembled.

Size: The top is about $1\frac{1}{8}$ inches thick, $28\frac{3}{4}$ by 89 inches on the surface. The total hight is $34\frac{1}{4}$ inches, this proving that there could not have been balls at the bottoms of the legs. Thirty-four inches is the usual hight for

698. Carved Communion Table with Original Feet. 1650–60.

699–700. Sculptured Door Bar, 1778; Coach Horn, 18th Century.

701. WALNUT LIBRARY TABLE. 1700–20.

702. WALNUT LIBRARY TABLE, SCOLLOPED SKIRT. 1700–20.

703. PENNSYLVANNIA KITCHEN TABLE. 1710–50.

704. WALNUT LIBRARY TABLE, BULBOUS TURNED. 1700–30.

705–708. Four Quaint Lanterns of Various Dates.

709–712. Kitchen of the Hale Mansion. Early 18th Century Furniture.

communion tables so far found. The frame is 26 by $71\frac{1}{4}$ inches. There is thus an overhang at the ends of about nine inches. The posts are $3\frac{1}{2}$ inches square. The square of the posts at the bottom is $11\frac{1}{4}$ inches long, six inches of this being below the stretchers. The square of the posts at the top is 7 inches long. The top members of the frame are 4 by $1\frac{1}{2}$ inches. The bottom members are 3 inches deep by $2\frac{1}{4}$ inches wide.

The restriction of brackets to the front of a table frame is not unusual in smaller tables. In this instance the table was intended to show but one front. There were no mortise holes found in the posts to receive brackets, except at the front.

Nos. 699–700. We are familiar with the wooden door bar, but here is a door bar of iron on which scrolls appear, as well as the initials C. W. and the date 1778. The length is 57 inches. As one sees, this bar is really a huge hasp, the slot of which was slipped over a staple and secured by a pin. The long trumpet below is of the sort used on coaches to announce their approach. It is about five feet long. It requires a man with good lungs and some skill to use it. By adept blowing it gives out a varied musical bar that is very pleasing. Both of these articles were found in Pennsylvania.

No. 701. A walnut library table. This type seems to be found only in the Pennsylvania and Jersey region. These pieces are sometimes called kitchen tables, and their drawers often bear evidence of rough usage. No doubt the type was used in more than one room. The side overhang of these tables, about three inches, is to admit of sitting at either side very comfortably. The tops of these tables are all made removable, by four hand dowels. The overhang at the ends is always generous, and in some cases, more. Examples are found in pine also. If we presume that the pine pieces were for the kitchen and the walnut pieces for the parlor, perhaps no one can show that we are wrong. A characteristic feature is the large size of the knobs. The drawers usually, if not always, overlap, and more often than not they are in different widths in the same frame.

The stretchers sometimes run around the outside and sometimes there is a medial stretcher, as here. As a rule the stretchers are in a square section and not turned, but they are frequently found molded.

Size: The top is 31 by 66 inches; the frame is 25 by 53 inches. The total hight is $29\frac{3}{4}$ inches. There is the unusual feature of a third drawer.

No. 702. A walnut chair table with a scalloped skirt. Of late, since these tables came into demand, not a few have been found with the scalloped skirt. With the plain skirt, large numbers have been brought into the market.

Such a table as this, not as large as the previous number, might have been used for serving, but as a rule smaller tables of this sort would have been sought for the purpose, and such are found.

Size: The top is 32¾ by 48½ inches. The frame is 28¾ by 36½ inches. The total hight is 28¾ inches.

No. 703. A Pennsylvania table, of which the legs are maple and the other members pine. The drawers are not paired but the knobs are good of the type. The frame is beaded. The posts are 2⅛ inches square. The stretchers, as usual, are of a rectangular section, but larger vertically than horizontally.

No. 704. A walnut table with scalloped skirt and an end drawer. The turnings are much bolder than usual, approaching almost to the bulbous. The feet are quite characteristic. The table is large and handsome.

Nos. 705–708. A series of four lanterns, the property of Mr. Rudolph P. Pauly. The first example is hexagonal and is of tin, and the second example is octagonal and made of wood. The glasses, however, are divided into two parts with a lead joint. Fascinating little carved finials appear at the angles. This is one of the most interesting and important lanterns we have ever seen. The other pieces are of tin and of ordinary shape, that at the right being probably a sconce from which the reflector seems missing.

Nos. 709–712. The large living room of the Hale Mansion, South Coventry, Connecticut. It was built in 1776, by Deacon Richard Hale, father of Captain Nathan Hale, the "martyr spy" of the Revolutionary War, who was born in an earlier house which was demolished soon after the present house was erected, and which stood but a few rods from it. The maple gate-leg table on the left is one of the daintiest examples. It is very delicately turned and the frame on the end is scrolled. Its top is 41 by 52½ inches, and it is 23 inches high. The table on the right is a very rare specimen called in Connecticut a Windsor table, not from the Windsor chair, but from the town of that name. There is a larger example, which we do not show, in the author's collection. The table shown is of hickory, oak and maple. It was found in Hartford. The oval top is 21⅛ by 28¼ inches, and the hight is 24 inches. The room is well paneled on the fireplace side. A curious little bench stands before the fireplace.

Much credit is due to the owner of the house and contents, Mr. George Dudley Seymour, for the restoration.

No. 713. An extremely rare and important gate-leg example. One of the unusual features is that there are two gates on a side. Another is that there is a leaf on one side only. We may perhaps presume that the table is used in a public place like a court room. There is a good deal of wear shown on the back stretchers and a freedom from wear in front.

713. An Official Single Leaf Gateleg Table. 17th Century.

714. Walnut Table with Four Gates. 1690–1730.

715. WALNUT TABLE WITH FOUR GATES. SOUTHERN STYLE. 18th CENTURY.

716. WALNUT TABLE WITH FOUR GATES. 1690–1730.

717. GATELEG TABLE. EARLY 18th CENTURY.

718-719. GATELEG TABLES. EARLY 18th CENTURY.

720. Heavily Turned Gateleg Table of Maple. 1690–1720.

721. Cross Stretcher Gateleg Table. Early 18th Century.

B

This is proof, since the parts are all original, that the table was used at the ends and back only. The back would not have shown wear had the table been kept against the wall. The nature of the wear would preclude the supposition that the table was used for communion purposes. There is no wear on the rule joint of the leaf, showing that the table was used standing, that is, that the leaf was regularly raised. There is a fine molding on the stretchers, and the stretchers of the gates are molded on all four corners. The front stretcher is chamfered, as clearly seen.

The joint in the front rail is cut on a radius to permit the turning of the leg. There is a legend on the back rail: "Chas. Hosmer, Hartford, Conn." This gentleman has been called the father of the Historical Society in that city. The legend is probably a shipping direction. We are no doubt indebted to him for this splendid specimen, which has now been brought out from the obscurity of a basement, and placed in public view. His date was 1785 to 1871.

The wood of the table is cherry, except the upper frame rail in the back, which is pine, with a molded edge. The legs, as well as the front stretcher, are $3\frac{1}{2}$ inches square. The back stretcher is $2\frac{1}{2}$ by $3\frac{1}{2}$ inches. The table is 78 inches long and 30 inches high.

Our attention has been called, by the kindness of Mr. Lockwood, to the existence of other tables with gates on one side only, which tables were intended for use in pairs, in the same manner as, at a later period, the famous cabinet makers arranged their tables. The specimen before us could hardly have been used in that manner, or the wear would not be found in the portions indicated, although of course we do not know the original intention of the maker.

The massive squares of the legs and the generally large dimensions really give this table a place with the great refectory and communion tables. Nevertheless, the fact that the leaf has a rule joint precludes the naming of a date as early as we would otherwise give.

No. 714. A four-gate table of walnut.

Owner: Mrs. Lewis Sheldon Welch of New Haven.

The existence of twelve-legged tables, otherwise called four-gate tables, or tables with two gates on a side, has not even been suspected by some collectors. Some six or eight examples are known in America. Possibly the most important is that at the Albany Historical Society, which is the only one that has come to our attention having its gates swing from the centre, and giving a star or raised effect when the gates are all opened. That method of swinging the gate is commoner in England. It is a much wiser design than that of the table before us for, when the gates swing from the centre, the knees of the sitter are not interfered with by the legs of the table.

The origin of the table shown is presumably Connecticut. Of course, the drawer handle is not original. The purpose of using two gates on a side was, of course, the additional stability required by very large tables.

It is important to glance at the question of the probable origin of the walnut used in New England furniture. There is little of clear direct evidence on the subject, but we know that there was a brisk coast trade between the North and the South, and there can be little doubt that Virginia walnut was brought into New York and New England. When we reach Pennsylvania we find there a red walnut closely like the Virginia walnut.

We know that in England walnut was not a commercial wood before the days of Queen Elizabeth, when it was planted under royal patronage to a great extent. When, therefore, the walnut age came in, England was able to use her own forests. She was stimulated to the production of walnut from the fact that it was a fashionable wood in Italy.

Great forests of Virginia walnut, furnishing very fine timber, were found. Of course it was shipped to England, and it would be unreasonable to suppose that it did not also go into New England. It is found in fine furniture here and in New York so frequently that we rest in this conclusion. Nevertheless there were two sorts of walnut native to the North; the black walnut, which is occasionally found in early furniture, and the white walnut, another name for hickory, which of course entered very largely into the Windsor chair and various other manufactures. It is rather misleading to use the term walnut of hickory, because only those specially trained in local appellations will understand the meaning. As a structural wood, the Virginia walnut was superior to our native black walnut, as well as being more fashionable.

The furniture wood of the North is, however, par excellence, maple. The soft maple is the sort most frequently found in furniture. Other names for it are swamp and water maple. It is distinguished from the rock or sugar maple by the fact that the rock maple is a heavier, harder wood, and furnishes even finer material for turning than the soft maple.

No. 715. A four-gate table of walnut. It was found by the writer in Richmond, Virginia, and is now owned by Mr. Chauncey C. Nash. It is somewhat small and low for a four-gate table. The turnings are more characteristic of the South, where we are more likely to find the stretchers in square sections, as here, rather than turned. This table is practically all original except a small mend on the top.

722. Spanish Foot Gateleg Table. 1690–1720.

723. Boldly Turned Gateleg.

724. Turned Frame Table, Flat Gates. 1790–1810.

725–729. Hominy Mortar, Beehive, Hand Wrought Mortar.

730. Dainty Small Gateleg Table. 1690–1720.

731–739. Styles of Shovel and Tong Heads.

740.   SMALL GATELEG, GROOVED JOINT TOP.   1690–1730.

741–742.   SPLIT GATELEG TABLES.   1680–1710.

No. 716.   A walnut four-gate table found in southern New Hampshire, near Dover.

The top is not original, being of pine as shown.   The author has now replaced the top with another of old walnut, in the oval form.

It is thought, where a table has, frankly, a new top, that circumstance detracts very much from its importance.   In the instance before us, however, the frame is of great beauty and perfection.   We think we have never seen a table with such a forest of legs in so fine a condition, every foot being so nearly intact as not even to suggest restoration.

The effect of these four-gate tables, when opened, in the centre of a room, is startling and impressive as to beauty and dignity.   Such pieces are the central objects of the walnut period, more attractive, at least in the author's estimation, than highboys.

The frame of this table is 20 by 51 inches.   The hight is 29 inches. As restored, the top is made 70 inches in its largest diameter.

No. 717.   A large gate-leg table with unusually fine turnings.

Owner: the Metropolitan Museum.   One notices the very long effect of the frame in proportion to the width.

The slot cut in the posts of the swinging legs and in the frame is a distinct blemish in any gate-leg table.   It is, however, unavoidable. These tables look best when closed.

Gate-leg tables usually have one drawer reaching about two thirds of the length of the table, and if a table is very large there may be a drawer at either end.   In the earliest types there is often under the drawer a central slat on which it slides.   We seldom find grooved runs on the drawers of gate-leg tables, their period being rather late for this feature.   As a rule, the examples have a beaded member on the frame as seen here.   Of course the heavier type afforded more room for ball turnings.   If one contrasts these turnings with those of the two tables at the bottom of the same page, he sees less character in the latter.

Nos. 718–719.   Two gate-leg tables belonging to the Metropolitan Museum.

In the construction of gate-leg tables, the swing of the leg should not extend beyond the edge of the leaf, nor, indeed, come very close to it. In the example shown at the right, No. 719, the close approach of the gate to the edge of the leaf is an objectionable feature.   Of course, the greater the overhang of the leaf, the less interference there is between the human and the table leg.   There is a considerable variation in this regard, the overhang ranging from four to six inches.

In determining the source of walnut, we have noted that English walnut has an occasional bluish streak, perhaps every inch or two, running through the grain. All walnuts, however, bleach with wear and washing to a pale gray, especially if they are in an exposed location. The color may easily be restored by the application of a coat of oil. In fact, one is sometimes disagreeably shocked by the great change in color caused by oil.

No. 720. A gate-leg table with somewhat heavy turnings. The wood is maple, including the top. The leaves have the tongue and groove joint, resembling the modern matched board, only less pronounced, and with broader members. This sort of joint is counted the earlier and more desirable, although fine specimens are found with the rule joint, which is denominated by modern cabinet makers a table joint. From the point of appearance the rule joint is better, because when a leaf is down, no opening appears between the leaf and the top.

Claim is often made for great age in the tops of some tables with plain square joints. The burden of proof is on the claimant. We have seen but one or two tables in respect to which it seemed at all likely that the plain joint was ancient.

This table has lost the balls of its feet, but is otherwise original. The pattern of the turning is called the vase and ring, and in this case, taking the center of the turning and proceeding each way from it, it is symmetrical or reversible.

This table is of moderate size, and we shall not annoy the reader with sizes in every case It is unhappily the very small and very large tables that are most sought for, and those are the examples in which it is more important to note the size. The gate-leg table of medium size is intrinsically as good as its smaller brothers, but sad to say, owing to the innate propensity of a collector to secure the unusual, it is not so much in demand as the small and large examples.

No. 721. A gate-leg table with a cross stretcher.

Owner: Mr. J. H. Stiles, York, Pennsylvania.

We do not remember having seen another example of a stretcher of this kind. The top, we presume, should be oval and not square. Possibly some gate-leg tables had rectangular tops originally, but none such have come to the author's attention.

This table has lost its feet. It has a good ogee scroll on the frame. In this connection we may remember that when this scroll or any decoration on the frame occurs, it of course shows on the end member rather than on the side, which is completely masked when the leaf is closed and largely masked when it is open.

No. 722. A maple gate-leg table with Spanish feet. The top on

743. SMALL WALNUT GATELEG. 1690–1730.

744. HAND-MADE BOWL WITH HANDLES.

745. Tuck-away Gateleg Table. 1690–1710.

745A. A Fire Carrier.

746. Folding Gateleg Table. 1700–1730.

747. Maple Gateleg.

748. FOLDING GATELEG, GROOVED SCROLLED TRESTLE ENDS. 1690–1710.

749. LONG FOLDING GATELEG. 1690–1710.

this table is of the proper size and has the grooved joint, but it is of pine and of course is not original.

Gate-leg tables with Spanish feet are rare. Some such tables have nearly all the scrolls of their feet new, and in no case have we seen one in which the feet did not require some repairs. The tables go well with Spanish foot chairs in the same room.

Size: The top is 45½ by 47 inches. The frame is 14 by 33 inches. The hight is 27½ inches. There is a drawer.

No. 723. A gate-leg table with heavy turnings In this instance, the stretchers are of a square section. The wood is all walnut. The frame is scrolled at the ends. The construction is without a drawer. All parts are original. There is a grooved joint and the ancient hinges. It is sometimes possible to decide whether a top is new or old by the style of the hinges. The table hinge, as the term is commercially understood now, came in about 1790. Earlier hinges were wrought, their edges being more or less irregular, and often in the butterfly pattern, or if not, in a cruder pattern than the fine hinges of the Sheraton period.

No. 724. A table with flat gates. This style is more generally found in England. Of course, the relation between the gates and the legs of the frame is lost by this method, but it is very early. The turnings here are handsome, and rather unusual. This table is walnut. Square stretchers are the rule with flat gates. It will be seen in this instance that they were beaded on the top and bottom, but that the beading on the top is mostly worn off.

One observes that with the heavy turning it is possible to use the single vase pattern, as here. With a light turning, the vase would be so attenuated as to lose its distinction. Therefore, the smaller the post, the more intricate must be the turning, and the more must it be composed of fine elements in order to retain its decorative features.

Nos. 725–727. A very high vase-shaped hominy mortar with its pestle. On the right is the old-fashioned beehive of straw. It is of the sort seen in the woodcuts in the "Old Farmer's Almanac." These beehives were used up to a late period in Pennsylvania, but as they are now prohibited by law, it behooves those who would possess one to be active. The bees, when taking possession of a hive of this sort, will first coat it carefully with wax to make it waterproof. The maker ran two sticks through at right angles to assist the bees in building their comb. Some of the specimens rise to attractive cone shapes. The hight is about 14 inches and the diameter 16 inches.

The owner of these three objects is Mr. Francis Mireau of the Fountain Inn, Doylestown, Pennsylvania.

Nos. 728–729. A huge mortar and a pestle formed by taking advantage of the crook of a limb. The material is apple wood. The peculiar merit of this piece is that while it is brought down to a turned form, the work is carved out by hand, because a section is left in the original size to serve as a handle. The piece is very heavy and large, so much so that probably a common straight pestle would be awkward to operate. This specimen is known to have been used for at least three generations. It was common for persons who were at a distance from a mill in the ancient time to make their own meal in such mortars.

It is owned by the Curtis Inn, Woodbury, Connecticut.

No. 730. A small and very delicately turned gate-leg table all in walnut. The turnings are striped with bands of red paint, which is old, but we suppose not original. The construction is excellent and all original. There is the tongue and groove joint. It will be noticed that on very small tables the walnut top is likely to be considerably less than an inch in thickness, as here. All in all, when the turnings and the size of this table are considered, it is most attractive. It will be observed here that the legs of the gate run to the floor, not only in the outside leg, but in the inside leg. That is, there is a fixed projection below the inside leg, like a leg terminal, though of course it is separated from the upper part of the leg. In this manner the harmony of the table is conserved and its beauty is much enhanced. Old tables are made in both ways, some omitting this complementary feature.

Size: Top, $24\frac{1}{2}$ by $28\frac{3}{4}$ inches.   Hight, $27\frac{1}{2}$ inches.   The leaves are 10 inches wide, and the center of the top is $8\frac{3}{4}$ inches wide.

Nos. 731–739. A series of nine shovel and tong handles. As a rule, the tong handles terminate in a ball. The better designs have a segmental swelled portion, for which there is no use further than the element of design. The best shovel handles are scrolled, as in the third example.

No. 740. A small gate-leg table.

Owner: Mr. G. Winthrop Brown.

It has a drawer and the tongue and groove leaf joint.

The frame of a gate-leg table sometimes, as in this case, is made to take the drawer directly under the top. In other cases, there is a cross member $\frac{1}{2}$ to 1 inch thick, on the frame, above the drawer. This member seems to add strength, but the greater part of the best tables do not have it. We mention the matter because this cross member has been challenged, but we feel certain that it was original in several instances. Of course a drawer very much weakens the frame. It was probably for this

750. CHERRY TRESTLE END GATELEG. 1680–1700.

751–755. TRENCHERS AND UTENSILS.

756. BALL TURNED SPLIT GATELEG. 1690–1730.

757. EARLY MAHOGANY FOLDING GATELEG. 1720–30.

758. A Corner Gateleg. 1690–1710.

759. All Turned Joint Stool or Stool Table. 1680–1700.

760. Birch Frame, Ball and Ring Turned Tavern Table. 1660-80.

761. All Turned Tavern Table. 1690-1710.

reason that a single drawer was used instead of a drawer at each end, on the smaller examples.

Nos. 741–742. The left-hand example has a single drop leaf, which is held up by a split gate; that is, the gate is slit in two longitudinally, in the same manner as the banisters of a chair or the applied spindles on oak furniture. The construction avoids cutting into the frame by a narrower slot. Nevertheless, the table, when open, shows the half leg and is not as attractive as the usual gate-leg form. It is, however, an interesting curiosity and is, as a rule, seen in the smaller tables. It will be observed in this example that there is a triangular frame, but that the stretchers at the base are in the form of a T, and do not run around the table as is usual in the triangular style.

The other example is turned in the knob or ball style, and in other respects opens like No. 741. One is shown open and the other closed in order to illustrate the method of operation.

The left-hand table has a heavy original pine top. The right-hand example is in hard pine, and is reputed to have come from Bilbao. The top is thin, as we often find it in small foreign tables. Nevertheless we see no reason why the table should not have been made in this country, as hard pine was common.

No. 743. An all walnut gate-leg table. All the legs extend to the floor and there is an agreeable wear of the turnings. It is all original except the back leaf, and has the grooved joint. The legs are in a fine state of preservation. The leaves have the fine large original butterfly hinges. The table was found in southern New Hampshire.

Size: Frame, 11 by 29 inches; hight, 28 inches; top, $41\frac{1}{4}$ (with the grain) by $39\frac{1}{2}$ inches. It is an odd instance of a gate-leg table which is actually longer than it is wide! Ordinarily speaking, these tables are larger across the grain; that is, owing to the spread of the leaves, arranged in reference to the swing of the gate leg, the diameter is larger than the length. In this case that is not true.

No. 744. A bowl worked out by hand and in the shape of a cocked hat, or at least to suggest that form. The knobs are left as handles. The material is burl. Of course the object in cutting a bowl from burl was to escape the danger of splitting. The burl is the result of the loss of orderly impulse in a tree. Nature forgets herself and the grain becomes a tangle. The burl is not a knot; neither is it a crotch nor a root. It is a benignant tumor. Such burls are found on the maple, ash, oak and walnut, and probably on other trees.

Owner: Mr. Albert C. Bates of Hartford.

No. 745. A single gate table, otherwise called a tuck-away table.

This example is in maple with a thick pine top, which is chamfered away at the edge below in order to give an effect of lightness, as in the case of the Windsor chair seat. This specimen was found on Cape Cod. One notes the feet of the trestles, cut in an arch from below. These specimens are much sought for and are very rare. They were most convenient as tea tables, carrying out the thought of all the earlier furniture, to provide it in collapsible forms. It will be seen that the stretchers here are turned.

No. 745A. A fire-carrier. These articles, seen from above, somewhat resemble a corn-popper. There are holes in the top so that the coals could be supplied with oxygen. The handle in this instance is cast, but in better patterns it is found wrought. The object was to carry fire from one room to another, or from one dwelling to another. Carrying the fire from one room to another was a quicker and easier method than the use of the spark and tinder.

No. 746. A tuck-away or gate-leg table in which the top swings down so as to present its longer diameter horizontally instead of vertically, as in the instance previously discussed. This table has a history attached to it by a metal plate. It descends from an ancient family. The wood is maple. One notes that the stretchers are not turned.

Size: the top is 20 by $26\frac{1}{2}$ inches — a very small table. The hight is $26\frac{1}{4}$ inches.

No. 747. A good example of a New England type of the gate-leg table, all in maple. It was in the former collection of the author, and in the Webb House, Wethersfield.

No. 748. A gate-leg table of pine, in which the usual method is reversed; that is to say, we have flat trestles instead of a flat gate. The trestle is crudely carved with an ogee scroll on each side, and it is fluted also.

One notices that the feet must have lost something from wear, as they formerly swept out in a longer curve and formed a more stable base. The flat stretcher, which forms, also, the foundation for the gates, is scrolled. We are unaware whether or not the top is original.

No. 749. A folding gate-leg table. The tuck-away tables are also called folding gate-legs. The term is here applied to trestle-post gate-legs which have a top of a very narrow section.

Owner: The Metropolitan Museum. The shape of the top is against the presumption of originality, as is also the extreme length of the leaf, but we are uncertain on these points. The table is extraordinary, being the longest folding gate-leg we have seen. It may have lost a half-inch at the base, so that the full contour of the shoe forming the foundation of the trestle does not appear.

762. Large Bracket and Drop Table, Original Top. 1670–90.

763. Heavy Small Tavern Table. 1660–70.

764. MEDIAL STRETCHER TAVERN TABLE WITH BRACKETS. 1690–1710.

765. MEDIAL STRETCHER TAVERN TABLE. 1700–20.

766. HEAVY HIGH STRETCHER TABLE. 1660–80.

767. BALL TURNED TAVERN TABLE, ALL LEGS RAKED. 1670–90.

768. Medial Stretcher Tavern Table. 1700–30.

769. Turned Table. 1700.

770. Cross Stretcher Table.

Size: The shoe is now 9 inches long and $2\frac{1}{2}$ inches square in the main section. The frame is $35\frac{1}{4}$ inches long. The hight is $27\frac{1}{2}$ inches. The legs are $1\frac{5}{8}$ inches square. The top of the stretcher is $5\frac{5}{8}$ inches from the floor. The center board of the top is only $6\frac{1}{2}$ inches wide, and its length is 43 inches. The leaves are each $10\frac{1}{2}$ inches wide. The thickness of the top is only $\frac{3}{4}$ of an inch.

No. 750. A heavy trestle gate-leg. The wood is cherry. It is all original with the exception of a very small section of one leaf, shown at the joint in the picture. This is an early example of the use of cherry. It would not have been necessary to have slotted the base for the flat gate, but so we find it. It would seem that the flat gate was sometimes used in order to avoid cutting out sections of the frame at top and bottom. The shoes are pretty well worn down on their uppers, as one might say! They were once scrolled with a cupid's bow; that is to say, a double ogee curve. They probably have lost about an inch. The joint is grooved.

Size: The top and the flat gates are $\frac{3}{4}$ inch thick. This is usual in small tables of hard wood. The posts are " stocky " for so small a table, being $2\frac{5}{8}$ inches, flush, square. The thickness of the table, closed, is about $15\frac{1}{4}$ inches; the leaves are $17\frac{1}{8}$ inches wide; and the length is 36 inches. Thus the oval is extreme, and it is considered in good style on this account.

Nos. 751–755. Three shallow vessels of burl. The little instruments between the bowls are Indian tools consisting of minute parallel knives for stripping up wood for basket work.

Owner: Mr. Albert C. Bates, Hartford.

No. 756. A gate-leg table with ball turnings and with two split gates. The material is yellow pine or, as some would say, piñon.

The turnings are very bold and interesting, but the members of the lower frame appear rather lean, as is frequently the case in tables of this kind.

No. 757. A folding gate-leg table of walnut. It originated in the South. The leaf has the rule joint. It is impossible to determine precisely when this type of joint came into use, but we find it well established by 1750.

This example is very compact, the thickness of the table when folded being only $6\frac{1}{4}$ inches. The top is 35 inches long and $42\frac{3}{4}$ inches wide — a very strong oval. The top has a fine thumb-nail molding. The hight is $24\frac{1}{2}$ inches. The piece has good style, with a long overhang and a large top in proportion to the base.

No. 758. A corner gate-leg table, with a triangular frame and a top which is square when opened, and in the form of two triangles when closed.

Owner: The George F. Ives Collection.

We have seen another table with a base precisely like this. The top had been restored in a round form.

Size: The top is 31 inches square and the hight is 27 inches.

Tables of this sort are important and attractive.

No. 759. With some hesitancy we insert this table at this point, at the end of the discussion of gate-leg tables. We may call this piece a stool or a table or, better yet, we may use the term stool-table. It was bought in Portland, Maine. All the legs are on a rake and not merely two, as is usual. All the members are turned. The condition is fine. The top is pinned on in four places at the center of each side, and the pin runs entirely through the frame. All parts are of maple.

The size of the frame at the stretchers is $13\frac{1}{2}$ by $16\frac{1}{2}$ inches.

The modern paint has now been washed off, and without the application of anything whatever, even of wax, the wood has a beautiful appearance.

771. HEAVY TAVERN TABLE. 1680–90.

772. HEAVY TAVERN TABLE. 1660–80.

773. Oak and Pine Tavern Table. 1690–1700.

774. Small Oak Tavern Table. 1670–90.

775. High Stretcher Tavern Table. 1680–1700.

776. Walnut Table. 1690–1700.

777. Walnut Table. 1700–30.

778. SCROLLED SKIRT TAVERN TABLE. 1670–90.

779. HEAVY OAK TAVERN TABLE. 1660–90.

TAVERN TABLES

W E NOW enter upon the discussion of the tavern table, about which something has already been said. In brief, we may state that it is always small, and was always, probably, originally without a leaf. It was designed to be moved about as wanted, especially in taverns, to serve guests wherever they happened to be sitting. Vast numbers of these tables existed, and a good many of them remain today.

No. 760. This ancient example of a tavern table has a frame which we think is birch. There are heavy turnings in the ball pattern, with incipient rings. It will be seen that the side stretchers are high, for what purpose no one has discovered. They are in the way of a person's legs. The only manner in which the table could be comfortably used was to sit at its end.

Owner: It was in the collection of Mr. B. A. Behrend.

Only the feet are restored. It was found in Milford, Massachusetts, in 1917. The top has a very long overhang, 17 inches or more.

The bases of these tables are usually in maple, and their tops are almost invariably in pine, sometimes yellow and sometimes white.

No. 761. A tavern table with rather meagre turnings, as is usual in the small types. Of course it was thus easier for the maids to move about.

No. 762. This handsome heavily turned table with brackets and drops, with its rare and original top, should perhaps not be classed among tavern tables. We have, however, a table a little too large for the tavern table and perhaps large enough for a breakfast table, but not for a dining table.

Owner: Mrs. G. C. Bryant, Ansonia, Connecticut.

One should compare this table with the heavy type preceding it in this book. There is an astonishing similarity between the brackets of these tables. The author has seen certainly a dozen, and perhaps twice as many, in which the brackets had practically the same contour, although some are slightly elongated to accommodate themselves to the length of the frame to which they are to be affixed. They are set into a thin mortise on the post, and attached to the frame below at their inside end by nails.

No. 763. A small, heavy tavern table.

Owner: Mr. H. W. Erving.

The frame is oak. The turnings are very early, and should be compared with those on the Robinson chair.

The size of the frame at the top is $14\frac{3}{4}$ by $8\frac{3}{4}$ inches, and it stands 21 inches high with the feet missing.

No. 764. A tavern table in which the stretchers are turned and a medial stretcher does duty for the two which would otherwise exist, one on either side of the table. There is an advantage in this method of construction, inasmuch as the posts are thus mortised in one direction only, and are left stronger. There is also a gain, to some minds, of an esthetic nature. This example is shown to have brackets worked upon the members of the frame, rather than applied. This method is carried around three sides of the table, but the back member of the frame is plain. The turnings are good. A portion of the feet is lost. The frame is maple, and the top is pine, and we believe original, though the drawer is renewed, and it would have been better with a knob of wood.

Size: Frame, 21 by 31 inches; top, $27\frac{3}{4}$ by $40\frac{5}{8}$ inches. Hight, $25\frac{1}{4}$ inches.

No. 765. A small tavern table with old black paint. It is all original.

No. 766. A rarely good tavern table belonging to the Metropolitan Museum. Its turnings are in the knob or ball style, and it has the distinction of well shaped brackets under the frame, and of high stretchers and a medial stretcher. We presume that there were drops. The top is so large that it comes under the class, as does Mrs. Bryant's table, of a breakfast or small dining table.

Size: The frame is $23\frac{7}{8}$ by $18\frac{1}{4}$ inches. The top is $36\frac{3}{8}$ by $36\frac{3}{4}$ inches, intended, of course, to be square. The square of the leg is $2\frac{1}{2}$ inches. The hight is $26\frac{1}{2}$ inches. There is a 4-inch drawer. It is $12\frac{1}{4}$ inches to the top of the high stretcher, and $4\frac{1}{2}$ inches to the top of the medial stretcher. This class of tables is, when we consider both date and style, the next most important to the refectory tables. Fine examples of this type are better than moderately good examples of the refectory type. This example lacks no feature counted strong and important.

No. 767. A tavern table belonging to Mr. Chauncey C. Nash. We count it of no small importance. All the legs are raked. The turnings of the stretchers are in the ball pattern. It has a wide overhang at the ends.

No. 768. An all turned tavern table with a medial stretcher. It is all original, unfinished, and lacks only a little of the feet. The drawer has an overlap, hence the date is not so early as the tables with the flush drawer.

780. MAPLE AND PINE TAVERN TABLE. 1700–20.

781–2. STAND AND PEWTER.

783–4. STAND AND HAT BOX.

785. ALL TURNED SCROLLED TAVERN TABLE. 1690–1710.

786. SPANISH FOOT TABLE. 1690–1710.

787. HIGH STRETCHER TABLE. 1680–1700.

No. 769. A little cherry table from Pennsylvania. Although so light and delicate, the drawer has the early side run which establishes a date of about 1700 or a little earlier.

Owner: Mr. L. G. Myers.

Size: 25 by 16½ inches. It is 27½ inches high.

No. 770. A walnut table from Pennsylvania. It has the rare and interesting feature of an X stretcher. The top is round. It is 29 inches in diameter. The hight is also 29 inches; very unusual for so small a table.

Owner: Mr. L. G. Myers.

No. 771. A heavy tavern table in walnut. The large cup turning is striking. It appears on one or two gate-leg tables. This example is too heavy for a tavern table, and most probably was used at the side of a dining room. There is the so-called stone mold on the upper members of the frame. The legs are massive and the drawer is on grooved runs.

Owner: The estate of William G. Erving, M. D.

Size: The top is 29 by 41¾ inches. The frame is 21 by 32 inches; the hight is 28 inches.

No. 772. A table resembling in its turnings and brackets No. 762. The posts are heavy, as in the early type, and the piece is, like the preceding, too massive to be moved about often. It lacks the cleats on the top, which is original, and measures 39¼ by 41 inches. The hight is 29 inches.

Owner: Mrs. J. Insley Blair.

No. 773. A tavern table with an oak frame and pine top. It is wholly original and never had a drawer.

Size: Frame, 20½ by 30½ inches; top, 26 by 40¼ inches; hight, 26½ inches.

No. 774. A small oak stand or table, the top of which is old but not original, and the feet of which are lost. It has, however, a fine sturdiness and a style of turning quite like that of the very earliest examples, as seen in the Salisbury communion table.

Size: Frame at the top, 17⅞ by 8⅝ inches. The top is 25 by 18¼ inches. The hight is now 22¾ inches, to which we should probably add 2½ inches to obtain the original hight.

No. 775. A walnut high stretcher tavern table.

Owner: Mrs. J. Insley Blair.

The top is also of walnut. The small size and striking turnings of this table render it very attractive. The turnings here are not the usual ball or knob sort, but the balls are separated by a considerable distance. The turned stretchers are most interesting.

No. 776. An all walnut table, all the legs of which rake. The meritorious brackets and corresponding central ornaments on this table, together with the delicacy of the turnings, afford a very satisfactory and complete result. Every part is original. There were never drops on the frame, there being scarcely space to receive them.

Size: The frame at the top is $10\frac{1}{2}$ by $17\frac{1}{4}$ inches. Just below the stretchers it is $18\frac{1}{2}$ by $21\frac{1}{2}$ inches. The top is $27\frac{3}{4}$ by $32\frac{1}{2}$ inches. The stretchers are very strongly molded for half their hight in a cyma scroll, usually called a stone mold. We do not know the origin of the table, but it was purchased in Boston in 1923.

No. 777. A small walnut table originating in Pennsylvania. On the drawer there is a crude scratch inlay, a scroll filled in with a white wood, none of which shows in the picture.

No. 778. An early tavern table with an oak frame. Although it has lost its feet, the molding on the frame and the brackets, and the early type of the turnings, make it interesting.

No. 779. A heavily turned tavern table of very early date. It was not the custom to use brackets on the smallest tavern tables, even when their style was otherwise counted good. In this example the frame is molded, and, above and below, the stretchers are marked by a double bead. The frame is oak. The top is pine. All parts are original.

Size: The frame at the top is $10\frac{1}{2}$ by $22\frac{1}{4}$ inches. Just below the stretchers the size is 14 by $22\frac{1}{4}$ inches, by which it appears that the splay of the legs is in one direction only. The size of the top is 20 by 34 inches.

This table originated near Greenfield. It was found by Dr. Miner.

No. 780. A tavern table with maple frame and pine top. The turnings are especially good. All parts are original. The drawer, as it appears, is not flush. A stretcher desk in this work has very similar turnings.

Size of the frame: $17\frac{5}{8}$ by $24\frac{5}{8}$ inches. The top is $23\frac{3}{4}$ by $37\frac{1}{2}$ inches. The hight is 25 inches.

Nos. 781–782. A stand or small tavern table. It is difficult to draw the line between the tavern table and the stand, just as it is difficult to draw it between the tavern table and the small dining table. We could make a division according to size, but it would be purely arbitrary. Curiously, the name stand seems not to appear in the early inventories. Table was made to do service for stand. We find standard very rarely, but its meaning is not the same as stand. We fail, in the published inventories at this time, to find a wash stand.

A discussion as to what was used for a wash stand cannot be dismissed by the flippant " they did not wash." Small tables like this were used, or larger tavern tables. We believe that there was no wash stand, so called or so designed, in the seventeenth century in America.

The pewter articles upon this piece do not belong to our subject. The wash-bowl and pitcher, generally in use, were of pewter, or, perhaps, sometimes of brass. We have an instance when visitors at a house of some pretensions washed at the pump.

This piece is from the collection of Mr. B. A. Behrend.

Date: about 1700 to 1781.

Nos. 783–784. A small, neatly-turned tavern table in black. It is all original.

The size of the frame is 14½ by 20½ inches, and the size of the top is 17¾ by 27 inches.

The box is intended for a hat. We have been informed that such boxes, in wood, with a handle snapping on somewhat like a blind fastener, are found in Sweden. This box was bought in America and we do not know its origin.

Date: about 1700.

No. 785. A tavern table turned with much delicacy. It has the additional merit that it is not only scalloped on the sides, but on the ends of the frame, and has a drawer. Enough of the balls of the feet remain to show what the contour was. We are always pleased to see so much legitimate wear on the stretchers. The reader's attention is called to the use of the word legitimate!

No. 786. A tavern table all the legs of which rake and terminate in Spanish feet. There has been much discussion as to the appropriateness of carving a Spanish foot in a slanting position. We believe that this table is, to the time of present knowledge, unique. It is certainly most interesting.

It is in the possession of Mr. I. Sack.

In dating a piece of this character we are of course governed wholly by the feet. The date is from 1690 to 1720.

No. 787. A high stretcher table, the skirt of which is scalloped. The ball turning is always distinctive. The frame is maple and the top pine. The date is about 1680 to 1690.

Size: The top is 28½ by 37½ inches — a very wide top. The great width in proportion to the length was probably intended to make a roomy table for four persons. One notes the odd absence of any medial lower stretcher.

No. 788. In this example we have a detail of style which, so far, is new in our description. This table is called a trestle tavern table. It is built in the fashion of the trestle table, with a tapering shoe corresponding to a tapering cleat above. The lower stretcher is turned to correspond with the posts, but the upper stretcher is a plain member. The frame is maple and the top is pine. This piece is altogether original and unrestored. It was found in Connecticut. The convenience of such tables, without any frame below the top, is quite obvious. They could be drawn close to the user. They were available as stands or tap room tables, or for any purpose where a light piece was required. The analogy of this table to the extremely early table board and trestle is at once suggested, and the pattern was no doubt derived from that source.

Size: Top, in one piece, $18\frac{1}{2}$ by 30 inches. The shoes are $15\frac{1}{2}$ inches long. The hight is $25\frac{1}{4}$ inches.

No. 789. A stand or small oval tavern table, painted black. It is all original. The frame just under the stretcher measures $12\frac{1}{2}$ by $15\frac{1}{2}$ inches. The oval top is $21\frac{1}{2}$ by 24 inches. The hight is 23 inches.

Date: 1680 to 1700.

No. 790. A stand in which all parts are original except the top. It is too small to be called a tavern table. All the legs rake and are neatly turned to correspond with the stretchers. One notices the cutting of the frame in the form of a bracket, which is one with the frame. We presume that the top is two or three inches too small in diameter. The frame of this little stand is exactly square.

No. 791. A trestle tavern table belonging to Dr. Mark Miner of Greenfield. It differs slightly from the table already figured, in having the upper as well as the lower stretcher turned. It is noted also that the shoes are wider than the square of the post.

Nos. 792–798. Wooden utensils for the table, together with a goffering iron. The smaller trencher in the foreground is a humorous example. The author remembers, when a boy, going on one occasion to a farmhouse for dinner where, after the meat course, the family, following the example of the head of the household, all turned their plates bottom up and received their pie on the new surface. Do not, gentle reader, criticize the neatness of this proceeding! Our ancestors were told to " lick the platter clean." This little trencher is frankly built to be used on both sides, being hollowed unmistakably for that purpose.

The large trencher just behind it is precisely in the shape of a modern soup plate, and is the finest piece of the kind that we have met with. The other pieces with covers may be called tankards or any one of various other names. The left hand piece is prettily inlaid in a diamond outline of white wood. It will be seen that in both instances one of the staves is made very narrow and so shaped as to provide a handle. The

788. Trestle Frame Tavern Table. 1670–90.

789. Small Tavern Table. 1700–30.

790. All Turned Stand. 1690–1700.

791. Trestle Tavern Table. 1670–90.

792–98. Flounce Iron, Trenchers and Noggins.

goffering iron is cast and set on a brass standard. One heated the removable interior and then, thrusting it into the pod, secured a rounded surface for ironing the flounces and furbelows of that generation.

No. 799. An oval stand or small tavern table with all legs raking. It is of maple and belongs to Mr. Edward C. Wheeler, Jr.

Size: The top is $18\frac{3}{4}$ by $25\frac{1}{4}$ inches. The hight is $21\frac{3}{8}$ inches.

No. 800. A table with a triangular frame and a circular top. The cabinet work of a triangular table was more difficult than that on a square frame. Such a piece, however, has esthetic uses and, practically, the long segment of a side affords a greater overhang than is usually found in small tables. Such tables as a rule have no drawers.

Owner: Mr. Chauncey C. Nash.

Size: $28\frac{3}{4}$ inches in diameter of top. Hight, 25 inches.

The date is about 1700.

No. 801. A triangular table frame with raked legs. This is a light example, the property, with its furniture, of Mr. B. A. Behrend. One sees hanging from the edge a double bowled Betty lamp, the lower section being built to catch the drip of the upper part. There is, above, a candle stick with a curious handle which would allow it to be hung on a hook as a sconce. The other piece is a sand glass. The date of the table is about 1700–1720.

No. 805. A larger and heavier triangular table with the round top. It was in the author's former collection. It is all original. In many cases feet have to be restored. Of course, the advantage of raking the legs was found in increased stability. One sees that the stretchers are molded, as is also the frame.

Nos. 806–808. We have our first example of the adjustable candle stands. The arrangement by which the central shaft could be lifted was a ratchet and pawl. The base is a large block of wood made frankly in this shape to secure stability. The candles were of course placed at the ends of the crossbar. The lower standard is of pottery, from Virginia. It is of red clay with a coarse black glaze, and is from the old pottery, formerly at Morgantown, now West Virginia. It is similar in texture to the folk pottery of New England and Pennsylvania. These three articles are the property of Mr. H. W. Erving.

No. 809. This is a very quaint ratchet candle stand on stick legs. The candle is set immediately on top of the small shaft.

Owner: Mrs. J. Insley Blair.

No. 810. A stand of delicate turning and a series of ogee scrolls. The drawer is false, and the knob is original, the table never having had a drawer. While this stand boasts no remarkable feature as a whole, it is very attractive, being quite perfect, and in maple, the wood we best love for such purposes.

Owner: Mr. Edward C. Wheeler, Jr.

Size: The top is 16 by 25 inches, and the hight is 24½ inches.

Nos. 811–814. In the first of these reproductions we show two iron latches. Plate latches with springs were in use from about the year 1740 down to 1790. As a matter of fact they are found in use for the simpler rooms of many fine dwellings.

No. 812 is a little candle stand with a heavy X base and with candle bar in the form of balls. A third candle was set on the top of the shaft.

No. 813 is a small embroidery frame. There is a very perfect universal joint, or ball and socket joint, as it is sometimes called, with a wooden screw to set it. The feet are attached like the legs of a Windsor stool. The frame could be swung at any angle toward the operator, and the hands could reach under the piece to be embroidered, which was placed over the frame, previously covered, as we have seen, with cloth; and another hoop was placed over it to hold it taut.

No. 814. The most interesting of all the pipe tongs which have come to our attention. They are made in a square section and not round, as are several of the other similiar examples. The shape of the scroll and of the thumb piece for pressing down the tobacco, and of the nail which was a guide for the cleaner for the bowl, are all clearly shown. The tongs bear on their side a legend stating that they were captured at Fort William Henry. They are shown here as they hung in the old Williams House, South Easton, Massachusetts. They are understood to belong now, by inheritance, to Mr. Fred H. Williams of Boston.

No. 815. An oval maple stand.

Owner: Mr. Edward C. Wheeler, Jr.

Size: The top is 18¾ by 27¾ inches. The hight now is 20¾ inches, to which we should add some two or three inches for the feet, which are lost. The turnings are delicate. One sees in this table the usual cleat which runs across the frame of oval tavern tables, and is set its full size into the frame. It is to prevent the breaking off of the edge of the top, and is very necessary. The heavy stretchers are plainly early.

No. 816. A burl bowl, remarkable for its size, although there are larger; but more remarkable for its shape, worked out by hand. The burl often grew so large that the side of it next the tree was of a hollowed section. The maker of this piece took advantage of that fact to carve ears.

The wood is probably maple, though others in the author's possession,

799.　Splayed Tavern Table.　1680–1700.

800.　Triangular Table.　1690–1710.

801–4.　Raked Triangle Table.

805. HEAVY TRIANGULAR TABLE. 1720–1740.

806–809. RATCHET AND POTTERY STANDS.

810. MAPLE TABLE WITH FALSE DRAWER. 1690–1720.

811–814. IRON LATCHES, WOODEN STANDARD, EMBROIDERY FRAME, PIPE TONGS.

815. Oval Maple Table. 1690–1710.

816. Great Burl Wrought Bowl with Ears.

with nearly the same figure, are pronounced ash by such good judges of wood as Mr. Henry Ford.

The diameter of this piece is 23 inches.

Mr. Luke Vincent Lockwood has a bowl, turned, of a diameter of about 29 inches, from the author's former collection. These are the largest we have found. A few years since, these bowls were knocked about as encumbrances. The author found the largest specimen at a shop conducted by a person notorious for getting the full value for his goods; nevertheless, he was willing to be rid of the bowl at a ridiculously small figure. Those were the happy days!

No. 817. We have previously shown several tavern tables with high stretchers corresponding in design to the medial low stretcher. In the example before us, we have a very aristocratic specimen. In addition to the usual ball turning, it has at the centre of the turning a double vase motive. A molding carried about the frame is another refinement. The skirt or valance, as it is indifferently called, on the frame, is cut in very handsome brackets and scrolls. The drawer is provided with the side grooves.

This table is from the Prouty Collection, and has been previously illustrated.

Nos. 818–820. A remarkable, and as far as we have learned, unique set of hardware in the tulip-bud pattern. In a decorated chest of drawers shown we have a tulip-bud of precisely the same contour as that which is here wrought in iron. The scroll of the latch-bar is a large spiral. The bar, indeed, is altogether the most remarkable we have ever seen. We see here for the first time that, in the best early hardware, there was a purpose to match the hinges with the latch, carrying the same motive through all.

We are not aware that attention has previously been called to the matching of the design of latch and hinge.

No. 821. A high stretcher tavern table with ball turning and pierced brackets. This fine example is practically all original. It is the property of Mr. Chauncey C. Nash.

While a trifle simpler in some respects than the example preceding it, this table has the unusual feature of the pierced bracket. As an amusing instance of the rapid increase of appreciation in such a piece of furniture, we may say that this table, as soon as found, changed hands five times in five days, the owners being in three states. It has since been sold twice. Were it supposed to be on the market, undoubtedly buyers would stand like dogs at a woodchuck hole for an opportunity to seize it.

In this connection, we have an opening to answer the question so often asked, why there are so many antiques. The answer is to be found in the death of collectors and the consequent dispersal of their treasures. It is also to be found in the occasional financial embarrassment of collectors, for they are not all millionaires. Some of us have court cupboard tastes and pine cupboard pocketbooks. Another explanation is to be found in the unwisdom of collectors, which often permits them to resign pieces whose importance they are not keen enough to know. While this is an unusual circumstance, it is more apt to occur in the case of the more important pieces, as in that of some we could mention, but, frankly, we would not dare. Again, dealers sell, the small to the great, and so the process goes on, until at last, little by little, such things are caught in the drag net of the museums. But be it understood they are not bought by the museums, who either never have funds for such a purpose, or, if they possess the funds, they lack the quickness to seize their opportunities. They achieve their greatness through the gifts of their friends.

Thus, through the reasons we have mentioned, and by sickness and by accident, and by cupidity, the same piece sometimes comes often into the market. In this manner one of the best articles known has changed hands nine times in four years.

No. 822. A beautiful and rarely outlined little table belonging to the estate of George F. Ives. Except for the loss of its feet, it is in fine condition. The turnings are bold for so small a piece, the stretchers beautifully agreeing with the legs. The scrolls on the frame are different on the legs and on the side. The narrowness of the frame and the depth of the scrolls forbade a drawer.

No. 823. A walnut table.

Owner: Mr. Edward C. Wheeler, Jr.

The frame is scrolled, and we find a molding run about it, adding to its importance. Though the feet are missing, the bottom stretchers still stand up well from the floor. The turning resembles that of No. 817, and the scrolling on the skirt is slightly suggestive of that, as is also the molding. One can see from that example how the feet of this appeared.

Size: The top is 13¾ by 23¾ inches, and the hight is 25 inches. Probably, in modern phrase, the table would be called a stand.

No. 824. A bobbin reel. We moderners should distinguish between this and the spinning wheel. It was merely to wind the bobbins for the loom, and was used in the seventeenth and eighteenth centuries.

No. 825. A small table with a square frame and an octagonal top. The piece is very perfect and has neither been tampered with nor restored, nor does it require it. The paint, however, might be washed off, as it shows now in two colors. The points of merit are the boldly scrolled, though simply shaped skirt, and the unusual shape of the top. There is

817. High Stretcher Scrolled Skirt Tavern Table. 1680-90.

818-820. An Unique Tulip Bud Door Set. 18th Century.

821.   High Stretcher, Pierced Bracket Tavern Table.   1680–90.

822.   All Turned Scrolled Skirt Tavern Table.   1690–1710.

823. High Stretcher, Scrolled Skirt Tavern Table. 1690–1700.

824. Bobbin Wheel. 17th and 18th Centuries.

825.   Octagon Scrolled Skirt Plain Stretcher Table.   1690–1700.

826–828.   Harpsichord and Cane Chairs.

much satisfaction in a piece of furniture that may be left wholly as found. We discovered this piece in Plymouth in 1921.

Size: Top, 27¾ inches across. The frame is 21½ inches square. The hight is 26¼ inches and the table was probably not more than about half an inch higher originally.

Nos. 826–828. Large musical instruments of our period perhaps cannot be counted American. They were, as we suppose, imported, but their frames are American. We merely glance at the subject, and show two or three examples.

No. 826 is called a harpsichord. It is in the great room of the Benning Wentworth house at Newcastle, New Hampshire. One sees that the base is of a simple character. It is flanked by a good pair of chairs. The right-hand one has unusual and very interesting carving on the stretcher.

No. 829. A spinet which the author bought at Haddam, Connecticut, from the family in which it had been from time immemorial. The instrument was made in London by Jacobus Kirckman, about 1690. One should take note that the numbers on spinets have been mistaken for dates. The frame of this spinet is simple. The instrument was made to lift off from the base, and was not attached in any way. There were small spurs, like nails, filed to a point, on the frame, which so far engaged the body of the spinet when it rested upon the frame as to prevent its slipping. The shape of this instrument is quite like that of a small grand piano. It is light enough to be lifted and carried by one man. It is said that it belonged to the niece of David Brainard, a missionary to the Indians in Connecticut.

No. 830. An interesting spinet because of its extremely elongated Spanish feet, cut in very good pattern when their length is considered. This spinet, formerly in the author's collection, is, we believe, now the property of the Brookline Public Museum. It was made by Thomas Hitchcock. The date is about 1690. The wood is walnut with inlays in front.

The tops of these instruments were so thin that in many cases warping cannot be prevented in a modern house. The only method of overcoming this permanently is to make a series of very fine parallel cuts on the under side, and then to bring the top to the proper shape and glue it. The method of straightening curved woods by flame is very unsatisfactory. After a while the ancient warp will reassert itself. Old wood is like an old man — practically impossible to reform. We have seen so much useless effort put forth in the straightening of warped boards, that we are induced to make this remark.

SLATE TOP TABLES

STILL more rare than a chest-on-frame, and with less reason for existence, is the slate top table. The top consisted usually of an oblong surface of slate with chamfered corners, which was set flush into a frame of veneered walnut. The object of the slate top was to provide a surface for tea things, and so to save the disfigurement of a wood top. The veneered edge, however, was about five inches wide and was particularly susceptible to injury through wetting. The designers, therefore, of these tables placed their patrons in a worse plight than would have been the case had they never owned them.

It is said that the tops were made on the Continent, perhaps in Switzerland, or in Italy, and that the frames were made here. Very few examples, possibly a half dozen, are known in America. We presume that owing to their lack of appeal to common sense, and also owing to their extreme delicacy, few were made, and that when they were made they were not preserved for any length of time.

In one respect, however, we are quite thankful to the makers, because the style of these tables showed exquisite taste, and indicated that Americans in the seventeenth century knew what was what in the matter of elements of style. We cannot point to anything made since that period more charming, airy and dainty in outline.

No. 831 illustrates such a table, owned by the Antiquarian Society at Worcester. The turning is in the fashion of the gate-leg or of a very dainty tavern table of the period.

No. 832 is the top of the same table. It appears that a portion of the slate is new. The inlay is of an intricate and delicate pattern. Of course, we do not certainly know that the tops were not made here. There were cabinet makers capable of doing the work, since the method was similar to that in use on the walnut veneer highboys. The pattern, however, is more involved than that in use on highboys. This example has been shown in other works.

No. 833 is quite a different pattern of a slate-top table. The trumpet turning is especially delicate and fine. The feet, attached below the stretcher, which is a double lyre shape, are scrolled in bold curves and are doweled to the post through the stretcher. There was a finial at the intersection of the stretcher arms.

829. Spinnet Formerly Owned by Niece of David Brainard. 1690–1700.

830. Spinnet with Spanish Feet. 1690.

831. Slate and Veneer Top Tea Table. 1690–1700.

832. The Top of Table Shown Above.

833. WALNUT TRUMPET TURNED X STRETCHER SCROLLED FOOT TEA TABLE.

834. SLATE AND VENEER TOP OF TABLE SHOWN ABOVE. 1690–1700.

835. Scalloped Skirt Tea Table. 1690–1700.

836. Slate and Veneer Top of Table Shown Above.

No. 834 is the top of the same table. The inlay is a very intricate and minute design, and has suffered through wetting, as we have indicated that it was likely to do.

The original slate entire is in place, although it is cracked. Below the slate there is a series of slats to rëenforce the back. The slate is so very thin that we presume the slats are original. Otherwise the top would have broken under slight pressure.

The wood is walnut, except, of course, the portions of the veneer, which are of other colors. This table is reputed to have been found near Boston, where it was bought, in 1923.

One notices at once the analogy between the turnings of these pieces and those of the six-legged highboy, and its lowboy to correspond. There is so little data on which to generalize that we cannot be certain where such a piece as this would be kept in a dwelling. In size, it is not very different from a lowboy. In the same room, the two pieces would complement one another and add very much to the charm.

Size: The top is $24\frac{5}{8}$ by $34\frac{7}{8}$ inches. The hight is $26\frac{5}{8}$ inches.

No. 835. This specimen of a slate top tea table is in better condition than the others.

Owner: Mr. Daniel Staniford of Boston.

Its turnings are similar to those in No. 831, but just a trifle heavier. We believe that in spite of the fact that we show two of these tables with gate-leg turnings, a greater number of them are found with the highboy turnings.

This specimen has a symmetrically scalloped valance under the drawer. The original handles assist us in forming conclusions as to the date.

The top has its original slate, which is far heavier than that in the last example described. The veneer in the design on this piece, however, is confined to one section of the top as seen. The veneer appears to be in apple wood. The stretchers are deeply and delightfully worn on three sides. The fourth side shows practically no wear. The grandfather of the owner of this table taught school, it is said, using the table for a desk.

Size: Top, 25 by 40 inches, the width of the board outside the slate being $5\frac{1}{4}$ inches. The frame is 25 by $19\frac{1}{2}$ inches. The hight is 28 inches.

Of course the rarity and the beauty of these tables make them desirable in the eyes of collectors.

LOWBOYS

THIS is another term for dressing tables. It is supposed to have arisen in jest, with a sly slur at the legs of these pieces and their corresponding pieces, the highboys. Lowboys are usually found in solid or in veneered walnut, when in the type of turning which corresponds with the earliest period of highboys. It was the time of the brass drop handle. The pieces are rather delicate and, as in the case of the highboy, they have for the most part been destroyed. Strangely enough, they are much more rare, and therefore more highly valued, than the highboys. It is very seldom nowadays that an example comes to light.

No. 837 is a lowboy with very curious and interesting turnings. Owner: Mr. John H. Halford of Norristown, Pennsylvania.

We notice an extra member in the turning of the legs which is quite different from that in the usual lowboy, and follows no recognized type. It is quite as if a larger urn were superimposed upon a smaller one. It is characteristic that the feet should be large, as here. In fact, the diameter of the turning on the foot is as large as the largest section of the leg above.

We presume that this piece originally had drops on the spaces which correspond above to the positions of the legs on the six-leg pieces. Of course, the object of omitting the two extra legs on the lowboy was to allow the knees to go under the piece. For the same reason the X stretcher was employed. As in the case of the highboy, there is a lining of walnut about ⅛ inch thick on the intrados of the arches, with an astragal molding on the outside. Of course, the object of this was to give a fine finish everywhere and to avoid the appearance of any end wood. The drawer scheme in this piece, a narrow drawer at the center and two deep drawers at the side, is the usual arrangement. One notices a cupid's bow or double ogee mold on the frame at the ends and an ogee arch in the center in front. This central arch was as a rule cut higher than the side arches, for the sake of leg room.

Nos. 838–843. The parlor of the Alden House at Duxbury. An important element of interest in this room is the flat arch over the fireplace. This is quite unusual, so much so that we have been guilty of stating that it never occurred. We have now found at least two examples, the other being in a house in Hanson. Of course the panel work was not

837. X Stretcher Walnut Lowboy. 1690–1700.

838–843. "John Alden House" Parlor, Duxbury.

844. Cross Stretcher Cup Turned Lowboy of Walnut. 1690–1700.

845. All Turned Stand. 1700.   846. Turned Stand. 1690–1710.

847. Bowl Turned Lowboy with Drops. 1690–1710.

848. Carved Foot Stove. Early 18th Century.

849. X Stretcher Trumpet Turned Lowboy. 1710–20.

850. Lacquered Cross Stretcher Table. 1690–1700.

original with the house, a bedroom of which we have already shown, and the date of which is supposed to be 1653. Panel work was added in dwellings of this sort beginning about 1720.

The pieces of furniture shown might have been in the house about 1720. The floor candle stand, with its inverted and weighted funnel base, is a type frequently found.

No. 844. A lowboy from which the drops on the front skirt are missing, but which has its finial at the intersection of the scrolled stretchers. The turning here corresponds with that of highboys of the inverted bowl or cup turning. The veneer is walnut with herringbone border. A single arch mold (astragal) was used a little earlier than the double arch mold. The bail handles with ornamental surfaces are of somewhat later date than the drop handles. This piece was bought not far from Boston. Certainly New England did possess a good number of lowboys.

Nos. 845–846. We insert here, for convenience, two stands, both of which are owned by Edward C. Wheeler, Jr. The turnings are dainty. That on the left has a drawer. We believe the top is too small. This stand is only 31 inches in hight. The piece on the right is of maple, in beautiful condition, and has plain stretchers. The top is oval and measures 17 by 23¾ inches, and the piece is 23½ inches high. The dates of both pieces range between 1690 and 1710.

No. 847 is a walnut cross-stretcher lowboy.

Owner: Mr. Edward C. Wheeler, Jr., of Boston. The huge middle drop is a striking feature and an amusing instance of how style dominated and pushed convenience to the wall in those days, as now. The basal scheme of a lowboy was to afford room as a dressing table. Of course one could not sit at such a table as this, and although we have named it a lowboy, we are more inclined to believe, since it has a single long drawer, and this peculiar conformation on the front, that it was merely a small table. This judgment does not at all detract from its importance. We shall later show another table of this type, certainly not designed as a lowboy. It will be seen that the larger drop is simply a reversed finial, a duplicate of that on the intersection of the unusually elaborate cross stretcher.

No. 848. A carved footstove, the top rosette being pierced for the sake of ventilation.

Origin: Pennsylvania.

Footstoves like this, carried in vehicles and taken into church, are still common enough because they are curious articles and, being small, they could easily be preserved. In this elaborate form, however, they are rare. We have seen another somewhat similar to this. It has a slide in one side to insert the tin container for the charcoal.

The top measures 9 by 8½ inches, and the hight is 7½ inches. It is of walnut. The date is uncertain, but probably in the eighteenth century.

No. 849. A trumpet-turned lowboy of walnut.

Owner: Mr. G. Winthrop Brown.

It has the double arch mold. The finials are interesting, being rather different from those we have seen. In fact, we hardly understand the motive. This is the first example in which the scroll stretcher has been at all simplified. The feet here are somewhat smaller than the other examples shown.

One should note that even in the walnut furniture the legs, especially in the highboys, are often of a lighter wood than walnut; basswood or poplar being often found. The turned section was sometimes painted, and naturally, being ornamental in its nature, it did not require the veneer which was applied to flat surfaces.

One sees here the thumb-nail molding, as is usual on the top of these pieces.

No. 850. A cross-stretcher table in maple. There is a label on the back of the drawer: "Table made 1700. Gilt 1847." The author was advised to remove the lacquer. The attempt, however, to do lacquer work in America at so late a period is thought to be sufficiently interesting to be allowed to remain, especially as it is rather successful.

We believe that the turnings are in pine. The drawer bottom is of pine. Obviously, this table was not made as a lowboy. It is much rarer than the lowboy. It forms, with the cross stretcher desk, stools, lowboy, slate top table, highboy and chair table, one of a large series of cross stretcher objects of sufficient number to furnish a room.

Size: Frame, 17¼ by 24½ inches. It is 28 inches high.

No. 851. A beautiful little lowboy of cherry.

Owner: Mr. Chauncey C. Nash.

This piece is one of the few of the period in cherry, with which we are acquainted, and it is the only lowboy we have encountered in the six-leg style. The turnings are odd and interesting. It was found in Stratham, New Hampshire, in the family with which it had always been. For a long time collectors declined to take it as the price was regarded as prohibitory. Any collector at the present time, however, would be only too glad to secure it. It was originally owned by Anna Rush, whose monument, erected by the women of Stratham, is in the cemetery.

The piece is all original, neither needing nor having had repairs.

Size: Top, 20½ by 34½ inches; hight, 30¼ inches. The frame is 17½ by 29½ inches.

One should take careful note of the shape of the scroll in the stretchers,

851. Unique Six Legged Lowboy of Cherry. 1710–20.

852. Tavern Table, Drop Leaf. 18th Century.

853. Unique Butterfly Table. 1690–1700.

854. Walnut Scrolled Skirt Table. 1710–30.

855. BUTTERFLY TABLE WITH DRAWER. 1700.

856. LARGE BUTTERFLY TABLE WITH PIERCED RING. 1700.

857. BUTTERFLY TABLE, CRANE BRACKET. 1700.

858. SQUARE POST TABLE.

859. TRESTLE FOOT STAND.

which is designed to follow the outlines of the skirt above. This is the proper style, followed also on the end stretchers.

No. 852. Placed here for convenience is an odd example of a light tavern table with a drop leaf, which, it is claimed, is original. It is in the same wood and color as the top leaf and it is possible that it may be original. Much discussion has arisen as to whether single, or in fact, any leaves ever appeared on tavern tables originally. The author doubts their originality unless some of these tavern tables were made along toward the middle of the eighteenth century, as perhaps this example was.

BUTTERFLY TABLES

THIS class of tables, about which a good deal of sentiment seems to gather, is a curious instance of the fact that some little detail of construction may make a certain class of furniture very much sought for. While these tables are thought by some to have originated in Connecticut, they are found in sufficiently large numbers in eastern Massachusetts and southern New Hampshire to induce the author, at least, to believe that they should not be confined to Connecticut origin.

The name of course arises from the outline of the bracket which supports the leaf. In the earliest types we think the bracket was rather simple. These tables are found with both plain and turned stretchers, the turned stretcher being very rare. A characteristic of most examples is the rake of the legs one way. In this respect these tables are like many tavern tables. The collector, therefore, should be warned that it is a favorite trick of furniture forgers to place a butterfly top on the splayed leg frame of a small tavern table. One needs to be somewhat keen in the matter to avoid the fraud.

We may not have a better opportunity in this book to point out the rapid increase of spurious pieces of furniture in America. Twenty years ago the values of this furniture were so small that there was no inducement for the unscrupulous to forge the originals. With the present very high prices, however, there is a powerful stimulus in the underworld to supply the buyer with what he wants. Within the past two or three years we have encountered pieces sought to be passed off, which were constructed with the utmost skill, so as to rival the English imitations. We have in the past looked across the water for the masters of this depraved skill. A school, however, is being built up in this country that may soon rival its co-workers in the Old World.

We have long been accustomed to look askance, habitually, at furniture from the Continent, especially from Italy. We may now proceed with the greatest circumspection in relation to American pieces, especially if they are of the class now counted valuable.

One needs to have very much more acquaintance with old furniture than that possessed by the average collector, to detect a good counterfeit. It is one thing to be deceived ourselves and an even worse thing for a person to buy and present to a friend a counterfeit piece, under the supposition that it is real. Such an instance came to our attention.

860–861. BALL FOOT TABLE CUPBOARD, AND BUTTERFLY TABLE. 1700.

862. BUTTERFLY TABLE, ORIGINAL TOP. 1700.

863. DROP LEAF TRIANGULAR TABLE.

864–867. SPLAYED SCROLLED TABLE.

868. BUTTERFLY TABLE WITH DRAWER. 1700.

869. LIGHT BUTTERFLY TABLE. 1700.

870. BUTTERFLY TABLE WITH DRAWER. 1700.

871. VERTICAL LEG BUTTERFLY TABLE. 1700.

872. TRESTLE BUTTERFLY TABLE. 1690–1700.

873. STRONGLY FEATURED BURL BOWL.

874. TRESTLE BUTTERFLY TABLE. 1690–1700.

875. OPEN BRACKET VERTICAL LEG BUTTERFLY TABLE. 1700.

876. BUTTERFLY TABLE WITHOUT DRAWER. 1700.

877-878. CURLING IRONS.

No. 853. A table supposed to be unique, and having elements that suggest the gate-leg.

Owner: Mr. H. W. Erving. The turnings, like the best gate-leg turnings, are carried out on the swivel framework used to sustain the leaves. There is a strut on a wedge shaped member which shuts into a slot in the frame, as shown. This piece is of the highest importance. It has been illustrated before. It suggests to us the style of the crane bracket, two examples of which will follow. It was, of course, necessary in this construction to make the bracket in the form of a T, cutting away the section that is to turn under the frame. The design is certainly of great interest, and quite successful.

Size: Of top, 33 by 37 inches.

No. 854. For convenience, we insert here a Pennsylvania tavern table, whose valance or skirt is cut in an odd series of curves, more attractive on the ends than on the front. Though the feet are lost, this table is an interesting specimen. One sees here the somewhat flat turnings, often characteristic in the legs of the Pennsylvania walnut tables, such as this is. It was in the author's former collection.

No. 855. A butterfly table with a good style of wing. One should here take note of the purpose of the raked leg, to form a wedge shaped frame. The wing or bracket which sustains the leaf is attached to the stretcher by the prolongation of the lower end, in the form of a dowel entering the stretcher. Above, in order to form a long bearing for the bracket on the leaf, the bracket is run past the frame up to the top, where, on the back edge, it engages with the fixed central board of the table with a dowel and bored hole similar to that below. Thus the bracket can be vertical, or nearly so, on the back. The turnings of this table are somewhat heavy, and may indicate an early period. The feet are partly worn away. One sees the overlapping drawer. The wood is maple, as usual.

No. 856. A large butterfly table, the property of the Rhode Island School of Design. It was in the author's former collection. It is the only example with which we have met having square leaves. We were never satisfied whether or not the top was original, but we have been assured that in this specimen it is. This table has an interesting detail in that there are sockets cut in the ends of the frame under the fixed portion of the top for the insertion of extended cleats to support an additional leaf. These sockets, however, are undoubtedly subsequent to the making of the piece. Thus a dining table of a good size was obtained. An interesting peculiarity of this piece is the cut out circle in the bracket, to give it a lighter effect, and some mark of ornament.

The wood is maple.

No. 857.   A curly maple butterfly table with crane brackets.

Owner: The estate of Mrs. Reinholt Faelten of Boston.

The design of the brackets is admirable, though of course the effect of a butterfly wing is lost.   Further, in construction there was a good deal of extra labor involved through the framing of the brackets.

Curly maple came into use, in some instances, before the close of the seventeenth century, we suppose.   It is a beautiful material, and deserves much attention, such as it is receiving in these days.   The principle of decoration is against the use of curly maple in a turning, as a turned piece of wood is decorative in itself and the double decoration at the same point is questionable taste, as well as being confusing to the eye.   As a consequence, a curly grain in a turning, while frequently seen, cannot be counted as a point of merit.   However, the makers as a rule avoided this curly grain because it was a very refractory material.   Even on a plain surface it is impossible to smooth it except by grinding.   Indeed, one of the charms of curly maple pieces is the ridgy effect apparent to the fingers when run over the surface.

Size: Top, 26½ by 35 inches; hight, 25½ inches.

No. 858.   A stand whose square posts are chamfered.   It came from the Churchill family, Newington, Connecticut.   The top and drawer are of pine, and the top has gouge carving at the ends like that seen on many chests and boxes.   It is the property of Mr. George Dudley Seymour, and is in the Wadsworth Atheneum.

Date: about 1700.

No. 859.   An interesting little table owned by Mr. Chauncey C. Nash. One might almost call the shoe an instep foot.   The openwork at the ends, cut in the form of a semicircle, is identical at the top and bottom. The material is pine.   It would be fair to call this little piece a trestle table.

Date: about 1700.

Nos. 860–861.   The former number is that of a small table cupboard with ball feet.   It is the property, with the table on which it stands, of the Rhode Island School of Design.   While we do not know the origin, we surmise it is from Pennsylvania.

The butterfly table below is small, and the curve of the brackets is plain.

No. 862.   A maple butterfly table of good size.   It has a drawer with knob and is all original, but lacks the balls on the feet.   The tongued and grooved joint at the meeting of the leaf and the joint of this table is counted desirable as a mark of date, yet the date is not to be precisely fixed.   We look for this joint, however, in furniture, before 1730.

879. Trestle Table with Leaves. 1690–1710.

880–883. Snow Shoes, Shovel, Churn and Hollowed Barrel.

884. ALL SPLAY LEGGED, SCROLLED SKIRT, DROP LEAF TABLE. 1690–1700.

885–886. TWO TURNED STANDS, PLAIN STRETCHERS. 1690–1720.

887. SMALL CROSS STRETCHER STAND. 1690–1700.

888–889. DARK LANTERNS.

890–891. IRON FLOOR STANDS.

892. SCREW CANDLE STAND. 1690-1740.

893. SCREW STAND.

A feature of these tables, which we have not pointed out, could nevertheless be deduced. That is to say, the sides of the drawer slant inward to match the slant of the frame. Under the drawer there is often a thin rail or slant running lengthwise of the drawer to sustain it. The handles should always be small wooden knobs. When the table is very small there may not be room for a drawer.

Size: Top, $40\frac{1}{2}$ by $45\frac{3}{4}$ inches. The width of the central board is $14\frac{1}{2}$ inches. Hight, $25\frac{3}{4}$ inches, to which we suppose an inch and a half should be added for the lost feet.

No. 863. A table with a round top and three drop leaves and triangular frame. It is owned by the Metropolitan Museum.

A feature of much interest is that the top is set on a swivel and that, when it is swung, the three leaves, being relieved from their supports formed by the angles of the table, fall as soon as they have reached the sections made parallel with them by swinging. We have never seen another table of this character, though we have heard a report of one or two. In this instance, one notices two ball turnings at the feet, a rare thing. The posts here are vertical. In some of the previous examples they are raked. The date is about 1700.

Nos. 864–867. A square table with all legs raking. On two sides there is a scroll on the skirt. These tables are considered somewhat important and are not usual. Resting on the top are a noggin, a canteen, and a small tub.

No. 868. A butterfly table belonging to Mr. George Dudley Seymour. Curiously, the drawer seems never to have had a handle. One notices here a greater degree of elaboration in the contour of the butterfly wing. This specimen is of cherry. It is from the Captain Churchill House, Newington, Connecticut. It may have belonged to his forbears. The table is absolutely original, including its feet. The leaves are hung on large butterfly hinges. We should note, when we mention these hinges, that their name has nothing to do with their use in connection with a butterfly table. Mr. Seymour has a companion cherry butterfly table, also from the same house, which table has a rectangular top.

No. 869. A small butterfly table of good design, though simple. Owner: Mr. H. W. Erving.

The long pear shaped feet correspond with the turning.

No. 870. A butterfly table from the collection of Mr. B. A. Behrend.

The wear of the stretchers is especially noticeable. The table is small with the usual oval top. The wood is maple.

No. 871. A butterfly table which varies from those we have shown in having a vertical frame. It was necessary therefore to change the construction of the wing, the upper part of which must engage with the under side of the frame, owing to the vertical construction. We have here, then, a wing suggestive of the first table shown under this heading.

No. 872. A combined butterfly and trestle-table. These are among the rarest of all American furniture specimens. The trestle foot is cut here in the form of a simple arc, and the stretcher is turned. The butterfly wings are not contoured, but are cut in a perfectly simple triangular form. It will be noted that on the upper part of these wings a portion of the triangle is cut away, and the part left is thinned to a bevel, so as to admit of the closing of the leaf. When the leaves are down, the table is only $7\frac{1}{2}$ inches across the top.

The source of the table is eastern Massachusetts, near Boston.

Size: The top is 31 by 26 inches. Hight, $23\frac{1}{2}$ inches. The spread of the trestle shoe is 14 inches. The square of the posts is $1\frac{3}{4}$ inches. It is $8\frac{1}{2}$ inches from the top of the stretcher to the floor. The width of the frame is $18\frac{3}{4}$ inches.

The hinges seem ancient, very. Nevertheless, the joint of the leaves is plain.

No. 873. A large, beautifully featured bowl of burl, one of fourteen in the collection of the author.

No. 874. A trestle and butterfly table.

Owner: Mr. Dwight Blaney.

The feet are somewhat more ornamental than in No. 872, and the butterfly wings have their usual curve. We do not at this date know of any other examples than these two, though there are many spurious pieces.

No. 875. A crane bracket table, a variant of the butterfly. One observes here the vertical frame. The turnings are all the same size. The crane bracket is framed. We have seen one or two other examples like this table. They are all painted black, as is this one, which was found in Westboro, Massachusetts.

It is from the author's former collection and is owned by Mr. Harry Long.

No. 876. A small butterfly table in curly maple.

Owner: The estate of George F. Ives.

The top is very narrow, being only 6 inches outside the frame, leaving no room for a drawer. The top is $23\frac{1}{2}$ by 33 inches. The frame at the base is 14 inches wide at the ends, showing a rapid spread.

We should call attention to the fact that in all the butterfly tables the wings are thin, varying from $\frac{1}{2}$ inch to $\frac{3}{4}$ inch. We have seen some restorations made with thicker boards for the wings.

Nos. 877–878. A curling iron and love-lock iron.

Owner: Mrs. De Witt Howe.

894–897.   Candle Stands and "Hired Man's" Bed.   18th Century.

898–899.   X Base Candle Stands.   1690–1730.

900–906. Pine Settle, Carver Chairs, Roasting Jack, Candle Box.

907. Double Top Stand.

908. Embroidery Frame.

909–910. Spoon Rack and Stand.

911–913. Pipe Box, Stand, etc.

914. Six Branch Chandelier with Wood Hub. 18th Century.

915–916. CROSS BASE STANDS. 18th CENTURY.

917. CHANDELIER WITH GLOBE CENTER. 18th CENTURY.

No. 879. A very rare table of which we have seen only one other example. It is built in the trestle pattern, but has leaves, which are held in place by a double-ended tongue, swiveled at the center and holding up both leaves. The type is most interesting and important.

Owner: Mrs. De Witt Howe.

Nos. 880–883. The snowshoes on the left have leather leggings attached. We may presume that the owner devised this scheme because he could not remember, like some other boys of a subsequent generation, where he had left his belongings. The shovel is all quartered oak in one piece, and is very sturdy as we can testify, it having served in the case of a recent great storm.

The churn was presented to the author by Mr. Stephen Alden of Brockton, and it came down in the Alden family. The barrel at the right is hollowed out of a single log, and has a bottom board nailed in. These barrels were sometimes of hornbeam. We suppose this one to be in maple.

No. 884. An unusual drop leaf table in which all legs rake, and with a scrolled skirt on the side. The wood is maple. This table is difficult to classify, and we have therefore placed it in this position. It is somewhat larger than a tavern table, and somewhat smaller than a dining table. The feet are missing.

It was in the former collection of the author.

Size: 44 by 52 inches, the long dimension in this case being with the grain, as the leaves are narrow.

Nos. 885–886. Two stands of similar but not identical turning.

They are the property of Mr. Edward C. Wheeler, Jr.

That on the left has an oval top. The hight, as it stands, is $21\frac{3}{4}$ inches, but it, as well as its companion, has lost the feet. The top is 20 by 31 inches. The table on the right one might say was a joint stool, so far as the size is concerned. It is 19 inches high and the legs slant or rake one way, as is usual in a joint stool. The rectangular top is 12 by 18 inches.

No. 887 is a very rare little stand, the photograph of which was furnished the author by Mr. Henry V. Weil. A feature of special attraction, of course, is the turned cross stretchers combined with the raked legs.

Nos. 888–889. Two little dark lanterns belonging to Mr. H. W. Erving. They are of much interest, though we suppose the date to be at least as late as the eighteenth century.

Nos. 890–891. Two candle stands with cast discs for bases, and with plain rods for standards. One of these has a bracket, for the lamp, in the toggle joint or folding pattern. The other stand is shaped to receive a Betty lamp. The origin is Pennsylvania, and the date unknown. It is probably somewhat late, and may be the nineteenth century.

CANDLE STANDS

W E HAVE previously, for convenience's sake, in the arrangement of the volume, inserted a number of light stands or candle stands of wood or iron. We wish now to discuss separately a number of these pieces which of late have come to occupy no small share of the collector's attention. They are found perhaps more often than otherwise with tripod bases. Sometimes, however, there is a heavy, clumsy block as a base, and sometimes there are four legs. Again there is a turned disc for a base. The greater part of these stands which we shall now show are adjustable for hight.

No. 892. This is one of two maple stands of this character found. The characteristics are a disc in the shape of a threaded washer on a wooden screw, to afford a small work table or a rest for implements. Above it is a cross member sustaining a candle at each end. The disc table has a slight raised edge like a tray. A peculiar feature of merit is the pair of wood screws below the candles. The object was to force the candle up as it burned. It is a touch giving completion to the piece and greatly enhancing its importance. The turning of the cross bar is very good. The hub, as we may call it, into which the post enters, has three wide straddling feet of simple turning. The main post finishes in a simple handle or finial. The candles are kept in place by tin candlesticks slit at the bottom so as to be attached to the crossbar.

Origin: Concord, New Hampshire. The condition is perfect. The surface is in the original natural color of old maple, a very pale yellow.

No. 893. A candle stand in the George F. Ives Collection.

The collector is warned that among all the spurious pieces of furniture now found, probably there is no subject oftener counterfeited than the candle stand. The author saw no fewer than a dozen, all absolutely of recent manufacture, in one shop, at one time. They might easily deceive a novice. They have also been so well done as to deceive experienced collectors. It is a favorite method to take the legs of Pennsylvania spinning wheels and insert them in the re-turned posts of old beds.

Nos. 894–897. A series of candle stands in the Nathan Hale mansion at Coventry, Connecticut. Mr. George Dudley Seymour is the owner. The stand on the left is a good example of its kind, being all turned. The diameter of the top is $16\frac{1}{4}$ inches, and the hight is 28 inches.

918–920. Tripod Screw Stands. 18th Century.

921–929. Coffee Grinder, Lamps, Nursing Bottle, Etc. 18th Century.

930. SCREW STAND.

931–932. STAND AND SNUFFERS.

933. PIERCED TIN LANTERN.

934. SMOKE JACK. 1760.

935–936. Tripod and Ratchet Stands. 18th Century.

937. Hard Pine Triangular Table.

938. Triangular Table.

939. Tripod Screw Stand.

940. Pod Stand.

941-945. Noggin, Lamps, Sconce, Etc.

The remote stand by the side of the bed has a cross base, arched, and supporting a maple shaft, mortised to receive a profiled cleat sustaining the round pine top. It is 16 inches in diameter and 27 inches high. To the right is a T base stand, so made that the part supporting the shaft is between the feet of the user who places his feet on the cross stretcher. The post is maple. The bed is of oak, an unusual material.

The diameter at the top is 17¼ inches and the hight is 25 inches. It is presumed that these stands are of the eighteenth century.

No. 898. A stand from Henry V. Weil. It is made so that it is difficult to overturn. One notices the notches carved on three sides of the stubbed feet. The top is octagonal.

No. 899. A stand with a massive post, chamfered, with stops. It will be noted that the ends of the cross members are notch carved. It is almost impossible to date these pieces, but they may be late seventeenth or early eighteenth century.

Nos. 900–906. A room showing seventeenth and eighteenth century furniture. In the distance, against the plaster on the left, there is a tall iron candle stand. Over the fireplace hangs a bar on iron hooks. It was used to air ironed articles; sometimes a checkered apron, perhaps, was allowed to hang there as sort of momentous warning to the youngsters.

On the right is a pine stool which is of a later period. Over the head of the grandfather, against the wall, there is a tin cylindrical candle box. The feet of the young lady are on a braided rug all made of corn husks, said to have been used in this form by the Indians. We doubt, however, whether the knowledge of braiding and rug making came to our ancestors from that source. No doubt some of their basket work was learned from the Indians.

One sees in this picture the huge proportions of a summer beam, the great beam overhead at the left sustaining the floor timbers. The room is the kitchen of the Iron Works House, Saugus.

No. 907. A very rare, possibly unique, candle stand belonging to Mrs. J. Insley Blair. The shaft or movable post at the center is guided by a crossbar with slots at the ends. When the shaft is elevated it can be fixed at any position by a small pin inserted in one of the holes at the elevation of the fixed mortised member near the top, through which the shaft runs. On the top of the shaft is a small square platform for the candle. The larger table top has a rim about it.

No. 908. An embroidery frame. A very neatly shaped arched trestle foot supports it. The cross arms above are made as screws on which the large wooden nuts turn to make the work taut. A pair of end screws on the posts are also used to give the work the proper slant.

Owner: Mr. Edward C. Wheeler, Jr.

The date may be the eighteenth century.

No. 909. A square base stand in which the cross members are gently rounded to the floor. On the stand is set a very excellent spoon rack with simple carvings between the racks and a tree decoration above, at the top of all being a knob. These pieces probably originated among the Knickerbocker inhabitants of the banks of the Hudson, where several others have been found.

Owner: Mr. B. A. Behrend.

Nos. 911–913. A boldly-turned stand with turned tripod feet. On the stand is a pipe box with pierced heart ornaments, and a drawer for the tobacco. On the right, with an iron standard and a bowl below it, is an adjustable Betty lamp. They are owned by Mr. G. Winthrop Brown.

No. 914. A chandelier of wood and strips of tin terminating with scalloped saucers of tin, in which the candle is placed. The style is excellent and such articles are rare.

Owner: The estate of George F. Ives.

Nos. 915–916. Two similar candle stands; that on the left, though more ornate, is perhaps not so good as that on the right, massiveness in these old stands being a point of merit. Both stands are shaped with raised bases terminating in bracket feet. The right hand stand has a chamfered shaft with stops. They belong to the eighteenth century.

No. 917. A tin chandelier in the George F. Ives Collection. At the center of the tin hoop from which the arms extend is set a large globe, and the sustaining chains are sufficiently obvious.

No. 918. A tripod candle stand, the hub of which is decorated with scratch carving. The table is set on a turned base and, while movable, is not adjustable for hight, as is the crossbar above it.

Nos. 919–920. Candle stands, the lower one of which has a rim and the upper one of which is designed to be set on a table, being small and therefore very unusual. These three pieces belong to the George F. Ives Collection.

Nos. 921–929. Household utensils of hardware belonging to Mr. Francis Mireau, Fountain Inn, Doylestown, Pennsylvania. The large piece above in the shape of a boat is sharply slanted toward the center, where the sides meet at an angle. The disc with handles was rolled back and forth and coffee was thus ground. The piece is cast. The heart-shaped flat iron speaks for itself, and so does the miniature fluid lamp. On the left below is a quaint padlock. The next on the right is a vessel of tin with a handle and a snout which served as a nipple for a nursing bottle. The tube extends to the bottom of the vessel, so that the infant could

946-947. Two X Base Stands. 1690-1730.

948-951. Four Candle Stands. 18th Century.

952–955. CANDLE STANDS AND SCRAPER CANDLE. 18th CENTURY.

956–958. TRESTLE STAND AND ADJUSTABLE STAND.

959–961. Three Lanterns. 18th Century.

962. Large Ship Lantern.   963. Glass Reflector Lantern.

964–970. Bed Room with Odd Chest and Early Rocking Chair, etc.

971. Camp Meeting Lamp.

972. Carved Spoon Rack.

get the last drop. It is a most interesting little piece, but not half so much so as another which we have seen, with a nozzle going out from either side; and which was obviously intended to feed twins!

The next articles are pretty well known, being probably the earliest forms of candle molds, before their time candles being dipped. On the right is an ink well.

No. 930 is a quaint candle stand with crudely shaped feet, something in the form of a hoof.

Nos. 931–932. This candle stand belongs to Mr. J. Stodgell Stokes. It is most quaint in the shaping of the feet, and their attachment to the hub. It is very unusual, in being provided with only one candle instead of one at either end of a crossbar as usual. There depends from the end of the knob on the candle holder a pair of wrought iron snuffers.

No. 933. A large lantern now named for Paul Revere who, we doubt not, would have repudiated it. Such lanterns were used in the nineteenth century and perhaps in the eighteenth.

No. 934. A smoke jack which the author took out of the kitchen chimney in the Wentworth Gardner house in Portsmouth, repaired, photographed, and returned to its place. It fitted into the flue of the chimney so that the draft revolved the mechanism with its worm gear. The shaft protruded through the face of the chimney, and to the end of it was attached the small chain belt that turned the jack. A most interesting and fascinating contrivance, and extremely rare, if not unique, in this country.

No. 935. A simple candle stand with legs almost like sticks.

No. 936. A ratchet stand with four stick legs. The piece is odd in that the whole mechanism to which the pawl is attached rises and falls with the crossbar.

Owner: The George F. Ives Collection.

The date of these pieces may be the eighteenth century.

No. 937. A three-cornered table of yellow pine. It is very heavy, exceeding the weight of most oak pieces. It was purchased in New York, but is probably derived from a point somewhat farther southwest.

No. 938. A three-cornered rake legged table belonging to Mr. Frederick K. Gaston of New York. It is a most interesting piece. It follows the lines of the earliest Windsor turnings, so much so that one of its legs might be compared, except for length, with a Pennsylvania blunt arrow turned chair leg. One notices that the round stretchers are placed at different elevations in order not to weaken the wood. The posts at the top are run into a block on which the beveled circular table is fixed.

Size: Diameter of the top, $14\frac{1}{4}$ inches. Total hight, $22\frac{1}{2}$ inches.

No. 939. A stand in which the hub and the miniature table seem to be turned but are really worked out on a bench. The legs and the post, otherwise called the shaft, are turned. The crossbar is decorated by gouge turnings. The piece is attractive, partly owing to the size of the table, which is only $6\frac{3}{4}$ inches in diameter.

The hight is $31\frac{1}{2}$ inches.

No. 940. A ratchet candle stand with pods or sockets of wood into which the candle was dropped. A small block within this socket is moved up and down by a little metal clip extending through a slot in the side, and thus enabling one to regulate the hight of the candle. The base is formed of a slab through which the posts are mortised. It is the quaintest of all stands so far known to the author.

Nos. 941–945. A series of articles in the George F. Ives Collection. The second is a magnifying lamp. The sconce with three candlesticks is very good. Next we have a swivel, otherwise called a ship lamp, which can be carried or hung on the wall; and last is a tinder box.

No. 946. An excellently done stand with an especially good base, not so much for its artistic properties as for its sense of stability and quaintness. The heavily turned post is good.

No. 947. This is the best stand we have seen, in design. The piece is walnut. The shaft, which is fluted, is set on at a diagonal. The feet are well molded. The base was arched at one time more markedly than now, before perhaps an inch of wear occurred. The left hand piece is $26\frac{1}{2}$ inches high and 12 inches in diameter. The right hand piece is $25\frac{1}{2}$ inches high and 12 inches in diameter.

They date from the earlier part of the eighteenth century.

Nos. 948–951. Four stands of various outlines. That on the left resembles one we have shown in having a T head, on one member of which, the chamfered post, stands. They are from the collection of Mr. B. A. Behrend, and are of various dates, probably all of the eighteenth century.

No. 952. A candle stand with an arched cross base and an adjustable crossbar.

Owner: Mr. Hollis French.

No. 953. An adjustable stand of odd construction. The lower part of the base is hollow, and the smaller post rises and falls within the base.

Owner: Mr. B. A. Behrend.

No. 954. A candle stand with a stick leg base, and a candle-stick which is hooked upon a bar. The bars afford a range of elevation.

Owner: Mr. B. A. Behrend.

The three last described are of the eighteenth century.

973. WOOL-SPINNING WHEEL. 17th AND 18th CENTURIES.

974. HUTCH TABLE.

975. FLAX WHEEL. 18th CENTURY.

976–979. Yarn Reels. 18th Century.

980–983. Great Room of Ipswich Historical Society, Yarn Reel, etc.

984. Raked, Scrolled Table. 1690–1710.

985. A Rag Rug Loom. 17th and 18th Centuries.

986–989. Burl Bowls, Mortar and Toddy Stick. 18th Century.

Nos. 956–957. A small trestle stand similar to two others which we have shown. It is a rare piece. The lantern is of a late type.

Owner: Mr. B. A. Behrend.

Date: 1660–1690.

No. 958. A rarely odd candle stand the feet of which are merely stubs inserted in bored holes. The shaft is adjustable for hight, by a screw in the base. The photograph is furnished by Mr. Henry V. Weil, who owned the piece.

Date: 1700–1750.

Nos. 959–961. In these lanterns we have various types of the eighteenth or early nineteenth century. One or two of them are rarely good.

Nos. 962–963. Two heavy and quaint lanterns which perhaps do not require description.

Nos. 964–970. A late seventeenth century room arranged as a bedroom. The bed is of oak and the chest on the left is one which we have not illustrated although we have shown one similar to it. The portrait belongs to the early nineteenth century. The walls are properly done for the simple period of the eighteenth or the finer period of the seventeenth century. The rocking chair on the right is one of several discovered within a few years, having an enlarged post at the bottom bifurcated for rockers. We think that the bed has been cut down from a high-poster. It must have been a wonderful specimen in its day.

The chair against the wall in the background over the table has a slat back and square posts. We do not otherwise feature it, as its American origin is questioned.

No. 971. A camp-meeting lamp throwing light to every quarter, and not two-faced, but four. It is of tin.

No. 972. A spoon rack and knife box. It is carved in the Friesian design on the front and ends of the box, and with checker work in the back, and above with a pine tree. Its condition is wholly original.

No. 973. A spinning wheel for wool shown in operation. Such wheels are not rare and occupy a good deal of room. The garret is the place for them. Those who spun for hours used a spoke stick or wheel stick to whirl the wheel and avoid blistering the fingers. A good spinner would do perhaps six hundred yards of linen in a day, but we are not aware how much the wool wheel, deftly handled, would produce.

No. 974. An amusing little hutch table which is sketched here rather than photographed. The top swings so that the piece could be put against the wall. The cubby under the top was thus open.

No. 975. The usual type of the spinning jenny on which linen thread was made, the distaff being of especially good construction with turned ends connected by bowed ribs.

Nos. 976–979.   Four forms of reels, all of them having some method to warn the user by a click when a skein had been wound, so that count might be kept, or the skein cut off at that point.

No. 977.   This is adjustable on its shaft for winding hanks of the different lengths, for what purpose we do not know.

Nos. 980–983.   The great room of the Saltonstall House, used by the Historical Society of Ipswich, Massachusetts.   It has been called, by those competent to judge, the best seventeenth century room in America. It has the crossed summer beam which has sprung from the great weight attached so as, in the center, to hit the head of a man of average hight. Those who study such matters tell us that the stature of man has increased since the seventeenth century.   The cross summer beam was a poor method of construction, as the mortise on the huge cross timber weakened the main beam.   The beautiful quarter round chamfer of the main beam, with its good chamfer stop, here appears quite plainly.

On the right, attached to a table edge, is a collapsible reel such as was used in the nineteenth century.   It was very convenient.   We do not elsewhere show a tin oven or jack.   They did not come in until the quainter, heavier early type, resting on the andirons, went out.   Neither do we at all like them, as when they are used, they cumber a room and prevent a view of the fire.   They are removed after use.   They belong to the last part of the eighteenth century.

No. 984.   A stand with odd turnings.   It is meritorious from the shaped bracket, which is, of course, cut on the skirt of the frame.   It rakes on every side.

Owner: The George F. Ives Collection.

Size: Top, 24 by 31 inches.   It is 27 inches high.   It probably belongs late in the eighteenth century.

No. 985.   To carry through illustrations of most of the occupations of the early days, we illustrate a rag carpet loom in operation.   The lady wears one of the quilted petticoats, which she is ambitious to have us know she possesses.   She is weaving the sort of carpet on which she stands. The house is that formerly owned by " Ole Bill Spear " in North Pembroke.

Nos. 986–989.   Bowls of burl and a mortar of the same.   To collectors who are just beginning, a mortar has some fascination, but unless it has some special features, as in this case, it is of little value.   The stick lying on the table, and with a bulbous end, is to crush sugar and, undoubtedly, was sometimes used for making toddy.

990–992.　Three Fine Types of Pipe Tongs.　18th Century.

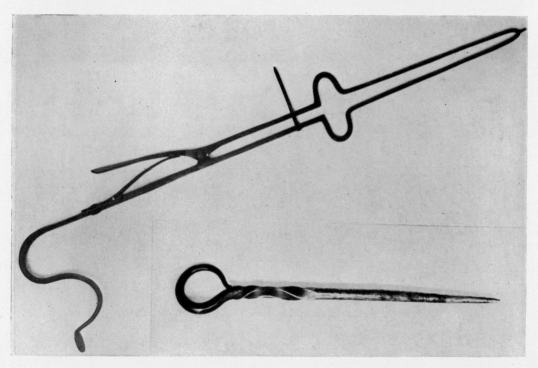

993–994.　Fine Pipe Tongs and Ornamental Skewer.　18th Century.

995. STUMP FRAME LOOKING GLASS. 17th CENTURY.

996. Looking Glass with Inlay. 1710–20.

997. Looking Glass, Frame with Molded Lining. 1690–1700.

998–1002. Horn Lantern, Sparkers, etc. 18th Century.

1003–1004. QUILL WORK SCONCES. 1720.

1005. PETIT POINT NEEDLEWORK PICTURE. 17th CENTURY.

1006–1007. A PAIR OF TIN CHANDELIERS. 18th CENTURY.

1008. A QUILL WORK DOUBLE SCONCE. 1710–20.

1009. LOOKING GLASS FRAME. 1700–20.

1010. LOOKING GLASS AND FRAME.

1011. LOOKING GLASS. 1700–10.

Nos. 990–992. Three remarkably good pipe tongs belonging to Mr. Henry Ford. The pair at the top is quite like one in the author's collection, and in that of Mr. Erving. The piece at the bottom was slightly repaired in its thumb-piece. It is otherwise original, and of very delicate contour. The central piece is most quaint. We have never seen anything else like it.

Nos. 993–994. No. 993 is so nearly like the one illustrated above that only by taking the articles in one's hand can the slight differences be seen. It is at the Wayside Inn, South Sudbury, and belongs to Mr. Henry Ford.

No. 994 is a decorated ceremonial skewer with reversed spiral. It was intended, no doubt, to withdraw the ordinary skewer on the top of the roast in the kitchen, and to insert this skewer when the meat went onto the table. It thus served not only to hold the roast together, but could be used to steady it in carving. It was presented to the author by Mr. Chetwood Smith, and was found in the attic of the General Eliot house in Sutton. General Eliot was a Revolutionary officer, and no doubt used this skewer.

LOOKING–GLASSES

IT HAS not yet been possible to ascertain definitely the origin of the finer looking-glass frames found in America before 1720. This remark applies particularly to the veneered walnut frames which were used during that period. We have every reason to suppose, however, that many of the frames were imported. At the same time, we believe it probable that some of them were made in this country.

Regarding the glass, which was as a rule, and perhaps always, plate, with a very soft bevel, scarcely observable in some lights, we know that that was invariably made abroad in our period.

In showing a few looking-glasses, therefore, it should be carefully understood that the only claim made for them is that they have been in America a great while. This remark would not apply to the obviously American simple small pine frame made in imitation of the finer walnut frames.

No. 995. A bead work frame in yellows, tans, greens and blues. The initials M. B. and the date 1660 are wrought in among the beads. The flower forms seem not to be emblematic, though the conventionalized rose may be so regarded. The flower in the lower right hand corner is unmistakably an iris.

This frame has its original beveled plate glass. In order to exclude objectionable reflections, it is covered in this picture.

Owner: Mr. L. G. Myers.

The so-called stump frame is the earliest of which we have any examples in America. They are very rare indeed.

No. 996. A looking-glass of satinwood with a walnut outside edge. The top has three inset panels of corresponding design. Originally the inlay covered the entire top. The veneer between the panels is now missing.

Size: The frame measures 3 inches across the molding. It is inlaid with Thuya and tulip wood. Size of glass, $13\frac{1}{4}$ by $16\frac{3}{4}$ inches.

Owner: Mr. Francis Hill Bigelow.

No. 997. A heavy looking-glass with its original glass, from which, however, the silvering has been cleaned off. The glass is now used to cover a coat-of-arms. The frame is beautifully decorated with marquetry of the period of 1700. This glass was sold from the Wayside

1012. LOOKING GLASS. 1710–20.   1013. LOOKING GLASS. 1710–20.

1014–1015. Looking Glasses. 1710–20.

1016–1017. Looking Glasses, Cut Glass and Painted Tops. 1710.

1019. Sconce Glass. 1700–30.   1020. Looking Glass. 1700–10.

1021. Warming Pan with Decorated Brass Lid, Iron Handle. 18th Century.

1022. LOOKING GLASS. 1700–20.　　　　1023. GLASS, CUT TOP. 1710–20.

1024. DOUBLE GOOSE YOKE.

1027. Spinning Jenny.

1025–1026. 17th Century Bed Posts.

1028. Cupboard Latch.

Inn, Sudbury, at the auction of its contents some fifty years ago. It had been painted so that when it was sold, its character as a walnut and inlaid frame was not suspected. The cresting is missing, but the condition of the frame is otherwise quite perfect.

Owner: Mr. George W. Hunt of South Sudbury, who inherited the glass from his father, who in turn purchased it at the auction. The arms are those of the family who for many generations conducted the Inn, but are a copy.

Nos. 998–1002. The first object is a horn lantern. The author has one quite like it. The name lantern, formerly lanthorn, has no reference to the horn of which its transparent substance was composed. The word is not of English derivation. The object, of course, in using the horn was to secure a material at once transparent and unbreakable. We do not know when glass was first used in lanterns, but we should probably not date an example like this earlier than the beginning of the eighteenth century.

The next three objects may or may not be American, but the presumption is strong against the scrolled candle stick, which has to us an Irish suggestion. The fire-makers or sparkers were no doubt made in the simple forms here. The more elaborate forms are usually foreign. The fat lamp is discussed elsewhere. The lantern at the right is an interesting, but not an early, type.

Owner: The George F. Ives Collection.

Nos. 1003–1004. A remarkable pair of quill work sconces. The frames are in all respects similar in styles and material to looking-glass frames of the period. The obvious reason is that the looking-glasses themselves were often used as sconces. The designer of these sconces fitted his frames with decorative materials designed to catch the light in front. The frames are of walnut. The vase design, with rosettes and border, is of paper gilded on the edge. The flowers, principally carnations and tulips, are made of wax which is perhaps mixed with mica. Each petal is edged with silver wire. The colors are red, blue, purple and white, of varying shades. The whole sparkles from the light of the candle below.

They were made by Ruth Read, daughter of the Hon. John Read, a lawyer of distinction in Boston between 1722 and 1749.

In " Gold and Silver of Windsor Castle," 1911 (p. XXXI), Mr. E. Alfred Jones refers to this pair of simple scrolled candle brackets as being typical of such in use in England during the reign of Queen Anne. None of the English specimens seem to have survived the melting-pot. Similar brackets may be observed in Hogarth's engravings, " The Laughing Audience " and " The Analysis of Beauty." This pair of brackets was made by Knight Leverett of Boston (1703–53), and is engraved R R 1720.

We distinguish here between the sconce brackets which hold the candles, and the sconce, which is the portion against the wall — the framed section.

The pieces are supposedly unique. Their effect is excellent.

In not a few instances glasses probably had sconce brackets which have been lost, the sockets even being removed, so that there is scarcely a trace of their former location. The effect of looking-glasses with candles was not overlooked by the designers of the period. The fashion of using such candles was continued into Chippendale's time and even later, only in the later time the candles were placed at one side rather than below the glass. We may suppose that the fashion of cutting the surface of the glass in ornamental forms was a persistence of the decorative idea such as appears in the pair of sconces before us.

Owner: Mr. Francis Hill Bigelow.

Size of each: 9 by 21 inches.

The frames are veneered, apparently in walnut, $\frac{3}{4}$ inch wide, and are now painted black.

No. 1005. A framed petit point needle work picture of the seventeenth century. With its rich coloring, quaint drawing and perspective, it is characteristic of the period, and is of particular interest owing to the fidelity of the costumes displayed. It is introduced here, however, on account of the frame, which is of pine, well molded and with a wide gold line. In order to show the cloud effect, the top is made with a double arch, and should be compared with sconce No. 1008.

Owner: Mr. H. W. Erving.

Origin: Probably American.

Nos. 1006–1007. A pair of tin chandeliers. They were bought in New Haven. They were the first instance we have come upon of a pair. One notices that the word chandelier is derived from the old spelling for candle. Compare chandler, a dealer in candles. These pieces are in their original condition. The measurement across the arms is 21 inches. The middle disc is $8\frac{1}{4}$ inches in diameter, and the saucer bases of the individual candles are 4 inches in diameter. All edges are crimped. They are suspended by a wire.

No. 1008. A sconce in quill work. One sees at the bottom the bases upon which the arms of the candles are attached. This piece, together with No. 1003, is the only one of the sort known. They were of much importance and involved a vast degree of labor. One sees in this

1029–1033. Court Cupboard Posts. 1640–1700.

example an arrangement of flower and leaf design with birds in the foliage.

Owner: Mr. Francis Hill Bigelow.

No. 1009. A decorated looking-glass. The frame is small and is painted in scrolls, which do not show at all clearly. The frame is said to have belonged to Peregrine White, though we do not know what the evidence is. It will be remembered that he was born on the Mayflower in Provincetown Harbor, and that we are supposed to have his cradle at Pilgrim Hall, Plymouth. He lived to a great age. Many articles have come down to us from him. He was the only original member of the Pilgrim band who lived into the eighteenth century. We believe this looking-glass to be American.

[*Continued on page 635.*]

1034–1037. 17th Century Table Legs.

1038–1042. 17th Century Table Legs.

1043–1048.   17th Century Table Legs.

1049–1053. HIGHBOY AND LOWBOY LEGS, 1690–1720.

1054–1071. CUPBOARD AND CHEST AND TABLE DROPS. 17th CENTURY.

1072–1078.   17th Century Table and Couch Legs.

1079–1085. Stretchers. 17th and Early 18th Centuries.

1086–1106. Chair Finials, Cupboard and Chest Knobs. 17th Century.

1107–1111. 17th CENTURY TABLE AND CHAIR LEGS.

1112–1116. TABLE AND CHAIR STRETCHERS. 17th AND EARLY 18th CENTURIES.

1117–1119. 17th CENTURY COURT CUPBOARD PILLARS.

1120–1129. Chair Stretchers. 17th and Early 18th Centuries.

Owner: Mr. Mark M. Henderson of Norwalk, Connecticut.

No. 1010. A looking-glass dating from about 1700. It is all original, but there was a decorative crest, which has been lost. We presume all the fine looking-glasses of the period to have had crests. Most of these, however, are now missing. The reason for this is that the crest was separately made and attached by dovetailed cleats on the back. It is not until we have the crest made as a unit with the glass that we begin to find such crests still attached quite generally. The glass in this frame is original. We do not know why this method of grinding ever went out. We understand there is some practical difficulty in grinding

1130–1140. Chair Spindles. 17th Century.

modern glasses in the same faces. The effort now is seemingly, by a sharp bevel, to emphasize the grinding. This is partly owing to the greater thickness of modern plate. In the old days, however, there was an effort made to hide the junction of the bevel with the main face of the glass.

It will be seen, as we proceed, that the earliest looking-glasses were nearly square. In this form the glass was less expensive. Later, for the same reason, we often have looking-glasses in two parts, with one glass under the other, a scheme devised for the same reason of economy.

We do not know how the ground bevel originated, nor why it was used. In this connection we should notice the shape of the earliest frames. They were very wide, like raised panels, and the molding retreats in a soft ovolo to the outside. This is directly opposite from the type of frame used about 1850.

Size: $27\frac{3}{4}$ by $31\frac{1}{4}$ inches outside. The glass is $18\frac{1}{4}$ by 22 inches. The wood is walnut veneer on pine, as usual.

1141–1149.   Finials, Drops, and Stair Banisters.   17th Century.

No. 1011.   This glass, also, evidently had a top which has been lost. The inlay here is very like that on No. 1009, only here it is visible.   The inlay is in satin and tulip woods.

Size: The glass is 16 by 19¾ inches.   The frame is 4 inches wide in addition.   The width of this frame is important, as it indicates great age in this style of molding.

Owner: Mr. Francis Hill Bigelow.

No. 1012.   This is the first instance of a looking-glass in which the cresting is an integral part of the frame.   The decoration at the top, which shows indistinctly, is a very good inlaid design in tulip wood.   The glass is not original.   There were two glasses.   The frame is walnut.

Date: 1710–1720.

Size: The width of the frame is here reduced from the other examples we have seen, indicating a later date and an increase in delicacy of treatment.   It is 1¾ inches in width.   The outside measurement of the frame is 18½ by 48½ inches.   The adaptability of walnut for furniture making was recognized in the south of Europe at a period somewhat remote.   All record of the matter is lost.   In the early veneers it was sometimes too thick.   It was laid on in cross sections, as in this frame, and the joints sometimes open.   The modern method of the use of very thin veneer is designed partly for economy and partly from the supposition that the veneer will stand better.   The tendency to curl is noticeable in most heavy veneers.   The use of pine as a basis of veneers is proof positive that pine was commonly used, in English furniture at least, in this connection.

No. 1013.   A walnut frame with convex molding.   The style of the top is frequently seen in English looking-glasses.   The pierced work sometimes outlines a design of heraldry.   During the reign of William and Mary, when these glasses were made, the loyalty of the colonists was such that royal emblems might easily have been cut here.   We remember such a loyal emblem in pine as the keystone of the finish of a window in a dwelling house in Portsmouth, New Hampshire, as late as 1760. But the builder was a Tory!

One should carefully distinguish between these fretted or pierced frames in walnut, of the period we are now treating, and the later scrolled and fretted frames of the Chippendale period, when the work was done on mahogany, and extended all about the looking-glass.   In our period, the decoration is, for the most part, at the top.   If this rule is transgressed, we find it at the top and bottom only, but never at the sides.

Size: Of glass, 11⅞ by 17⅛ inches.

Date: 1710–1730.

Owner: Mr. Francis Hill Bigelow.

1150–1153. 18th and 17th Century Chair Finials.

1154–1156. 17th Century Chair Finials.

1157–1163. HOUSEHOLD UTENSILS AND FROE. 18th CENTURY.

1164–1166. 17th CENTURY CHAIR FINIALS.

1167–1175. Various Iron Utensils. 17th and 18th Centuries.

1176–1186. Iron Utensils. 18th Century.

1187–1193. GLASS AND PEWTER SCONCE REFLECTORS. 18th CENTURY.

1194–1195. A LAMP AND A CANDLE CHANDELIER.

1196–1198. FLOOR STAND AND CANDLE STICKS.   1199. TWO TIER CHANDELIER.

1200–1205. RUSH LIGHTS AND LAMPS. 17th, 18th AND 19th CENTURIES.

1206–1212. Tulip Blossom, Tulip Bud, Scrolled Chest and Buck Horn Hinges.

1213–1216. An Attic of 1752 with Various Furnishings.

No. 1014. A flat walnut frame. The glass is beautifully engraved, in the upper section, in a floral design, with birds and conventional scrolls. At this date the cutting of the upper glass in imitation of flowers and birds became popular. It would have seemed better to have left the glass free for the use originally intended in a looking-glass. We see, however, that the use of a looking-glass itself is in the direction of luxury, and invariably must accompany the development of taste and the ramifications of style.

A glass as large as this forms an important part of household decoration. The use of looking-glasses for this purpose from this point on is important. They not only served their original purpose, but added light and brilliance to the rooms in which they were placed.

Size: Of glass, $13\frac{7}{8}$ by $33\frac{7}{8}$ inches.

Date: About 1710.

Owner: Mr. Francis Hill Bigelow.

No. 1015. This frame is in a convex molding in burl walnut. One begins to see here the scrolled lines at the top, as we reach the Queen Anne period.

Size: $15\frac{3}{4}$ by $43\frac{1}{4}$ inches. The frame is $2\frac{1}{8}$ inches wide.

Date: About 1710.

Owner: Mr. Francis Hill Bigelow.

No. 1016. A walnut looking-glass in two parts. The bird cut in the upper glass is sometimes called a phoenix and sometimes a pheasant, but is not always recognizable by any of Audubon's illustrations. It is at least a bird, and a touch of mystery is rather an advantage. In this instance one sees clearly the method of the time, in lapping the upper glass over the lower. The object, of course, is to blend the two glasses as much as possible. It was at a later date that the division was frankly made by a section of the molding.   In that case, the upper glass was often used to frame a design. Here the original idea still prevailed, of continuing the reflecting surfaces as a unit. The rabbet in the frame, into which the upper glass fitted, was made deeper; the rabbet in the lower section being more shallow, the glasses came together nicely. Old glasses, becoming a little shaky, are very likely to give trouble at this point, and permit the upper glass to slip down. Hence many were broken. The wood of this frame is somewhat bleached, showing how light walnut may gain a quite charming but very different color from that intended by the maker.

Size: The full hight is 37 inches.

Date: About 1710.

No. 1017. An interesting looking-glass, with painted section.

The upper section is a panel of wood on which is represented a ship in full sail. The colors are now very quiet, but entirely distinct. All parts are original. We see here a tendency toward the abandonment of the use of the upper section as a looking-glass, giving it over to decoration entirely.

The use of wood as a ground for pictures is extremely early, some of the great paintings of the ages being done on wood. At first thought it seems not to be a suitable substance, yet the work done on it has often proved more permanent than that on canvas.

Date: About 1710.

Owner: Mr. Chauncey C. Nash.

No. 1019. A looking-glass which was, of course, designed to carry a sconce on the central projection at the bottom of the frame, which is very closely similar to the projections on the frame of No. 1008. The plain semi-circular top is unusual. Very narrow glasses of this character were often in pairs, and it is probable that this specimen once had a mate. One should compare the molded frame of this glass with a similar molding which runs around the backs of walnut chairs of the same period. The design was a favorite one of the cabinet makers of that day, who were also capable of getting into ruts, like those of the present time. "We refer," as the Rev. Dr. Hawes of Hartford used to say, "to those to whom we allude."

Size: $7\frac{1}{2}$ by $20\frac{1}{4}$ inches.

Date: 1700–1730.

Owner: Mr. Francis Hill Bigelow.

No. 1020. A looking-glass with a stained maple frame. Maple, as of less value than walnut, is more likely to indicate American origin when found in a looking glass. Nevertheless, we should be very careful of this conclusion. There is much maple in England and it was used more or less in furniture.

This glass, though rather simple, is of very pleasing design. The odd button ornament, or boss, and the somewhat wandering, uncertain lines of the scroll are interesting gropings after beauty.

Size: The narrow part of the frame is $1\frac{1}{8}$ inches, and is convex, as quite generally in this period. The glass is $11\frac{1}{4}$ by 17 inches.

Owner: Mr. Francis Hill Bigelow.

No. 1021. A warming-pan with an iron handle and a curved portion of the top to form a hook. These hooks were more often turned sidewise, and in the form of a shepherd's crook. The warming-pan with the iron handle is earlier than that with the wooden handle. One sees here the brass cover pierced in a decorative design.

No. 1022. A looking-glass with a handsomely scrolled crest. We like this type of scroll better than the usual pierced scrolls in the English looking-glass. Further, we are more inclined to believe in the American origin of looking-glasses with simple scrolls. The frame has the extra-ordinary width of $4\frac{1}{4}$ inches. The veneer is in apple wood, showing the end grain. In this case the glass is covered to avoid confusing reflections. Of course the glass is beveled.

It is the spirit of the true collector to value the glass as much as, or more than, the frame. He resists even the re-silvering of an old glass, yet many old glasses are re-silvered, but the result is not entirely satis-factory. It seems impossible to secure a perfect amalgam. Formerly, mercury was used in an alloy with tin. Pure silver is sometimes used. The direct rays of the sun would soon ruin the silvering on a glass. It is for this reason that old glasses passing through so many experiences are usually in so bad a condition. The suspicion arises that new plate is sometimes submitted to direct sunlight to secure the old effect. It is easy, however, by noticing the softness of the bevel on the old glasses, to distinguish them from the new.

Size: The glass is $15\frac{1}{2}$ by $18\frac{1}{4}$ inches.

Owner: Mr. Francis Hill Bigelow.

No. 1023. A looking-glass of Japanese design. The scroll is very tasteful. The glass is cut above in a foliage pattern.

Owner: Mr. L. G. Myers.

No. 1024. This so-called goose-yoke which is 9 inches long and has a large ring, is connected with the following tale, upon which the reader may pass his own judgment. It is said that a tame goose was yoked here with a wild goose which had been winged and caught for this purpose. The ring was then used to attach a cord, fastened to a stone thrown to the bottom of the goose pond, as a tether. The pair of geese could then sail about within a certain radius and served as a decoy for bringing down wild geese. The yoke is precisely like a reduced ox yoke. We have the single goose yoke, which is very commonly found. It is a triangular section.

Owner: Mr. Chetwood Smith.

Nos. 1025, 1026. These bedposts are believed to be of Spanish origin. We show them here because of the remarkable beauty of the turnings, which are found in almost identical form on some American chair finials. The wood of these posts is extremely gnarled, and difficult to work, so that below the frame it is left entirely rough, the thought being that as it was to be covered by a valance, it was not worth while to smooth. We show these turnings here as an interesting example of the universality of motives, at least in western Europe. These turnings may be suggested as indicating how, from the Spanish Netherlands, the turn-ings of the Brewster and Carver chairs may have come to America.

The large diameter of the turning is about 3 inches. The small diameter is about $1\frac{3}{16}$ inches, and the greatest length of a finial is about 10 inches.

No. 1027. A spinning jenny with the frame somewhat resembling that of a chair. This type is often found in Connecticut. There are, as one observes, two treadles which are intended to make the operation of the wheel simpler and steadier. Another feature of interest is that the spinning head, which hangs over the side of the frame, can be swung up out of the way by loosening the hand screw on the front of the frame; also, whenever it is set for spinning, it can be given just the proper tension by the set of the screw.

No. 1028. A wrought maple leaf latch. This remarkable and handsome example, no fellow of which we have so far seen, was probably intended for use on a cupboard door, as it is molded on the edge, apparently to match the mold on such a door. It is supposed to have caught by a snap, and to have been reversed from the usual latch position on this account. Size: $5\frac{1}{2}$ by 9 inches.

TURNINGS

CAREFULLY outlined drawings which were done on a full size scale, and reduced, are here exhibited. They will give an accurate idea of most of the forms in which the furniture of our period was turned. All but one of these drawings were done from the furniture. That one was done from a photograph on which we had the dimensions.

Nos. 1029–1033. The posts on court cupboards. No. 1029 is the upper post in the Parmenter cupboard.

Size: $20\frac{1}{8}$ by 4 inches, the latter dimension being the square of the top. The large part of the turning is only $\frac{1}{16}$ inch short of this dimension; the smallest is $1\frac{5}{8}$ inches.

Nos. 1030 and 1032 are the humbler turnings of pine court cupboards. No. 1031 is the reversible turning of the Prince-Howes cupboard. The turnings on the other cupboards of this style all vary somewhat from this one, but they are all about the same size. The size of this turning is $17\frac{3}{4}$ by $4\frac{7}{16}$ inches. The smallest diameter is $1\frac{3}{8}$ inches.

No. 1033 is the post of the Connecticut sunflower and tulip cupboard. These posts are practically the same on all the cupboards, with one exception. In fact, their similarity is so great that they are more like modern products in the sense of being almost interchangeable.

Nos. 1034–1037 are the heavy legs of the earliest tables. No. 1034 is the bulbous leg of the great Andover square table.

Size: $31\frac{3}{4}$ by $4\frac{1}{8}$ inches. The smallest diameter is $1\frac{3}{8}$ inches. The square of the leg is only $2\frac{3}{4}$ inches. At the top one sees the extension, which is a tenon entering into the mortise in the table top, which is, however, left unpinned so as to permit of lifting off the top.

Nos. 1036–1037 are respectively the legs of the Sudbury and the Salisbury communion tables. Each has a diameter of $3\frac{1}{2}$ inches.

Nos. 1038–1042 are table legs which come more in the range of common experience. No. 1038 is the leg of a trestle-board gate-table. Size: 26 by $2\frac{5}{8}$ inches.

The other turnings on this plate are all gate-leg table legs.

Nos. 1043–1048 are legs of various pieces. No. 1043 is the oak post of a chest-on-frame. No. 1044 is the oak leg of an early tavern table. No. 1045 is from a gate-leg table. No. 1046 is the post of an American turned settee. No. 1047 is the raked oak leg of a tavern table, and No. 1048 is the raked oak leg of a stool table.

Nos. 1049–1053 are the legs of the William and Mary and Queen Anne period, of the highboy and lowboy type, except that No. 1053 is the leg of a stool having a cross stretcher.

Nos. 1054–1071 are cupboard and chest half spindle turnings, drops, and bosses.

Nos. 1072–1078 are table, desk, or couch legs. No. 1076 is a very fine representation of the best type of the Pennsylvania turning, showing the ball of the foot larger than the rest of the turning, and the so-called blunt arrow with which the leg terminates at the floor. The chaise longue from which it is taken is in the author's collection. Heavy turnings like these are called fat. The ball of the foot is $3\frac{5}{16}$ inches in diameter.

Nos. 1079–1085 are the stretchers of chairs, the first two being especially heavy and fine, and such as are found on the best types of the Pennsylvania chairs, or on the ram's horn arm New England type. The No. 1080 is $3\frac{5}{16}$ inches, whereas the smallest diameter comes down to $\frac{7}{8}$ of largest diameter of the turning on No. 1079 is $2\frac{11}{16}$ inches, and that on an inch on this latter piece.

Nos. 1086–1106 represent, on the upper row, the finials of seventeenth century chairs, though No. 1086 was probably not found until the very end of the century, and is a distinct decline from the others. No. 1087 is one of the best Pilgrim turnings, and No. 1090 is the oddest turning. Nos. 1091 to 1095 represent the mushrooms on the front posts of chairs, except the last which is the conventional ball on most Pilgrim chairs before the mushroom period.

Nos. 1096 to 1106 show the knobs on drawers and doors of the period, though the first is a flat-headed screw for a candle stand, and the next is the foot of a desk box, and the last is a knob running through a cupboard door, and having an inside button attached.

Nos. 1107–1111. Chair legs, No. 1108 being the oak leg of the X stretcher Jersey chair table. Its large diameter is $2\frac{3}{8}$ inches. No. 1109 is the leg of the Robinson wainscot chair.

Nos. 1112–1116 are table stretchers, except the last, which is a chair-rung of a New England type.

Nos. 1117–1119. The first is the walnut post of a court cupboard from Durham, Connecticut. Most likely it should be reversed. It is not so fine a type as most others on court cupboards. No. 1118 is a court cupboard table leg, $3\frac{1}{2}$ inches in diameter. No. 1119 is the bulbous turning of the Virginia court cupboard. Just above and just below the great bulb there is a dowel. This central section of the turning is 6 inches in diameter, and 8 inches long.

Nos. 1120–1129 are Brewster, Carver, and mushroom chair rails. These are among the most interesting of all.

Nos. 1130–1140 are the spindles of beds and chairs; mostly, of course, of chairs. The five short turnings at the right are all back spindles of Carver chairs.

Nos. 1141–1149 are miscellaneous turnings, the second line of four above one another being the drops or finials of seventeenth century stairs, and the next two in line being seventeenth century banisters. Nos. 1148 and 1149 are finials on the cross stretchers of lowboys.

Nos. 1150–1153. Photographs of finials, the first two being of chairs of the date of 1700 or thereabouts, and the last two being from a Brewster and a Carver. The diameters of the last two are a little more than $2\frac{1}{2}$ inches. Before the shrinkage they were probably $2\frac{5}{8}$ inches.

Nos. 1154–1156. These are turnings on Carver chairs, except the last, which is from a Pilgrim slat back. Sizes, in their larger diameters, are $2\frac{1}{2}$ inches.

Nos. 1157–1163. These illustrate household utensils. The shovel is wrought from one piece and has a curled-over handle. It rests on a great mortar which is all a man can lift. The little handled tool in front of it is called a froe. It was used to split clapboards. A stick of oak about 16 inches in diameter and 4 feet long, and of very straight grain, was stood on end and marked at the center. The froe was then set with its point at the center and was struck with a maul or an ax successively as the froe was moved about the circle, as we would cut minute pieces of pie — war-wedges, so to speak. This accounts for the thinning of the clapboard from the butt. The clapboards were then roughly shaved to remove any prominent ridges of the grain. Some dwellings still remain with these clapboards in place, where protected by a lean-to roof on the back.

Nos. 1164–1166. Chair finials of the Carver and Brewster type. Shown here in half-size.

WROUGHT IRON IN AMERICA

WITHIN a recent period much interest has been aroused in this subject. The author has sought far and wide for all good specimens of wrought iron. He has not confined himself to the earliest types. We have hinges which probably date from 1640, and possibly a few latches from the same period. The best period of wrought iron was not, strangely enough, the seventeenth century, nor even the early eighteenth century, although we have many remarkable pieces included within those dates. Some of these pieces are also, owing to their rarity or quaintness, very much to be desired. If, however, we consider the subject fully from the standpoint of style and design, we should say that from the time of the Revolution to the end of the eighteenth century was the best period. After 1800 there was a rapid decline, except in Pennsylvania. There the traditions of the blacksmiths continued. We find, astonishing to relate, that good Betty lamps, which are classed in Pennsylvania under the large term fat lamps, in the same category with standing fat lamps, were made up to and beyond the middle of the nineteenth century!

In our treatment of this subject, we make no apologies for having scattered through the work, in the nature of small cuts at the bottoms of pages, a good many specimens of iron, which could not otherwise be included. We have sought to make the showing of lamps in iron and in tin as full as our resources permitted. We have excluded all except one or two fortuitous pieces of pewter, not that the subject lacks interest, but because of our limitations and the fact that other publications discuss that branch of household decoration.

We exclude from our lists the cast latches which came in about 1835. They are neither good in themselves nor in sufficient variety to attract attention. We exclude also, almost entirely, brass latches and other fixtures, because that is a large department of its own, and merits separate treatment. Indeed, brass has been thought of sufficient importance to feature largely and continuously in the work of the best English makers.

The fine and characteristic American wrought latches and hinges, however, went out completely from use and from the attention of American architects and decorators. In this department we have sought to give a very much fuller setting forth of those subjects than has hitherto been attempted.

Nos. 1167–1175. A series of articles belonging to Mrs. J. Insley Blair. The heart motive skewer holder, from which one skewer hangs, is the best we have seen. It is dated 1729. These skewer holders are now much sought for. The highest piece on the plate is an odd shaped waffle iron, and dates 1748. The three-pronged fork is inlaid with brass initials " J. D.", and with a star.

The large central piece, a spit on a rod, has a foreign aspect but it is supposedly American. The next two pieces are pipe tongs. The pipe box of tin carries a legend " Peter Thatcher, Yarmouth, Aug. the 28, 1813." It is the only pipe box we know with a legend, or constructed of tin.

Nos. 1176–1186. Utensils in the collection of Mr. Francis Mireau. On the left is a crude early thermometer. The spiraled trivet is interesting. The horn shaped affair was to hook to the belt and insert the whetting iron, which lies below. The grapples are said to have been used in fishing the old oaken bucket out of the well when it cast loose from its moorings. There is a shaving mug of tin, a couple of odd shaped choppers and a Colonial rat trap!

Nos. 1187–1193. A remarkable series of sconces in glass and decorative stamped pewter forms, owned by Mrs. J. Insley Blair. The diamond shaped sconce is exceedingly rare, if not unique. All the others are much sought for and at the present time the pewter discs, which are covered with glass to prevent them from tarnishing, are almost as much cherished by owners as the style of the two at the top which are made in glass.

Nos. 1194 and 1195. Two chandeliers belonging to Mrs. J. Insley Blair. That on the left is for lard oil and is three-branched. That on the right, for candles, is most quaint in shape, the central portion or hub being formed of two cones, the bases of which are attached to one another.

Nos. 1196–1198. This pair of candle sticks is said to have been found in the ruins of a church in Manheim, Pennsylvania. They are unlike almost anything else that we find in America, but we judge them to be a true Pennsylvania product.

The tall candle stand is a good piece of a type fairly well established.

No. 1199. A double chandelier owned by Mrs. J. Insley Blair. This quaint piece, painted yellow, is said to have been taken from a church in Hebron, Connecticut. The church was built in 1762. The crenelated crown-like circles of different sizes, are very tastefully done, together with the scalloped shaped canopy. Tin chandeliers are now highly regarded. Not many of them remain, especially in as good a form as this example.

Nos. 1200–1205. A series of lighting fixtures owned by Mr. Anthony T. Kelley of Springfield. It is a mooted question whether the rush light

1217–1223. Sconces and Lamps. 18th Century.

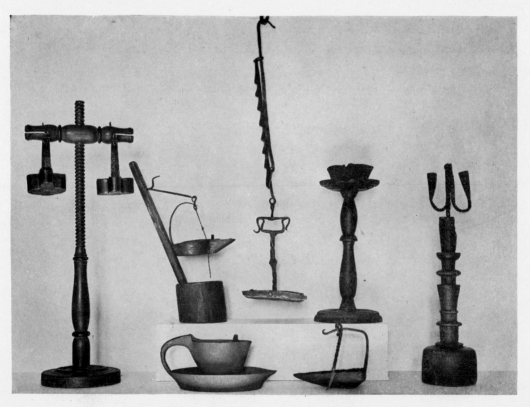

1224–1233. Lamps and Candle Sticks. 17th and 18th Centuries.

1234. TABLE CANDLE STAND.

1235. TABLE CANDLE STAND.

1236–1239. FOUR FLOOR STANDS WITH DOUBLE BRACKETS. 18th CENTURY.

1240–1241. Beacon Holders and Toddy Iron.

1242. Clock Work Jack.   1243. A Post Lantern.

1244–1245. Molded Brass Box Lock, Striker Restored. 1730–60.

1246–1250. Four Latches and Double Braced Striker.

holders were made in America. The two examples here are the first in the row, and the next to the last. It will be seen that the first has an iron tripod base, and the next to the last has a decorated wooden base.

In each case the arm which opens the nippers is a weight to hold them together with sufficient pressure so that the rush light shall not fall, but can easily be raised as it burns. We see no reason why these rush light holders should not have been made in America. The rushes were common and the use of the holders abroad was common. Of course, there was a greater abundance here, at least after the very first years, of tallow for candles, and of oils. We hardly believe the frugal Pennsylvania and Yankee settlers would have failed to provide their own holders, had they wanted them. It is possible that they were very little used in America. We are bound to say, however, that so far as we are able to trace any of these holders at all, they are traced to Europe. The other oil or fat burning lights in this row are sufficiently self-explanatory.

Nos. 1206–1212. These hinges, designed with a good deal of taste, are from Pennsylvania, except the single buck horn which was found in Massachusetts.

The tulip blossom hinge is the best example that has come to our attention, although we have recently seen a sketch of another almost as good. In this hinge we have the fully developed blossom, which the reader is asked to compare with the subsequent examples of the bud, and with the examples of the bud, the half opened blossom and the fully opened blossom used in various latches. We have not found a fully developed latch with a blossom as good as this and of large size. We think it quite probable, however, that such a latch existed. The long chest hinges in a fine fleur-de-lis pattern are also from Pennsylvania. There is an oddity about these hinges which may deceive the collector. Their edges were shaped by filing, and we can personally vouch for the fact that some hinges known to have been in place for at least one hundred years show the bright marks of the file on the edges, whereas the main surface has an oxidized appearance. It is known that filed surfaces retain their brightness longer than hammered surfaces. There is a great variety of designs in Pennsylvania chest hinges. Some of them which we shall show, are very attractive. There is scarcely any end, however, to the ramifications of design in this department of hardware. This fact is the more curious, since in the seventeenth century the chest hinges were quite simple, generally merely staples, otherwise called loops.

Nos. 1213–1216. The attic of the Webb-Welles house, Wethersfield, Connecticut, now open to the public. It was photographed as the author found it, except, perhaps, for the addition of a chair or two. Curious lanterns are hung about, together with herbs. There is a gallery, a small portion of which shows, which is reached by an open stair. People there could witness dancing on the main floor of the attic. The house dates from 1752.

Nos. 1217–1223. A series of lighting fixtures belonging to Mrs. J. Insley Blair. Above are plain sconces, which nevertheless are very rare, with their three candle sockets each. The sconce below, with a reflector, is somewhat of a puzzle, as it would seem that a reflector was needed directly above each candle. The other reflecting sconces are better known, being more or less typical, but are now highly regarded. The next to the last in line is roughly shaped in tin to represent a sunburst. The middle piece, with a long post, has a handle showing a series of candle sockets around it, and is most rare and attractive. It will be noted that we do not attempt to date these pieces very precisely. Doubtless some come down from the seventeenth century. Most of them are of the eighteenth century and a few, no doubt, date from the earlier part of the 19th c.

Nos. 1224–1233. The first piece is an extremely rare standard for Betty lamps, arranged with a crossbar and screw. It is important. The lamp to the right on the bottom is a cast Betty lamp, corresponding to the wrought sort next it to the right. At the top in the center is a light trammel with a most quaint device attached.

The standard to the right of it is of turned wood, another example of which we show. It has upon it, however, an earthenware open Betty lamp, which is extraordinarily rare.

The combined rush and candle holder at the right is of great interest.

No. 1234. A candle stand of iron on tripod feet, with a handle at the top roughly scrolled like a buck horn. The crossbar is adjustable. This is one of the rarest pieces we have ever seen, and it has great interest because it is a table type, the same general pattern as the tall iron floor stand.

The hight is 22 inches, and the outside measurement of the bar and attached saucers is $10\frac{3}{8}$ inches. The feet are scrolled in simple pattern.

It was found in Guilford, Connecticut.

Owner: Mrs. J. Insley Blair.

No. 1235. An adjustable table stand for two candles. The material of the post is iron, very nicely wrought, but terminated with a turned brass ring, the base of which is milled. The turned base of the whole affair is weighted and the reflectors as well as the candle bar are adjustable. An extinguisher is caught in a little socket provided for it. This was found in Boston.

Owner: Mr. John H. Halford.

Nos. 1236–1239. Four floor stands for candles, three of which have the conventional adjustable crossbar for two candles, while the last, on the right, has an adjustable bracket for one candle.   The third stand in line terminates with an iron finial hammered from the bow of the post, and the fillet lower on the post is also hammered.   In the case of the other examples the attached portions at the finial and on the stand are of brass.

No. 1240.   A torch-holder which was found on the North Shore, but of whose origin, of course, we are ignorant.   It swings on hinged sockets and is scrolled with English designs, but we believe it to have been long in America.

No. 1241.   Two articles, the left-hand one being a toddy iron.   One should distinguish between such toddy irons and the goffering irons which were toddy irons only by accommodation.

The other article illustrated under this number is a torch holder which was attached to a pole, and which swivels.   We name this article, like the preceding, a torch holder, but undoubtedly pitch pine was placed in the iron basket.   The name may be as good as any.

No. 1242.   An iron and brass clockwork jack, to which a pulley is attached to turn the spit rod which rests upon the andirons, to roast the meat.   We had always supposed these pieces to be American.   We have found two of iron and a third one in which the mandrel was of wood, all on the North Shore.   We have lately seen one of the same pattern that has come from England.   These pieces have at the top a kind of balance wheel, which was spun by hand when it was desired to start the jack.   The weight was so accurately balanced that it was intended to run slowly.   A worm gear is attached to the hand wheel.

These articles are among the most interesting and curious that remain to us from the older day, so that a fireplace fitted with them is of the greatest interest.   At the Essex Institute, Salem, a fireplace is so equipped.

We have also seen one at the Hancock House, Lexington, and at the Wayside Inn, South Sudbury, and the author has one.   There are probably others.

The mechanism is earlier than the clockwork jack invented by Simon Willard.   It is said that Queen Victoria's meat was cooked in Windsor Castle on a jack similar to this, which has been in use there from time immemorial.

No. 1243.   A lantern to be set upon a post.   It is of very good early design and terminates with a finial of turned wood.

Nos. 1244–1245.   A brass box lock which, owing to its material, is somewhat of an intruder in this work.   The author found the original in Portsmouth, New Hampshire.   Afterwards he found a similar one among the unlisted treasures of the Metropolitan Museum.   The striker and the key are new.   The molding of the lock is the unusual and meritorious feature.   Such locks were in use from about 1725 through the century.

Nos. 1246–1248. Wrought iron latches, the central one of which is 16 inches long and only 1¾ inches in width. It is on this account that it has five perforations for nailing. Undoubtedly it was set on a very narrow stile, and it was difficult to attach such a latch on a narrow plate so that it would be secure. The left-hand latch is of a somewhat crude heart shape, and that on the right is a ball and blunt spear design.

Nos. 1249–1250. An unusual latch, the spear of the top of which is broken, but faintly outlined. It was 19¾ inches long and 3¼ inches wide. The matter of most interest in relation to it is the catch, which may be seen to be braced by a scroll turning in two ways. We have seen several of these. It shows feeling for design and yet, perhaps, not a very early date.

Nos. 1251–1256. A series of latches of somewhat unusual interest. The first we may call a ball and diamond. The second is a scroll design apparently unnamed. The third and largest is one of half a dozen we have seen. It is 14½ inches long. The fifth in line is a tulip partly opened, and more opened at the top than at the bottom. The last is a tulip bud.

Nos. 1257–1268. A series of latch bars. The one at the bottom is no less than 25 inches long. The second in line is finished at the top in a spiraled cone. Its total length is 15 inches. With one exception, this is the most remarkable which we have seen. It was found in Pennsylvania, as was also the fourth from the right. This seems to have been the suggestion of the Pennsylvania locks with a hollowed ball. The third from the left must have had its lifting disc run through a slot in the door. The fifth in line is the latest form of latch that can be considered passable. It has the plate to attach it to the door. All early forms are nailed simply. This piece has a little lifting ball riveted to the latch bar, which is also another late type. The long latch at the top came from a church door and passed through a slot in the wood, which accounts for its opposite form. It has a fine spiral. It is 23 inches long at the hinged portion.

The origin is Connecticut.

Nos. 1269–1272. The left-hand latch is of a crude, simple pattern. The next is a curious, rather than an elegant design. The third is very like No. 1249, except that it is made without the spear terminals. The last is a somewhat crude ball and spear.

Nos. 1273–1275. The first latch is the heart pattern, and the second is of a less perfectly shaped heart. The last latch is the triangular pattern. There is shown at the top the ordinary simplest form of the catch or striker, which is always of a square taper section, driven into the jamb. Below are shown the faces or sides of the thumb pieces.

No. 1276. A latch belonging to Mr. L. P. Goulding, another of

1251–1256. Six Interesting Latches. 18th Century.

1257–1268. Twelve Styles of Latch Bars.

1269–1272. FOUR LATCHES. 18th CENTURY.

1273–1275. SIMPLE LATCHES. 18th AND EARLY 19th CENTURIES.

1276–1278. Latches and a Betty Lamp.

1279–1280. Cranes of Various Styles.

1281–1286. Six Scrolled Latches. 18th Century.

1287–1290. Four Scrolled Latches. 18th Century.

which is owned by the writer. It is a very good pattern called the ball and spear.

Nos. 1277–1278. An elaborate and important latch belonging to Mr. H. W. Erving. It is not always possible, nor perhaps necessary, that we should name these shapes, but we delight to try. In this case, however, we admit ourselves at a loss. At the right is a Betty lamp.

Nos. 1279–1280. A series of cranes. The small ones show a pair to be used one on either side of the same fireplace, and therefore is permissibly small. The large crane with an ornamental end and a spiraled brace originated in Pennsylvania. The other spiral crane is a New England piece. We would hazard the judgment that the frequent use of large trammels in Pennsylvania indicates their use on a lug pole rather than a crane.

The varieties of cranes are numerous. Their use is later than that of the lug pole, which was fixed in the fireplace at a point far above the lintel. It was not possible to swing out a kettle. The removal of a kettle was therefore a very awkward matter, and somewhat dangerous, the heat of the fire being intense unless one waited for it to die down, as was not desirable in the winter. The hanging of the crane symbolizes the setting up of a household, and the gallantry of the young husband, to enable his wife to swing out the pot where she could manipulate it without scorching her face.

Nos. 1281–1286. A series of six latches, some of which are quite important. The second is a very delicate heart pattern, with an attenuated spear point. The third is the pointed heart pattern. The fourth, we suppose, might be named from some flower, but we leave that matter to the botanists.

The size is $16\frac{1}{2}$ by $2\frac{7}{8}$ inches. It was bought in New York.

The last in line is a handsome pattern of extreme rarity.

Nos. 1287–1290. The left-hand example is merely a triangular plate with the corners cut off. The next is a crude heart pattern, and the third is a small ball and spear design. The last in line is one of the best we know for design, being of a flattened ball shape with the spear. One notices the ornamental cutting on the handle. In this connection, one should observe the handle decorations, because the style depends a good deal upon their character.

No. 1291. This might perhaps be called a thistle pattern. It is the most elaborate design we know. While only 14 inches in length, it succeeds in concentrating a good deal of decoration in a small space.

No. 1292 is a very large and simple latch, probably intended for a public door.

No. 1293 is said to be from a church door in Connecticut. It is 23 inches in length and while not elaborate, is a very dignified piece.

No. 1294 is the largest latch we have seen in an ornamental pattern. It is 26 inches in length and might perhaps be called a swordfish design. The spike at the top is hammered to a tapering cone. No doubt this also is a church door latch.

While foreign latches and hinges are, to a very great degree, more elaborate than our own, they would seem very inappropriate on American doors. Where they have been brought over and affixed to our doors they are much out of place. The charm of hardware is in its agreement with the simple architectural lines of the eighteenth century. Foreign hardware is spoiled by attachment to American doors, and the doors themselves are spoiled.

The thumb pieces of latches are sometimes held from dropping out of the throat or mortise through which they pass by splitting the section on the inside of the door, and swinging it out on a curve, making a kind of cusp. The other method is to attach it by an iron pin or dowel, passing through the throat and the thumb piece. We are inclined to believe the split thumb piece to be the older form. The thumb pieces are sometimes more or less elaborate, but in every case they should curl at the end and, in the best instances, a secondary short spiral terminates them. The small straight inside termination, such as we see on doors after 1800, gives no purchase by which to open the door, and we are often at a loss to know how they could have been used.

Nos. 1295–1299. The two examples on the left are Pennsylvania wrought combined locks and latches, the first with a rolled scroll and the second with a hollowed thumb piece. These latches spring. The third example is that of a native chest lock as found in Pennsylvania. It was attached on the interior. Some say these locks are foreign. Others maintain that they were made in Pennsylvania. They are very much like the intricately elaborate etched locks of Spain, except that they are simpler.

No. 1300 is one of two known. It is curious rather than elegant. The origin is Connecticut.

No. 1301 is another example of the ball and spear, with a looped latch bar.

Nos. 1302–1309. A series of eight latches, two of which are closely like others shown, whereas the fourth in line is a good type of the simple large heart latch. It has good design on the handle. The third from the right has the points turned over to be struck into the door when the latch is attached, and thus to form a secondary and additional means of rigidity. The second from the right is the simplest and commonest form of the latch as used at the last of the eighteenth and well into the nineteenth century, in which the plate is a simple disc or thumb-shaped piece. Many of these are still in place on houses of the period. Quite generally the thumb-piece is held in place by a pin. The last latch on the right is interesting because the handle is beveled, showing three faces.

Nos. 1310–1313. The left-hand latch shown here is possibly a reminiscence of a tulip bud, but we should rather call it a roll-pointed triangle. The example at the right has the fleur-de-lis above a ball at the top, and at the bottom an outline and an incised heart, of which we have noted no other examples. It was purchased in New York.

Its length is 17½ inches.

We elaborate later the use of the heart motive in hardware in matched sets for doors.

Nos. 1314–1318. Five latches, the first being a broad heart, the next a pointed heart, the third a rough triangle, the fourth a rather carefully outlined heart, and the last being the rare tulip pattern. We have the beginning of the opening of the bud below and a somewhat later stage above. This should be compared with No. 1255 and also with No. 1256 and other tulip bud patterns.

No. 1319 is a large and elaborate latch owned by Dr. Irving P. Lyon of Buffalo, New York. We may call it a swordfish design. The length of the entire handle plate is 24½ inches; of the handle proper, 8⅝ inches; of the latch bar, 17 inches. The measurement around the curves of the handle is 8⅝ inches, and the length of the spike is 5½ inches. The origin of the latch is not certain, but it is known to be American, and it probably came from Connecticut.

The special and perhaps unique design of the latch bar is very handsome. The catch also is braced by two scrolls, practically at right angles. It is all in all, perhaps, the most important example that has come to our attention.

Nos. 1322–1323. A large latch found in western Massachusetts, in which the ball element is repeated and the plate is terminated in a pointed triangular section. The scrolls cut to parallel the balls are a highly decorative feature. The thumb piece is of good design. The bar is flattened and scrolled at its inside termination beyond the ball. The guard, the bar, and the handle have the repeated molding to unite them in motive.

The size is 23 by 4¼ inches.

No. 1324 is the long section of a Pennsylvania chest lock, a kind of cock's comb.

Owner: Mrs. Edgar Munson of Williamsport, Pennsylvania, who has this hinge on an original Pennsylvania chest.

Nos. 1325–1326. A skewer holder with the original skewers. No doubt the skewer, being a small article, was quite likely to be mislaid. In well-regulated households, therefore, a skewer holder was hooked on the beam.

Nos. 1327–1328. A small trammel with Betty lamp base attached. This is a quaint and unusual piece owned by Mr. H. W. Erving.

Nos. 1329–1331. The pair of andirons on the left is an unusual American form. The rings are more common in English examples. On the right there are two single irons showing types of andirons, one with a bend over cone, the other with a scroll and disc. The piece in the foreground was an ash bar to place before a small chimney fireplace. There are four spirals at the corners to prevent its falling over, as it is flat and set on edge. The pieces with rings are two forms of griddles, both swiveled. At the right of them is a small charcoal stove.

Nos. 1332–1339. It is a great pleasure to find and to show so many different types of trammels. Until recently these interesting articles have been very much neglected. That which is dated 1697 is the oldest dated piece of iron we have seen of this kind, and also the quaintest and the largest. We therefore regard it more highly than any other. It could not have been used except on a lug pole about nine feet above the floor, in order to hang the great kettle on the hook at the base and have it come above a backlog. The etchings or scrolls have been filled with chalk in order to permit their outlines being discerned.

Next on the right is a chain trammel, the hight of which was changed by the use of the small hook at the top. All the links of this chain are twisted and the large hook at the bottom is elaborately etched on its outside.

The long trammel to the right of this has the heart motive and is quite ornate and attractive. It is all original except the wooden handle at the top, which had been lost or burned. It of course was used to change the hight of the trammel.

On the extreme left of the page is a very unusually shaped trammel with wrought scroll. The very short trammel has a heart shaped dated and initialed scroll quite like that found on a Betty lamp to be shown later. The other trammels with holes and hooks are the more ordinary sort, but all those shown here have some especial merit.

Trammels give much character to a fireplace, especially those in the serrated form. Of course, they are adapted only to the larger fireplaces. They connect us with the earliest period of fire making known to our branch of the race. The trammel of 1697, when extended to its full length, was about 80 inches long. Some of the chain trammels are almost as long. A great fireplace with its series of chains and trammels was most impressive. Trammels are very common still in Pennsylvania, but in New England they are rare, especially in their finer forms. The writer

1291–1294. Flower Blossom Latch and Three Church Door Latches. 18th Century.

1295–1299. Five Pennsylvania Locks. 18th Century.

1300. Quaint Church Latch.   1301. Ball and Spear Latch.

1302–1309.   18th and Early 19th Century Wrought Latches.

1310–1313. ROLLED TRIANGLE, HEART AND FLEUR DE LIS LATCHES. 18th
CENTURY.

1314–1318. HEART AND TULIP WROUGHT LATCHES. 18th CENTURY.

1319-21. Swordfish Latch.   1322-23. Decorative Latch.

1324. Bird Head Hinge, Pennsylvania Chest. 18th Century.

has searched far and wide to obtain the fullest possible showing compatible with our space.

No. 1340. A trencher of curly maple, 13 by 14 inches. The shrinkage is shown by the difference in diameter. It proves that these pieces were turned while they were green. Such a trencher, together with great burl bowls and smaller trenchers, one at each plate on a trestle-board, is an assemblage of articles that transports us at once into the Middle Ages, and affords a fine rich old flavor to human life.

No. 1341. A reflector composed of small decorated pewter discs set behind a sealed glass to prevent tarnish.

No. 1342. A Betty or fat lamp on a four-legged stand. All parts of this piece are beautifully wrought and the Betty lamp itself is most carefully done. The lamp is adjustable. The hook of the shaft at the top was, of course, for a handle. The hight is just under two feet. The saucer base is $7\frac{1}{4}$ inches in diameter. The feet are welded into a unit and a hand bolt attaches them to the stand and the stand to the saucer. A table lamp of rare merit.

Nos. 1343–1347. On the left, a simple pair of pipe tongs, $25\frac{1}{2}$ inches long and coming to a very delicate point. The fork and spoon are highly attenuated and are in the hight of the modern fashion! The spoon is ornamented with a delicate fillet and a hook. The ladle is all wrought, and has two pouring nozzles. The piece on the right is a flatiron holder. The two pieces at the right are owned by Mr. L. P. Goulding.

No. 1348 is a heart shaped skewer holder of very interesting design, it being stamped with entwined heart decorations.

No. 1349. A handsomely scrolled foot scraper with twisted standards. Owner: Mrs. De Witt Howe.

Nos. 1350–1353. Four lighting fixtures owned by Mrs. J. Insley Blair. Three of these have conical bases of tin designed usually to be filled with sand. The second piece is a trammel light. The third is a most unusual example, the like of which we do not remember having seen.

Nos. 1354–1355. A metal and a glass sconce belonging to Mrs. J. Insley Blair.

Nos. 1356–1360. Hinges found in the part of Pennsylvania where the Moravians did their work. We presume the small hinge showing a cross in a circle is a motive remembered by them from their old world home. The other scrolls are most interesting and are of a sort which they love to use on their homes and ecclesiastical buildings.

Nos. 1361–1372. The long hinges are of Pennsylvania chest types. The hinges on the right are forked or horned, or simply scrolled examples for doors. The pair of hinges with a butterfly at one end and an I at the other is very unusual.

Nos. 1373–1375. It is a great pleasure at last to assemble a complete latch set doubtless designed as such. It is in the open heart scroll pattern. The origin is eastern Pennsylvania. We do not remember having seen attention called to the fact that the hinge and the latch in the best designed American hardware were harmonized as we find them here.

The length of this latch is about 19 inches, and the disc has a diameter of 4 inches. The rise of the latch-bow is more pronounced than any other we have seen, being 3 inches. What an impressive entrance such hardware on an old and worthy door must have supplied!

No. 1376. A two-tiered chandelier of wood and tin, owned by Mr. Anthony T. Kelley. The openwork of the wooden scroll and the quaintness of the whole design, by which the upper tier, with a smaller number of lights, alternates between every other lower light, is most excellent.

Nos. 1377–1385. The hardware assembled from St. Stephen's Church, East Haddam, Connecticut, by Mr. Morgan B. Brainard of Hartford who interested himself, when the church perished, in seeing that this memorial was retained. The latch is somewhat different from any we have shown, and almost as good as any known. Most of the objects on the board explain themselves. That on the extreme right is of course the bolt corresponding to the piece immediately under the latch. One was pushed into the lintel and the other into the door stool. We have here an important date, as the edifice from which this hardware came was not completed until 1795, showing that the most decorative hardware used in America was found in the last quarter of the eighteenth century.

Nos. 1386–1389. We have sketched from old hinges these examples. The first are the scrolled HL; the next are the double L hinge. At the top on the right is a butterfly of the earliest style in which no pin was used, but a tongue was wrapped around a slot to form the parts. At the bottom on the right is an old shutter hinge such as has been found on the North Shore and examples of which are still known.

Nos. 1390–1410. This large board of quaint hinges exhibits many of the earliest and best varieties. In the precise center is a single one of the cock's comb hinges. This example is in iron. They are sometimes found on English furniture in brass. There is a house in Connecticut nearly all the doors of which are attached with this sort of iron hinge. Difficult as it might be to pry them from their original fastenings, it has been found utterly impossible to pry them away from their present owners.

A pair of scrolled HL hinges flanks the cock's comb. At the upper corners and elsewhere on the board are the three different types of gudgeons, one plain, one ragged and one with a hand screw roughly worked. The minute hinge on the lower left is the usual cotter pin, otherwise called a staple or wire or clinch or loop hinge, used on the earliest American chests and to some extent on simple small cupboard doors. The strap hinge, which is necked somewhat, that is, drawn in as it approaches the roll for the gudgeon, is of the better type. The hinges with battle-ax heads and discs are from Long Island, perhaps, but more likely from Pennsylvania, where we have seen many.

The curved hinge is called a fish tail. Of course the object of curving it was the same as making the L hinge or the H hinge — to secure strength through driving nails in different strata of wood.

The hinge on the extreme right is called a spear point strap and wedge. That at the bottom on the left is called the strap and butterfly, but the point of the strap is the commoner plain disc. There is also on this plate a plain H hinge and an offset H hinge, and a pair of strap and horseshoe hinges.

No. 1411. A twelve-light chandelier of tin, the center, of course, being hollow. The design was drawn for the author by Strickland & Law of Boston, who were acquainted with the original.

Nos. 1414–1415. The object on the left is a handsome mortar about 22 inches in hight. The pestle is made in the form of a great maul, and is also turned. It was found in Woodbury, Connecticut. The other object we of course had to inquire the use of, and we learned it to be a still. We did not know which end up to set it in photographing without investigation. It seems that it was used in the Ballard Tavern at Ballardvale, Andover, in the seventeenth and eighteenth centuries.

Nos. 1416–1426. A series of locks. That at the top on the left is a gate lock. The wooden locks are large and have quaint keys. On their under side is mortised an iron lock of sheet metal like the second lock on the left. The five examples at the bottom are brass box locks, except the two padlocks. These last are of Pennsylvanian origin, and the others were found in New England. We have shown the drop handles detached.

Nos. 1427–1441. A series of chest or door hinges, and five designs of shutter fasteners, all except the minute design of the latter being found in Pennsylvania. The hinges are somewhat crude and simple. The small plain pair of T shaped hinges, one of which is broken, was presented to the author by Mr. Chetwood Smith. They are probably as early as 1700.

Nos. 1442–1443. A pair of sconces with their wooden bases, from which the sconces may be lifted and carried about. They are brass tipped and very quaint and old. It is unusual for American candles to be set on spikes. They were found near Guilford, Connecticut.

No. 1444. These long tongs with teeth are so far unique in our experience. They are supposed to have been used to take up coals and place them in warming pans. They are owned by Mr. Mark M. Henderson.

Nos. 1445–1450. On the left are a pair of Pennsylvania chest hinges. The next pair are odd in respect to the fact that at one end there is a staple. The next example is one of a pair, whose mate is missing. It is very tastefully scrolled.

Nos. 1451–1455. A pair of interesting pronged hinges bought in Boston. On the upper right corner is a pair quite resembling ox shoes.

Nos. 1456–1462. On the left is an interesting little hinge with a crown decoration on one side of the disc. It was presented to the author by Mr. Charles R. Stauffer, Norristown, Pennsylvania. The next pair of handsomely scrolled hinges were perhaps made by the Moravians. The next is an odd single hinge, the application of which is doubtful. The next pair is a variant of the other large pair, but here the ends of the scrolls terminate plainly, and there they are like mouths.

Nos. 1463–1470. All the hinges here shown are various types of chest hinges, the bottom piece being the most interesting as it is scrolled asymmetrically. The pair on the right are unusual gudgeons; that is to say, they are attached to the outside of a door to carry the hinge end.

Nos. 1471–1488. On the outside is a pair of hammered H hinges terminating in arrows and with rolled ends to receive the gudgeon. One should note that this hammered and tapered H hinge is much earlier than the usual H and HL hinges, which are cut from sheets. At the center there is a scrolled T hinge, one end of which is like one side of an H or an I hinge. It is flanked by a very handsome pair of butterfly hinges. The long and delicate straps terminating in arrow ends are good.

Just inside the two outside hinges are a pair of hinges with offsets to strengthen the attachment. The other examples may explain themselves.

Nos. 1487–1491. The long shovel is otherwise called a peel. It was used to handle bread, pies, and pots in the bake oven. The other objects are obvious.

Nos. 1492–1494. A single huge butterfly hinge 14 inches in length. It was found in Connecticut. The pair of strap and butterfly hinges is of the sort often found in seventeenth century houses, some of them running back to the middle of the century.

Nos. 1495–1496. Two tall candle stands of good and unusual design, owned by Mr. Edward C. Wheeler, Jr. It will appear that the legs are beveled from the center to a thin edge. The left hand stand contains the sixth example we have seen of this sort of pipe tongs, and the right hand stand is designed for a Betty lamp with a base to fit the lamp.

Nos. 1497–1498. These little affairs are called bird trammels. They are small and light and if wrought iron can ever be called dainty, they are so.

No. 1499 is a small bracket with a secondary shelf slotted to serve as a support to prevent the over-setting of a candle. It is said to have been found in North Carolina, and is quaintly carved, and we imagine belongs to the early part of the nineteenth century.

No. 1500 is a very fine Betty lamp reported to have been found on Cape Cod. It has a heart-like escutcheon with the legend "Th. A.," below which are crossed axes. The quaint feature of this Betty is that the hook is straightened at the end to form a spike, which could be thrust into the wall, instead of having the spike in a separate scroll.

No. 1501 is an unusual trivet. Of course the word "trivet" suggests an object with three legs. This, like various trivets, has four legs. It has a handle which was perhaps at one time the basis for attaching a wooden handle. This piece is reversible.

No. 1502. This is the original device of the double boiler. It is quaintly arranged so that the protected water kettle can be swung from the downward scroll of the bar of the larger kettle on a pothook. Two pothooks, in turn, attach the upper bows to a crane. We have a second kettle in better condition than this.

Nos. 1503–1511. A series of eleven hasps, some quite simple, and others like the largest, with the scrolled ends, rather elaborate, being etched or covered with a stamped and scrolled design throughout its length. The second perhaps was used on a chest. Most of them were for doors, and they date from about 1700 to about 1900.

Nos. 1512–1514. On the left is a large disc latch found in Connecticut. It is most quaint. The size is $13\frac{1}{2}$ by $5\frac{1}{4}$ inches. The outside margin is cut in fine scallops by the use of a file.

No. 1515. The piece on the right is a spoon rack such as we find along the Hudson. It was used by the Knickerbocker settlers, who designed a considerable number of shapes, several of which we show and some of which have been shown in other volumes. Its length is 24 and its width is $8\frac{1}{4}$ inches. In each crossbar there are four slots, so as to hold a dozen polished pewter spoons, the joy of the Dutch housewife.

Nos. 1516–1521. Forks, skimmers, ladles, spoons and a boat-shaped wrought vessel for dipping wicks. This last might also serve as a dripping pan. On the right is a pair of pipe tongs similar to others shown. These large forks were called tormentors. Let those who do not know what this means remember their old theology.

Nos. 1522–1526. A series of trammels and pothooks, the bottom one of which is a swiveled hook.

Nos. 1527–1528. A pair of andirons which scrolls outward and upward, and then outward again in its terminating octagonal ball. A very interesting example. The right hand andirons have a double set of hooks, on which was laid a roasting spit. Either set of hooks could be used to adjust the roast from the fire as desired.

No. 1529. A pair of Hessian andirons belonging to Mr. J. Stodgell Stokes of Philadelphia. They are the most remarkable pair we have seen, being puddled in the early style and designed quite differently from the usual Hessian type. The mustaches are caricatures, being carried to the ears. The entire attitude is one doubtless purposely outlined to excite derision. They are very heavy and substantial.

No. 1530. An interesting wall sconce belonging to the George F. Ives Collection.

Nos. 1531–1533. Iron floor candle stands, the property of the George F. Ives Collection. We are not certain about the left hand pair. They have a foreign look, but we think Mr. Ives was not able to verify the matter.

Nos. 1533–1539. The stag horn hinges are of Pennsylvanian origin. The handles are early iron examples and the escutcheon is struck up from a die, probably by hand.

Just under the pair of hinges is an attenuated strap and heart hinge. We are glad to illustrate this as showing another correlation between hinges and latches, which latter are often found in the heart design. The largest hinge is an L with a serpentine short arm. It is found in eastern Massachusetts. There is another pair of these known in Sudbury. We count this hinge important.

The length is about 38 inches and another has been found of about 40 inches.

No. 1540. A table stand of iron, rather elaborately wrought and with an extinguisher attached. All the elements indicate a good deal of thought on the part of the designer, although the piece fails of that simplicity which we like to see in Colonial hardware.

Nos. 1541–1547. A series of candle-sticks and sconces in the George F. Ives Collection. The stand on the left is for setting the Betty lamp upon. The two pieces are disconnected when desired.

The long fishhook-like piece is said to be a loom light. They were commoner in England.

Nos. 1548–1552. The hinges here sketched are attached to furniture in the author's possession and it was not feasible to photograph them on that account. The two examples at the left are variants of the so-called rat-tail hinge. The upper section is mortised into the wood and the pin section is clinched. The three hinges first in line are from cupboards. The last is from a lady's vanity box. The hinge at the bottom is on the table cabinet earlier shown.

We know that sometimes elaborate hinges were brought from abroad for use even in the seventeenth century. It is now impossible to know whether this hinge is American or not.

Nos. 1553–1555. Tall candle stands, two of which were bought in New York and the third is said to have come from the South.

Nos. 1556–1557. Candle stands of wood owned by Mr. Edward C. Wheeler, Jr. On the right it appears that the candle is simply hooked by its thumb-piece over the end of the crossbar.

As we began this book with chests, it may be appropriate that we end with the same class of objects, in the nature of a valedictory.

No. 1558. The chest at the top is owned in Pennsylvania. It dates from the middle of the eighteenth century, and is therefore very old for a walnut chest. The series of handles indicate a coming in of the Chippendale style. The picture does not show the initials nor the date.

No. 1559. A pine carved and scrolled chest belonging to Mr. Horatio C. Armstrong. The ogee cut of the legs on the ends, the notch carving on the ends of the front boards, the heavy molding, the initials and the ornamental scroll at the center, and the brackets together with the central skirt ornament combine to render this piece, though of pine, interesting and striking.

METHODS OF COLLECTING

ADDRESSING ourselves now to the collector with a conscience we may suggest profitable methods of search. Pictures of desirable pieces shown to small dealers now and then will bring out the knowledge of and perhaps result in the securing of similar examples. The dealer is himself often surprised at the desire of the collector for a particular piece, a picture of which is shown. He may know of its existence and has not, perhaps, thought it worth while to buy. We have not found advertising for particular pieces a very profitable method of securing results. With one notable exception the effort has so far proved useless. That exception, however, was so important that it was worth all the effort made. Probably persons whose eagerness is great and who are willing to spend freely may find advertising an attractive method.

We have considered, though we have never attempted, circularizing the householders of districts where ancient furniture is likely to be found, using illustrations.

Those who wish to search personally from house to house will do well to meet householders at their doors with pictures concerning which concrete inquiries can be made. Householders who would perhaps resent or at least be annoyed by inquiries of the ordinary sort may be interested in seeing pictures of unusual pieces.

The large dealers ultimately secure a great portion of the finest examples. One who seeks to collect should not neglect the large shops especially since it is found that objects not wanted in one part of the country are eagerly bought in another part. It may, therefore, be that it is possible to secure in Pennsylvania what could not be found in New England or one may see in Boston what is scarce in New York.

Of late dealers are advertising a great deal. The number of such dealers probably runs to several thousand and there are some hundreds who are really living from the proceeds of their business. It is to be noted, however, that important pieces are seldom advertised. It is scarcely necessary to advertise them. Almost every dealer has a waiting list, as we may say, of customers who have bespoken any rare article that may come into his possession. Nevertheless there is now and then a dealer who thinks that by making a rare piece known he may secure the attention of an important customer. All large dealers try to hold a few important pieces to make their places of business attractive to the collector. They do not like to let their last important article go.

It will be found that as a rule when a rare piece comes on the market the price of it is fixed at a round sum because there are generally eager collectors who are willing to pay handsomely for a piece that fills a gap in a collection. If, however, the dealer has miscalculated as to his market and the one or two whom he had in mind for his " find " do not buy he is then thrown upon the broader public who perhaps have not yet grown to feel the importance of the article in question. It is, of course, always dangerous to leave a " find " in the hands of a dealer if a collector really wants it. Any day a very wealthy or a very shrewd collector, not by any means always the same person, may snap up the treasure. One must coolly determine whether he will take his chances on securing the piece at a lower price or buy it when found. Responsible dealers with capital who are willing to wait may perhaps hold to their original figures for a long time.

It is in one sense unfortunate that there is no market value for antiques. In another sense much of the zest of collecting arises from the recognition of importance. The gullible are being taken in every day by spurious articles or by extreme prices. It is not worth while to waste pity upon them because they have not thought it worth while to follow methods of ascertaining values.

The values set on furniture by their original owners are often most absurd. To all who have not made a study of early furniture an antique is an antique. Ten times the value of an article is sometimes asked by an owner. In fact more often than otherwise the original owner asks higher prices than the dealer.

1325–1326. Skewers and Holders.

1327–1328. Betty Trammel.

1329–1331. Andirons, Griddles, and Charcoal Stove.

1332–1339. Eight Types of Trammels. 1697–1770.

1340. Curly Maple Trencher.

1341. Pewter Disc Sconce.

1342. BETTY STAND.   1343–1347. PIPE TONGS AND OTHER UTENSILS. 18th CENTURY.

1348. SKEWER HOLDER.   1349. TWISTED SCRAPER.

1350–1353. CANDLE STANDS OF UNUSUAL DESIGN. 18th CENTURY.

1354–1355. A METAL AND A GLASS SCONCE.

1356–1360. Pennsylvania Moravian Hinges. 17th and 18th Centuries.

1361–1372. Chest and Door Hinges. 18th Century.

1373–1375. An Open Heart Motive Door Set. 17th or 18th Century.

1376. A Wooden and Tin Chandelier. 18th Century.

1377–1385. A Church Door Set.

1386–1389. H, HL and Rapped Joint Butterfly Hinges. 17th and 18th
Centuries.

1390–1410. American Wrought Hinges. 17th and 18th Centuries.

1411. A Tin Sconce. 18th Century.

1412–1414. Mortar and Still.

1415–1426. Locks of Wood and Brass, etc.

1427–1441. Hinges and Shutter Fasteners. 18th Century.

1442–1443. Double Purpose Sconces.　　　　1444. Ember Tongs.

1445–1455. Various Pennsylvania Wrought Hinges. 18th Century.

1456–1462. Late 17th and Early 18th Century Pennsylvania Hinges.

1463–1470. Pennsylvania Chest and Door Hinges. 18th Century.

1471–1486. Various New England Hinges. 18th Century.

1487–1491. Fireplace Utensils.

1492–1494. Odd Hinges.

1495–1496. Floor Stands.

1497–1498. Bird Trammels.

1499. Carved Bbacket for Candle.

1500. Betty Lamp.

1501. Double Ended Trivet.   1502. Double Boiler.

1503–1511. Types of Hasps. 18th Century.

1512–1515. A Disc Latch, and Carved Spoon Rack.

1516–1521. Utensils.

1522–1526. Trammels, etc.

1527–1528. ODD PAIRS OF ANDIRONS. 18th CENTURY.

1529. VERY UNUSUAL CAST HESSIAN ANDIRONS. 18th CENTURY.

1530. WALL SCONCE.

1531–1532. FLOOR STANDS.

1533–1539. A SERPENTINE H HINGE, STAG HINGES, HANDLES, ETC.

1540. An Elaborate Table Sconce.

1541–1547. Various Candle Sticks.

1548–1552. Five Unusual Hinges.

1553–1555. Three Floor Stands.

1556–1557. Wooden Stands.

1558. A Walnut Pennsylvania Chest. First Half 18th Century.

1559. Fine Carved and Scrolled Chest. 1690–1710.

INDEX

INDEX